Communication

Oral
Communication
Message and Response

Larry A. Samovar
Jack Mills
San Diego State University

Third Edition

ωcb

Wm. C. Brown Company Publishers
Dubuque, Iowa

Copyright © 1968, 1972, 1976 by
Wm. C. Brown Company Publishers

Library of Congress Catalog Card
Number: 75-27608

ISBN 0-697-04147-6

Fifth Printing, 1977

Printed in the United States of America

Contents

Preface   ix

Introduction—Purpose and
Preview   x

1   **Preliminary**   1   **Communication—How It**
         Considerations   **Works**   3
              1   The Communication Process   3
                            Ethics—The Responsibility of
                            Communication   12
                            A Preview of Principles   14

         2   **Your First Speeches—**
              Getting Started   21
              Formulating a General Purpose   21
              Formulating the Specific Purpose   23
              Choosing the Method of
              Speaking   24
              Analyzing the Audience   27
              Empathy   35
              Choosing the Title of the Speech   38

         3   **Sound and Action—**
              Presenting the Message   40
              Visual Dimensions of
              Presentation   41
              Aural Dimensions of
              Presentation   50
              Taking Stock of Needs   54

         4   **Listening—Evaluation and**
              Criticism   57
              Purposes of Listening   58
              Barriers to Effective Listening   60
              Improving Your Listening   64
              Listening to Speeches   67
              Listener Responsibility   72
              Speaker Responsibility   73

2   **Your Ideas**   5   **Evidence—The Foundation of**
              77   **Your Ideas**   79
              Verbal Support   79
              Visual Support   91
              Finding Material   91
              When to Use the Forms
              of Support   95
              Detecting Fallacies   96

v

6   Organization—Assembling
    Your Ideas   101
    The Core Statement   102
    Formulating Main Points and
    Subpoints   103
    Patterns of Relationship   106
    General Purpose Patterns   106
    Logical Patterns   109
    More Considerations of Design   111
    Outlining the Message   113
    Preparing the Introduction   116
    Preparing the Conclusion   124

7   Language—The Medium of
    Your Ideas   128
    Language to Represent Reality   129
    Language to Induce Desired
    Responses   134
    Improving Our Language Habits   139

3   Having an Influence
    143

8   Informative Speaking—
    Being Understood   145
    Types of Informative Speeches   146
    Steps in Preparation   146
    The Materials of Informative
    Speaking   148
    Organizing the Speech to
    Inform   156
    Visual Aids   162

9   Persuasive Speaking—
    Changing Beliefs, Attitudes,
    and Behavior   170
    The Targets and Topics of
    Persuasion   172
    Types of Persuasive Speeches   174
    Preparing the Persuasive
    Speech   175
    Choosing the Means of
    Persuasion   180
    Expectations   198

4   Changing Environments
    201

10 Special Occasions—The Unique
    Communication Situation   203
    The Entertaining Speech   203
    The After-Dinner Speech   206
    The Impromptu Speech   207
    Making Introductions   210
    The Manuscript Speech   211
    Answering Questions   213

11 Discussion—Group
    Communication   218
    Types of Group Discussion   218

Preparing for Discussion   222
Utilizing Reflective Thinking   225
Communicating in Small
Groups   228
Styles of Leadership   232
Barriers to Discussion   234
Evaluating the Discussion   235

Appendix   237

Index   253

Preface

In undertaking a third edition of this book we suffered something of the anguish that parents experience as their child grows: "We know he needs to grow up, but we hate to see him get any bigger." A quick comparison with the previous editions should show that our "child" is not much bigger, but we hope you will find that he has grown up.

We have attempted to retain those features of the previous editions which readers claim they have found useful and to supply additional features where the need has become apparent. A major realignment of materials was undertaken in certain areas. The treatment of nonverbal communication has been moved from its original setting in the chapter on language to the chapter on presentation. The treatment of factors of attention has been distributed through sections of several chapters rather than compartmentalized into a single chapter, and the materials on persuasion have undergone substantial rearrangement and augmentation. All chapters have been updated with new illustrative materials; outlines and examples have been added at a number of points. The inclusion of sketches in this edition hopefully will offer the reader's eye a bit more variety than before.

In assembling this edition we have been guided by the philosophy that communication is an *activity*—something we *do*. Accordingly, we have tried to present ideas that can be used rather than simply contemplated. If in our zeal to provide that which is useful we become too prescriptive, we hope the reader will recognize that our intention is to present a point of view, not *the* point of view.

We have tried, as before, to see things from the vantage point of the student. We hope that our arrangement of materials is such that the student encounters first principles *first,* then moves on to increasingly more sophisticated ideas.

Finally, we hope this edition provides the instructor with a flexible instrument that can be adapted to the unique demands of each teaching situation.

Larry A. Samovar
Jack Mills

The major question which logically confronts you at this point is, "Why should I take this course in speech?" As a history, chemistry, psychology, or an art major you are justly concerned with the question of taking a college course "outside" your special area of interest. Most majors, in this age of complexity and specialization, need all the experience they can obtain in their selected field. So, the query remains, "Why speech?" The answer, at least in its stating, is quite simple. **We live and function in a society based on communication.** Through communication, of which speech is one form, we are able to "keep in touch" with one another. One is able to tell others, and be told, how one feels, what one knows, and what one thinks. Without the ability to communicate (speak, write, listen, and read) each of us would live in isolation, set apart from our fellow human beings. The faculty of oral communication is virtually fundamental to our living process. Without speech we remain near seclusion, unable to communicate our thoughts, wishes, needs, or feelings to family, friend, or foe.

The ability to communicate through language symbols separates us from the other animals. Because of our ability to use language we can draw from the past and talk about it. The other animals cannot relate past experiences to one another, and hence cannot make ready for the present or the future. This principle of **time-binding** enables us to pass on our culture to others, to know what has happened to earlier generations and how to adjust our environment for future ages.

You need only take stock of your waking hours to see the importance of communication. Reflect on what you consider a "normal" day and you will discover that most of that day was taken over by communication. You were engaged in activities that attempted to share your internal state, at a given instant, with another human being. There are studies that estimate that we spend up to eighty percent of our waking hours engaging in some communication act.

Because communication so saturates our lives and because it is such a natural process, like eating and breathing, we have a tendency to take it for granted. Yet the pervasiveness of the act should not diminish or detract from its importance.

The uses we make of communication appear to range from the therapeutic to the pragmatic. You tell a friend how you are suffering because you failed an important examination, knowing full well your friend can't change the results of the test. Yet the sharing of that information seems to have some sort of therapeutic effect. On the job we use communication so that we can make a sale, explain a product, or persuade a client. After hours we use oral communication to persuade others to our point of view, such as trying to convince the County Board of Supervisors not to put the proposed trailer park in the middle of a wilderness area. The use of communication here is pragmatic.

Our gift of speech, and the fact that we make great use of it, does not benefit us much unless we have the ability to speak with reasonable effectiveness. History has often been called the story of people and governments trying to resolve their problems. It appears that to date we have but two methods of resolving our conflicts: we can talk them out or we can fight them out. The method of bullets and bombs, although used many times in recent history, seems far inferior to the method of words and reason. A democracy needs and utilizes the spoken word.

Whether on the public platform, on the job, or in a friendly conversation, we use speech as the central means of sharing our feelings and passing on our ideas. In short, we have answered our initial question of "Why speech?" We use communication as the principal instrument by which we function in our various and daily environments.

OUR PURPOSE

The purpose of this book is to help you solve your communication problems more easily and effectively. You have been exchanging ideas, emotions, and experiences with others almost since birth; hence, you have been solving communication problems with at least some measure of success. No doubt you will continue to do so with or without the aid of additional formal training. But the chances are, if you are like most people, your communication activities have become matters of habit. It is only through conscious study that you can improve your communication patterns, and it follows that you will improve from this study and practice only if you are motivated to improve. You must personally see a real need for communication if you are to gain and grow with this training experience. An attitude that reaffirms the axiom that **speech is important for our everyday existence** will contribute greatly to what you take away from this training encounter.

PREVIEW

When you begin a trip—say, to Aspen, Colorado—you may aim your car in that general direction, but it is the map that lies open on the front seat of the car that tells you how to get there. The map keeps you from driving about in circles or from eventually winding up in New York City. A preview of this book might well serve the same end as a map—a helpful guide for accomplishing a purpose.

It is the main task of this book to help you become a more effective communicator. Selecting the "road" to that destination has not been easy. We wanted to avoid listing our chapters in a sequence that might seem haphazard or purely arbitrary. In the best of all worlds we would present all the principles of speech communication at the *same* time, for in reality most of them are in

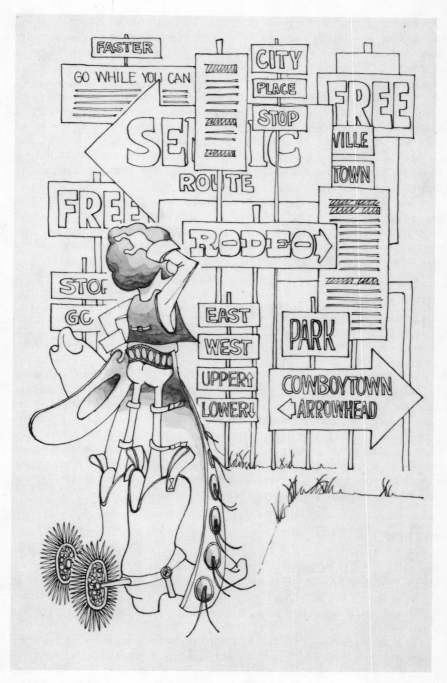

A preview helps us decide where we
are going.

operation during each communication encounter. However, because words and ideas must be uttered one at a time, with each waiting its turn, we were forced to make a series of decisions concerning which principles would be presented first and which would have to wait. We based our decisions on the philosophy stated in the preface of this book—to meet the student at his current stage of communication development. That development, like most evolutionary stages or learning processes, normally reflects a movement from the uncomplicated to the intricate. Thus we shall progress from the materials needed in the early stages of your training to the ideas and content necessary for more advanced instruction.

The book is divided into four closely related sections, with each section separated into several chapters. The first section, "Preliminary Considerations," is divided into four chapters dealing with those materials that are most germane to your initial exposure to training in speech communication. Underlying chapter 1 is the assumption that successful "doing" rests firmly upon understanding. Hence, the chapter opens with an explanation of what communication is and how some of its basic components function during interaction.

Chapter 2 presumes that you need some advice and information in anticipation of the speaking assignments that lie ahead. It offers some initial information on (1) how to select a general and specific purpose, (2) how to choose a method of speaking, and (3) how to analyze the people with whom we are to talk. Very likely your classroom instructor will offer other guidelines that relate to your specific group.

Chapter 3 is predicated on the notion that if you are to give oral presentations early in your training, you should have some knowledge about delivering a speech. This chapter looks at how your message is affected by the distance between you and your listeners, by your dress, appearance, and other visual factors, by your actions and movements, and by the way you manage your voice.

Chapter 4, the final chapter in the first section, looks at yet another activity that is fundamental to human communication—listening. Knowing that you will be listening from the first day of your training onward, we have placed our discussion of this activity early in our text.

Part 2, "Your Ideas," assumes that you have begun to master many of the skills discussed in Part 1 and that you are now ready for more advanced concepts and activities. Chapter 5 is typical of the general tenor of this section. It maintains that we need valid and concrete evidence if we are to affect the beliefs, attitudes, and actions of others. How, for example, can we convince an audience that vitamin C helps arrest the common cold if we have not researched and documented our claim?

Chapter 6 is concerned with the organization of messages. Even the best ideas, if poorly organized, will not hold an audience's attention at the desired level.

The final chapter of this section, chapter 7, focuses on language. A recognition of its capabilities and limitations is central to any substantial improvement in the quality of our oral communication.

By the time you have completed the first two sections of the book, you should be ready to cope with the complexities of two very specific communication situations in which you exercise an influence over other people. The concern of Part 3 is informing and persuading. Chapter 8 investigates those occasions when our purpose is to increase someone's knowledge. Chapter 9 explores those situations when our influence changes someone's behavior.

Part 4, the final section of the book, deals with some unique communication environments in which we may find ourselves. Chapter 10 sees us examining those instances when we are asked to present speeches on special occasions, such as after-dinner speeches, impromptu speeches, and the like. Chapter 11 concentrates on small group communication. It deals with those situations in which we interact with several others in searching for solutions to problems.

Having previewed the main features of the book and having suggested the rationale for the chapter sequence, we are now ready to accomplish the main purpose of this text—to make you a more effective communicator.

Preliminary Considerations

Part 1

Communication
How It Works

1

Admittedly this is a book on *how to* communicate. We are primarily concerned with the efficiency with which you share your opinions, ideas, and feelings with other people. Communication is something you do, and hence this book strives to have you do it well. However, it is our contention that understanding the processes in which you are involved is the first step to improvement. Therefore, this chapter is predicated on the assumption that *understanding* and *doing* are two sides of the same coin—they are interrelated. In this chapter we seek to point out that interrelationship by examining what communication is and how it works.

THE COMMUNICATION PROCESS

To understand the nature and function of speech, we must examine the process of which speech is but one manifestation—the process of communication. We use the terms *communication, oral communication,* and *speech* synonymously in this text simply because a speaker is primarily engaged in communication—that is, in affecting the behavior of others. We ask and answer questions, we take part in conversation, we exchange ideas in committees, and we take part in class discussions; we participate in situations for which we are prepared and in some for which we are not prepared. In short, we use "oral communication" and "speech" interchangeably because **the skills and concepts of successful communication are the same principles that apply to effective speech making.**

You will notice that the last part of the final sentence in the preceding paragraph is presented in bold-faced type. This added emphasis should suggest to you that the issue of speech communication commonality is an important one. As we have indicated, the components of communication are essentially the components of public speaking. In both cases, issues such as credibility, interest, motivation, clarity, types of responses, and the like, must be considered. Even the assumed differences begin to fade upon close examination. For example, although only one person tends to talk during public speaking, the "other person" is still sending messages. Nonverbal communication is present in all public speaking situations. The way the audience responds is a type of message. There is even commonality in the issue of preconceived purposes. In both public and private interaction we tend to have a purpose that has triggered our role in the communication process. We seldom engage in random behavior. So, although the number of people involved may vary and the time allowed for preparation may shift from occasion to occasion, public speaking and communication basically include the same elements.

WHAT IS COMMUNICATION?

In its broadest sense, the term **communication** includes all methods of conveying any kind of thought or feeling between persons. The telegraph operator is communicating when he taps out code meanings that are responded to by other individuals. Actors, artists, writers, and musicians communicate with their audiences by various methods including spoken and written words, actions, form, and colors; and audiences participate in the communication process by responding to the symbols sent by each communication source. The tired student who yawns in an early morning class communicates something to the professor and to those who sit around him. A smile is a communication act, and so is a frown.

It is easy to see that the term *communication* is indeed an enigma. Communication is something we all do, yet it is so very broad as to make it difficult to define. A recent article in the *Journal of Communication* revealed no less than fifteen working definitions of human communication. The problem of defining becomes even more difficult when we realize that in one sense inanimate as well as animate objects and things can communicate. Therefore, in any definition we must allow sufficient latitude to include the processes as well as the functions of the act. One such definition would suggest that communication is the process of sharing with another person, or persons, one's knowledge, interests, attitudes, opinions, feelings, and ideas. There is still another definition that would broaden the scope of the process to include verbal and *nonverbal* messages. Other definitions pose the issue of whether or not the message must be intentional on the part of the speaker.

Whatever definition is analyzed, two crucial characteristics seem to emerge. First, communication, when defined as the process of sending and receiving messages, implies that there will be a response to the message. Thus, communication is a two-way process. Second, the successful transmission of ideas is dependent upon mutual understanding between the communicator and the communicatee.

THE INGREDIENTS OF COMMUNICATION

Although every communication situation differs in some ways from every other one, we can attempt to isolate certain elements that all communication situations have in common. Every time you talk to your neighbor, or every time you deliver a speech, these ingredients of communication are present. What are they?

The communication act has to originate from a **source.** You, as the source, want to express yourself—to pass on your feelings, to convey information, to give directions, to obtain agreement, to get something done, or to relate an idea. You have something *within yourself* that you want to share with others.

The communicator's idea, which to this point has been privately held, is now **encoded**—that is to say, the feeling within you must be put into a code, a systematic set of symbols that can be transferred from person to person. The procedure of translating ideas, feelings, and information into a code is called encoding.

The idea, now represented by a set of symbols, is the source's **message.** The message is the essential part of the communication process—the subject matter to be communicated. It is the message, in written or spoken language, that is the symbolic representation for the source's idea.

The message must now be sent from the source. The carrier or medium of the message is called the **channel.** Channels can appear in such forms as graphic signs, light vibrations, and air vibrations.

Even though the message at this point has been "sent," communication has not yet taken place, for there must be another ingredient, someone to whom the message is directed, the **receiver.**

For the receiver to understand the message, to react, he or she must **decode,** or retranslate, the source's message, putting it into a code that the receiver can use.

Let us construct a very transparent situation and observe all of the ingredients of communication in operation. Suppose you, as the source, are running for class president. You naturally want to secure all of the votes you can; hence, you have an idea to communicate. You are going to talk to a small group of students and try to gain support. So you want to produce a message. Your nervous system orders your speech mechanism to construct a message to gain you the support you want. The speech mechanism, serving as part of the encoding process, produces the following message, "I will work hard to improve faculty-student relations on our campus." The message is transmitted via sound waves through the air so the receivers can hear it. The sound waves constitute the channel. The members of the audience, or receivers, employing their nervous systems, find meaning in what you said (decoding). They now *respond.*

A MODEL OF COMMUNICATION

Many researchers in the field of speech communication maintain that the six ingredients just explained, plus some additional considerations, can be understood best if they are placed within the context of a communication model. As you know, a model is simply a representation or analogue of an object or phenomenon. You have all used models in a variety of ways—airplane models, models of the human body, and even dolls. They are partial replicas of the real thing. Models are useful in communication for a number of reasons. First, they help us understand communication by reducing some of the complexities of this highly intricate process. Second, many communication models combine verbal descriptions with pictorial and symbolic representations, and hence add yet another dimension in their effort to explain and clarify. Finally, models are useful because they can abstract from the total phenomenon those features that the model maker wishes to highlight. That is to say, a model of communication can focus on the linguistic elements without including the role of the brain in encoding and decoding. Conversely, a model of encoding and decoding need not incorporate linguistic factors.

Having briefly established the utility of models, let us now present a model that will help us explain how communication works. Like all model makers we have selected those elements that we believe are most germane to our particular approach to communication. Therefore, the model will concentrate on those aspects of human communication that are usually found in the speech communication situation.

To begin with, you will notice that the model is divided into three large sections: two labeled "What We Bring to Communication" and one labeled "Taking Part in Communication." Each portion of the "What We Bring" section has individuals (Persons A and B) shown *before* the communication act occurs. They are the participants moving toward the encounter, but they have not made contact. Their movement toward communication (symbolized by the arrows marked "Time") helps demonstrate the notion of process that is so important to communication. It must be remembered that each person was doing something before communication began and will move into another activity ("Time" arrows moving both directions) after the encounter.

Starting our model with "What We Bring" forces an awareness of the fact that any communication experience is based on the unique features of the participants. If we are going to understand what is happening *during* the encounter, we must appreciate what has happened before the meeting. Hence, our model begins by pointing out some aspects of human behavior. Many of these factors are symbolized, while others are simply labeled. In the first stage of the model, Persons A and B are represented by irregular-shaped circles with light and dark outlines. These markings, in combination with the arrows surrounding the circles, serve to call attention to a number of important ideas concerning communication. First, the circle itself represents the individual's personality. This is the life space one occupies—the sum total of one's personal history. Second, the irregular shape symbolizes the various moods of which all of us are capable from minute to minute. We are apt to feel happy after receiving an "A" on a difficult examination, and then in the next instant feel grief as we see our dog being struck by an automobile in the parking lot. As potential communicators, we seldom know what our coparticipants were doing prior to their meeting with us. We can come into someone's life right after the "A" or the minute following the automobile accident. Hence, we are likely to find a variety of moods brought to a communication event. Moods may even shift as the event is taking place. Third, the light and dark lines surrounding each person are used to symbolize the many attitudes each of us holds. The dark lines denote a strongly held attitude, while a light line signifies an attitude that is not firmly held. The open spaces in the circle illustrate those few areas where we hold no attitudes. Finally, the arrows surrounding each person are used to indicate motion. This motion, yet another sign of process, highlights the fact that our moods and attitudes are constantly in a state of

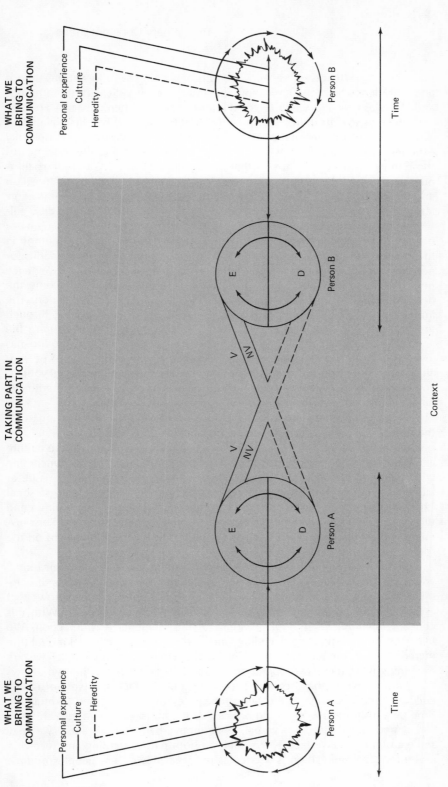

Figure 1-1 Model of Communication

flux. This means that each person we confront is going to bring various moods and attitudes to the communication encounter. As we indicated, these moods. and attitudes even change during and after the period when messages are sent.

Most of the attributes we bring to communication, be they related to disposition or attitudes, have their origins in *heredity, culture,* and *personal experience.* Therefore, you will notice that our model shows the influence of these three factors by the arrows that run throughout the person's life span. A number of relevant precepts of communication are symbolized by the position and direction of these arrows. To help you better understand communication, let us briefly discuss some of these ideas. In all three instances, heredity, culture, and personal experience, the information and potential impact originates outside of the person. In many ways these outside forces illustrate the notion that we are the products of outside forces, and the successful communicator need only discover those forces. Heredity, culture, and personal experience help determine our moods and our attitudes. In this way they become the determining factor in how we behave during and after communication. The influence of these components is symbolized by the arrows running through the life space of each person and eventually becoming manifest *during* the encounter. For example, let us assume that your personal background has given you some bad experiences with marijuana (arrow entering your personality), and therefore you bring this attitude (dark line and arrow in you) to communication. When a speaker tries to persuade you to legalize marijuana, he is confronted with this experience (arrow as part of transaction).

Three observations are in order before we move on to the next phase of the model. First, heredity is shown with a broken line instead of a solid line because its influence and impact are much harder to calculate than are culture and personal experience. Second, we will have much more to say concerning what we bring to communication in chapter 2 when we examine the issue of audience analysis. Third, the exact impact of heredity, culture, and personal experience is impossible to appraise accurately. Each one of us is unique and therefore subject to a variety of responses from the same stimulus. Person A might walk over and pick up a snake, while Person B would faint right on the spot.

Although the middle section is called "Taking Part in Communication," you should, from our earlier discussion, be able to see how all phases of communication are interdependent. This relationship is noted by the arrows that link preencounter activities with the portion labeled "taking part." With this concept in mind, let us look at some of the elements of interaction. We talked about encoding and decoding when we presented our verbal model (the ingredients of communication) earlier in this chapter. In the model we are examining now, these two operations (E and D) are linked by the two arrows that run through both processes. They point out the fact that we are usually encoding and decoding at the same time. We are receiving and formulating simultaneously. Next, you should notice that the messages being sent are both verbal and nonverbal (N = verbal, NV = nonverbal). For instance, we may smile and move as we talk. The model has both parties sending and receiving messages. Communication is a circular process. As we talk, people produce responses that become messages they are sending to us. It is also important to recognize in this model that the messages begin as solid lines but enter the life space of the other person in the form of broken lines. This shift of line structure is used to call attention to a very important axiom of communication. Simply stated, the message sent is not the message that produces the final reaction. There is not a direct stimulus-response relationship between what is sent and what is received. For example, if a speaker said, "Freedom is crucial as one gets older," he or she had an idea in mind when selecting those seven word-symbols. However, when you decode the message you will, because of your past history (what you bring to communication), have different meanings and responses for the words. Hence, the broken line calls attention to the principle that tells us that what is finally decoded and responded to is only an approximation of the actual and original abstraction.

On close examination you will detect that the message influences the person receiving the symbols. If you hear a speech on overpopulation, it is going to have an effect on you. When we receive fresh information, it may either produce a new attitude or alter an existing attitude. In either case, the response to a particular communication now becomes another ingredient that you will bring to the next encounter. More specifically, your reaction to the next speech concerning overpopulaiton will be influenced by what the first speaker had to say—it is yet another experience that is part of you. In chapter 2, when we explore the various types of speeches, we will have more to say concerning the classes of responses found in communication.

Although we have already mentioned that there is a response to a message, our model demonstrates this concept in yet another way. You say "hello," and your communication partner smiles in return. The smile, a response to your message, is sent back to you. In a very real sense our response to someone else's message is yet another message. In this way we can see that communication not only affects the receiver, but it also influences the sender—the originator of the message.

Finally, our model points out that interaction does not occur within a vacuum. The rectangle marked "Context" is used to portray the supposition that communication takes place within a particular context and setting. As you know from personal experience, the place of an act often controls many aspects of that act. The same words spoken at a party may take on different meanings if uttered in a classroom. The locale of communication, be it hallway or church, can influence such things as which channels we employ (speaking, writing, and so on), our purpose (persuasion, information, or enjoyment), and the roles we play (student at school, nurse at hospital, boss at work). Even the number of people present in the communication environment can have an effect. We often talk differently to one person than we do to one hundred.

Human activity is, of course, far more complex than the model just described. We would be derelict if we did not point out a few of the other ingredients that are inherent in communication.

A communication act does not take place in isolation, but rather as part of an ongoing process of sending and receiving messages. The speaker is not the only source sending messages to the receiver. Each situation is also characterized by what we might call *competing stimuli.* By competing stimuli we mean all those other messages that are vying for the listener's attention. Noise or talk coming from another source are examples of competing stimuli. It is a naive speaker who would assume that he held captive the listener's mind as he talked. Most of us as listeners are constantly attending to many messages at the same time. The successful communicator is one who realizes he is competing with other stimuli and works to overcome these obstacles.

We mentioned during the discussion of our model that as senders of messages we usually perceive the response people make to the messages we generate. They can respond with words, silent actions, or both. It matters little; what is important is that our message, as a stimulus, produces a response that we take into account. The perception of the response created by our message is called *feedback.*

The term **feedback** applies directly to (1) the reactions that you obtain from your listeners and (2) your efforts in adapting yourself to these perceived reactions. The term was originally used only in the literature of engineering and cybernetics to designate the feeding back of information to the machine so that the machine could adjust itself to changing conditions. A thermostat is an example of a device that employs the principles of feedback. As information related to the original message (heat) is fed back into the machine, there is an act performed that enables the machine to readjust—to shut off the heater when the air is hot and to turn it on when the air is cold. The source is having to make adjustments because of the information it is receiving.

Feedback provides the communicator with essential information concerning his or her success in accomplishing desired objectives. In so doing, feedback controls future messages. Whether talking to one or one hundred, the speaker has the two-fold task of (1) observing and interpreting audience reactions and (2) readjusting the next message in light of observations and interpretations.

Dean C. Barnlund, in his book *Interpersonal Communication: Survey and Studies,* offers perhaps the most succinct statement concerning the value of and the need for effective feedback in human communication. He writes,

> The timing and amount of feedback, the positive or negative value it
> carries, and the interpretation made of it—all affect the degree of
> understanding achieved through communication. The data suggests that
> when receivers are encouraged to respond with questions, comments,
> corrections, or even counter arguments, greater confidence and mutual
> respect are likely to result.

In short, an awareness and utilization of feedback increases one's communication effectiveness in all situations—both public and private. Being able to observe the reactions of others is one of the characteristics of a person who is "sensitive" to the urgency of understanding and being understood.

Due to limitations of space and the general nature of this book, we were forced in our model to reduce a number of highly complex operations to rather simple terms. One of our chief abbreviations was in the area of the responses produced by most messages. For example, it is folly to think of communication responses as single, one-dimensional entities. In reality there are *levels of responses*. This means that we usually respond in more than one way. Let us assume that someone tells you that driving a motorcycle is dangerous and that you should not purchase one. At one level—let us say the cognitive level—you agree with the person. Yet while that person is talking, you discover that you have some bad feelings about him or her—feelings that you keep to yourself. This is a type of conscious unstated response. When the person is finished, you reply that perhaps you should think the entire issue over. Here we have a verbally expressed response. A few weeks later you find that you have still other feelings about motorcycles. This is another level of response—your subconscious is reacting.

Our enumeration of the ingredients of communication could extend for the remainder of this book, for as we noted earlier, communication is highly complex and multidimensional—it is not subject to simple analysis. Factors such as perception, motivation, communication skills, knowledge level, social systems, and many others, all play a role in the process. We have attempted merely to isolate the factors that are most common and most dominant in the final response made by the receiver of the message. We will return to these elements, and others, as we weave our way through the principles and skills needed in successful communication.

THE NATURE OF
COMMUNICATION

From this introductory view of communication we see certain working principles emerging which should be kept in mind.

1. *Communication is a two-way process.* More than one person must be involved in any act of communication. Speech writers, authors, and musicians may compose in solitude, but there is no actual communication until an audience has reacted to the composition.

2. *Communication seeks to elicit a response.* Speakers communicate to accomplish a purpose. They know what reactions they want from listeners, and this awareness of purpose helps them to determine what to say and how to say it.

3. *Ideas and feelings are the materials of communication.* They must be specifically designed to accomplish your purpose. They must be effective ideas, ideas that, in the judgment of those who receive them, are worthy of expression.

4. *Communication is a symbolic process.* All communication entails the use of symbols of some kind to express ideas and feelings. When you use language to communicate your ideas, you do not simply transfer them to the passively receptive mind of your listener. Rather, you cause the listener to develop ideas that are approximately, but never exactly, the same as yours. The degree of resemblance between the ideas you want to express and the ones your listener develops depends largely upon how effectively both of you, as partners in the communication act, have made use of language-symbols.

Words are the basic symbols in linguistic communication; however, nonverbal elements also play an important part. For example, the sound of the speaker's voice, his or her appearance and actions are often as important as the choice of words. Communication calls for the use of a highly complex set of symbols including both verbal and nonverbal elements. Improving communication entails striving for greater habitual skills in combining and using all of these elements.

5. *Communication is a "real-life" process.* The outcome of any attempt to communicate always depends upon how well you adapt to the environment which surrounds and involves that communication situation. Among the factors which you must try to keep in mind are the occasion which calls forth your attempt to communicate; your relationship with the person with whom you are communicating; your appearance, mood, character, and personality; the knowledge, skill, and perception of the receivers of your communication; the most suitable style and form of speaking; the channeling system you use to bring that expression to your receivers' attention; and the response from that receiver which will achieve your purpose as a communicator.

To communicate is to do more than just send words. To communicate is to adapt your whole personality to the effort of arousing certain thoughts and feelings in the mind of another.

6. *The receiver's response is the test of the effectiveness of the communication act.* If the receiver responds in an unexpected fashion, one can suspect a breakdown of communication. In speech, the sender of the message knows the desired response *before* sending selected symbols.

7. *Communication is complex.* We can say unequivocally that as authors we have failed if, after you have read this first chapter, you do not agree with the axiom that communication is complex. Communication is complex because it is a process that calls for the simultaneous production of a number of intricate and interdependent activities. If communication were a linear phenomenon, with but one action producing but one response, the issue of complexity would not be so prevalent. However, communication is dynamic, not static.

Furthermore, communication is complex because it contains so many variables. In a sense this chapter has attempted to catalog a few of those variables, such as the many aspects of personality that each person brings to an encounter, the diverse forms that messages can take, and the influence of context on communication. Each of these components, when analyzed, offers us ample evidence for the assertion that communication is a complicated process.

ETHICS—THE RESPONSIBILITY OF COMMUNICATION

THE SENDER

The act of communication carries with it serious responsibilities. The perceiving of a message, by the very nature of our complex nervous system, involves in varying degrees changes of behavior on the part of both sender and receiver. Each party is gaining entry into the other's life space. Ordway Tead, in his book *Administration: Its Purpose and Performance,* observes:

> . . . the tampering with personal drives and desires is a moral act even if its upshot is not a far-reaching one, or is a beneficial result. To seek to persuade behavior into a new direction may be wholly justifiable and the result in terms of behavior consequences may be salutary. But the judgment of benefit or detriment is not for the communicator safely to reach by himself. He is assuming a moral responsibility. And he had better be aware of the area with which he concerns himself and the responsibility he assumes. He should be willing to assert as to any given new policy, "I stand behind this as having good personal consequences for the individuals whom it will affect." That judgment speaks a moral concern and desired moral outcome.

This responsibility is compounded as the group the speaker is addressing grows in size. In this day of the communication explosion, one's audience may range from a handful of friends to a large conference or convention. This social responsibility was never more important than in our own time, when television and radio facilities make it possible for a single speaker to influence the actions and the thinking of millions of people.

The power of speech to influence the minds of others has for centuries caused grave apprehensions about its use. The crux of the worry seems to be this: the means of changing behavior are so potent that in the hands of evil or ignorant people, they may be used to induce an audience to act in ways that are unwise or unjust. Perhaps one of the most astute rebuttals to this position was written by Aristotle over two thousand years ago. In *The Rhetoric,* Aristotle asserted that the art of persuasion (changing behavior) was good in itself, but could be used either for good or bad ends:

> If it is urged that an abuse of the rhetorical faculty can work great mischief, the same charge can be brought against all good things (save virtue itself), and especially against the most useful things such as strength, health, wealth, and military skill. Rightly employed, they work the greatest blessings; and wrongly employed, they work the utmost harm.

In talking about the ethics of communication we must understand that the evils, if they occur, are brought forth by humans, not by the processes of communication. The devices and means utilized by speakers are indeed their responsibility. The issue becomes one of speakers realizing that they have an obligation to their listeners as well as to themselves.

There are a number of indispensable questions that should be considered each time you are the initiator of a communication act.

1. *Have you investigated the subject fully before expressing opinions about it?* In your speech class and in this textbook you will discover that serious research and analysis is an important part of successful, effective, and ethical speaking. Because you should speak only from a sound background,

you have an obligation to be silent if you do not understand what you are called upon to discuss. "I don't know" is a valuable and too rarely used phrase. When you do speak, you have a duty to be morally thoughtful—to know what you are talking about before you try to influence the thinking of your associates.

2. *Do you respect the intelligence of the people with whom you are speaking?* The speaker should never distort or "readjust" the truth because he or she thinks the audience will not notice the distortion. Any misrepresentation can easily cause an audience to reject you and your cause. The audience's perception of you as a "good person" will greatly influence the success or failure of your communication act. There are volumes of experimental research indicating that what the audience thinks of you as a person can either hinder or aid your cause. Aristotle, Quintilian, and Cicero, the great speech theorists of classical Greece and Rome, agree—the speaker whose prestige is high in the eyes of the audience has a better chance of gaining acceptance for ideas presented than the speaker whose prestige is low

3. *Have you been ethical in the treatment of content?* Half-truths, outdated information, the lie, and unsupported assertions are some of the devices used by the unethical speaker. The unethical speaker seeks acceptance of his or her ideas but is unwilling to have them tested by the rules of solid logic.

4. *Are you aware that what you say will influence others?* As we observed earlier, you are altering and adjusting the attitudes and feelings of others. A constant awareness of this fact will allow you to revaluate your language and your goals.

THE RECEIVER

Ethical responsibility in the speech act is not borne by the speaker alone. The listener as well as the speaker shares in the moral issues of the speech act. Perhaps the most obvious area of ethical responsibility lies in listening itself. That is to say, if one is to judge, evaluate, accept, and respond to the remarks of others, he or she must first of all hear and understand those remarks. It is indeed unfair, as well as unethical, for us to act on a message to which we have not fully attended. We might say, therefore, that a listener's first obligation is to offer full attention to the speaker. Admittedly this is much easier to write about than to carry out. Each communication act is characterized by countless distractions, but these must be overcome if we are to fairly analyze what we hear. We will have much more to say about listening in chapter 4, but now our appeal to the reader is simply **try to pay attention.**

Once you have paid attention, you are better able to locate the techniques and devices of the unethical speaker. You will also be able to make valid decisions on what is being proposed.

A PREVIEW OF PRINCIPLES

We should alert you to the fact that we are about to make a rather sudden and abrupt shift in our emphasis. Up to this point, we have tried to explain some of the theory behind human communication so that you might have an understanding of what communication is and how it works. But communication is an act that people engage in; it is something we *do*. Therefore, we shall now focus our attention on those aspects of communication that deal with the practical phases of human interaction.

THE ORGANIZATION OF
YOUR IDEAS

Effective speaking, whether to one person or to a large group, demands careful thought and preparation. In your speech class you may face the problem of having to give speeches in the first few days of the semester before you've had an opportunity to study and absorb all the principles which are treated in this book. For this reason, we shall briefly look at some steps you should take in preparing your first speeches. *The steps of speech preparation to be examined at this point constitute the basic themes of entire chapters later in the text.* The order of the steps is not nearly as rigid as our listing might suggest. You may, for example, discover situations where analysis of the audience is the first procedure you decide upon instead of an analysis of the purpose of the speech. But regardless of the order in which you consider the six items listed, a thorough preparation should include them all.

1. *Determine the purpose of your speech.* All communication is purposeful—it seeks to elicit a response from the person who receives the message. This reaction can range from enjoyment at one extreme to direct, specific action at the other. Do you want your listener to understand a concept, agree with a concept, or act upon a concept? Think of your speech as an instrument of utility—a means of getting a reaction. A considerable amount of valuable energy and time can be saved by keeping your purpose clearly in mind. Knowing what you want your audience to do or feel will influence what you say and how you say it.

2. *Choose and limit the topic.* In speech class you may, on occasion, be assigned a subject area, but in most cases your instructor will let you make your own selections. In other speaking situations outside the class, the same procedure is often found. You may be asked to speak on a specific subject, or you may simply be asked to speak. In all of these situations the observance of a few basic principles will enable you to choose the proper subject and limit its scope to meet the demands of the audience, the occasion, and your purpose.

a. Select a topic that is worthy of your time and the time of your audience. No listener enjoys hearing about a subject that he or she believes is insignificant and trivial. Talk about subjects, issues, and controversies that affect the lives of your listeners.

b. Select a topic that is interesting to you. Unless you are interested you will not be sufficiently motivated to accomplish your purpose. Preparation will be a tedious task, and the delivery of your speech will mirror this apathetic attitude. But, pick a topic in which you're interested (or in which you can *become* interested), and you'll find that the results are apt to be contagious!

c. Choose a subject your listeners will find interesting and/or one you can make interesting to them. Think about your listeners, what they like, how they feel, and what they know. The effective speaker can, by knowing the audience, select topics that will interest them and also adapt new information to their interests.

d. Select a topic that can be dealt with adequately in the time you have at your disposal. It is obvious that the subject area of "Peace in the World" cannot be intelligently discussed in a five- or six-minute speech.

3. *Analyze your audience and the occasion of your speech.* We have seen that the listener is as much a part of the communication process as the speaker. A good speaker makes it a point to discover all he or she can about the people who make up the audience and the occasion that has brought them together. The speaker is then able to prepare, adapt, and adjust his or her speech to the specific communication situation.

The process of analyzing the audience and occasion is discussed more thoroughly in the next chapter. However, we may draw a few guidelines to assist you in your early speeches.

a. Learn all you can about the place where the communication will occur. How will the people be seated? Interaction will be influenced by the position you take in regard to the other members of the gathering. The size of the room, its shape, and other physical conditions will also affect the dynamics of the entire speech situation.

b. Learn the purpose of the gathering. Is it a regular weekly meeting, is it a special meeting, or is it a spontaneous gathering?

c. Learn as much as you can about the people to whom you will speak. Knowing their age, sex, educational background, occupation, needs, and attitudes will enable you to adapt your remarks to the demands of the specific listeners you are facing.

4. *Find the material for your speech.* There are basically two places to look for materials—within yourself for what you already know, and outside of yourself to discover what you don't know. You will soon realize that what you know, in many instances, may not be enough to accomplish your objective. In addition, we often are quite prejudiced in terms of the interpretations we give to our perceptions. Two individuals seeing the same situation may interpret what they see in different ways. It is therefore necessary to augment our observations with those from other sources. In chapter 5 we will talk about finding materials in books, magazines, newspapers, and other storehouses of information. At this point it is important to remember that the successful speaker is seldom the one who "talks off the top of his head."

5. *Organize and arrange the speech.* Now that you have the ingredients of your message—the materials—you must arrange them so that they can make sense to your listener. In most instances, if you are thorough in your search for materials, you will find far more than you can possibly use in the time

allotted to you. You will therefore be faced with two problems. First, you will have to decide what material you want to use. Second, you will have to make a decision concerning the organization of that material.

The purpose of your speech is the determining factor in selecting and arranging the materials you choose to talk about. You will want to include the material that directly relates to and supports the main idea of your talk as well as materials that add interest to your ideas.

Arrangement of materials centers around the three parts of the speech—introduction, body, and conclusion. The body of the speech should be planned first. This includes marshalling all of the supporting material designed to establish the central idea of the speech. The specific problems of selection and arrangement of the ideas which constitute the body of the speech will be discussed in some detail in chapter 6.

The main assignment of the introduction is to gain the attention and interest of the listeners, to put them at ease, and to help them focus their attention upon your speech. The material you select should accomplish those objectives.

The conclusion serves to end the speech gracefully and in a compelling manner. It may take the form of a summary, an illustration, an appeal, a challenge, or several other endings depending upon the purpose of your speech.

One of the chief organizational aids is the outline. It enables you to visualize your material in a clear and logical order. It lets you see what materials you have and aids you in sorting the relevant from the irrelevant. An outline helps you avoid the aimless, disorganized sort of thinking that is characteristic of many speeches.

6. *Practice your speech aloud.* If you desire to have your message understood and your purpose accomplished, you must practice aloud. You should deliver your speech three or four times before you present it to the audience. It is important that you avoid memorizing while you practice. *Learn* the main ideas of the speech, rather than trying to memorize, word for word, large sections of the body. Practice your speech aloud and allow time for changes if, after hearing it, you decide that you need to make alterations.

THE PRESENTATION OF
YOUR IDEAS

In chapter 3 some very specific principles and skills will be suggested as a means of improving the delivery of your ideas. At this early point we shall simply suggest some general practices that will be useful to you as you begin your speech training.

1. *Have a good mental attitude.* A good mental attitude toward the presentation of your ideas will make the job of delivering your speech seem much simpler and much more pleasurable to you and your audience.

Don't be unduly alarmed about stage fright. Nervousness is a common trait among beginning speakers. But even the "expert" experiences shaking knees, wet palms, shortness of breath, throat tightness, or increase in the

pulse rate. Perhaps the following suggestions may help to allay your apprehensions.

a. The realization that some nervousness is normal may, in itself, help
to minimize nervousness.

b. The attitude that the "audience is your friend" will also prove
comforting. In speech class you can be well assured that everyone is working
for you.

c. Come before your audience fully prepared. If you have doubts about
your speech and your preparation, it is likely to manifest itself in nervousness.

d. Try to "feel" confident. Some communication theorists suggest that
one's attitude toward oneself is the single most important variable in successful communication. Don't rush through your speech; have the notion that you
are "talking with your audience." Feel free to pause whenever you desire.
Don't be too embarrassed if you find that some of your words are not coming
out as you wish. In many instances you may be the only one to realize what
is happening. Oftentimes the acknowledgment of a "flub" will relax you and
your audience.

e. Finally, nervous tension can be reduced by having some meaningful
physical action in your speech. Try walking during your talk as a method of
relaxing and releasing nervous strain.

2. *Be direct.* Looking directly at your audience serves two vital and
necessary functions—both of which are briefly mentioned here but developed
in detail in later chapters. First, directness adds to a lively sense of communication. It indirectly tells the listeners that you care about accomplishing your
purpose and that you care about them. You know from personal experience
that the speaker who gazes at the floor or out the window reflects a lack of
interest and a lack of concern for the audience and for the entire speech
situation. Even in casual conversation it is helpful to look at the person with
whom you are talking. Establishing rapport between sender and receiver is
necessary if there is to be fruitful communication. Second, by looking directly
at the audience you gain invaluable insight into how your message is being
received. Successful communicators make use of the information they receive
by observing their audience and making adjustments based on the audience's
reactions. Whether you are talking to one person or a large group of people,
your perception of their reaction and response to your original message (feedback) will play a significant role in selecting, arranging, and sending future
messages.

3. *Be physically animated.* Try to avoid stiffness and a rigid appearance.
Your posture should be comfortable and natural. Many beginning speakers
develop mannerisms such as shifting their weight from leg to leg and resting
on the podium. These activities call attention to themselves and hence direct
attention away from the speech.

Gestures are quite useful in conveying thought or emotion or in reinforcing oral expression. They increase the speaker's self-confidence, ease
nervousness, aid in the communication of ideas, and help to hold attention.
Relax and be yourself, and you will learn that gesturing comes naturally.

4. *Use vocal variety.* Just as movement and gestures help to reinforce ideas, so does the animated voice. If there is sameness of rate, pitch or key, loudness, and quality, we have full-fledged monotony. Vary as many of these variable elements of the voice as you can, consonant with conveying the full meaning of your ideas and emotions.

Try to avoid unpleasant and distracting mannerisms such as "and-a," and "uh." These and other meaningless vocalizations call attention to themselves and detract from your message.

Good delivery is simply being direct, friendly, conversational, animated, and enthusiastic.

SUMMARY

In this chapter we have sought to introduce the fields of communication and speech and to present a few elementary principles as a means of providing you with the essential tools of effective speech-making.

Communication, in its broadest sense, is the process of sending and receiving messages. All communication involves the following ingredients: a source, encoding, a message, a channel, a receiver, and decoding. When these ingredients are combined in human communication, certain working principles seem to emerge: (1) communication is a two-way process, (2) communication seeks to elicit a response, (3) communication involves ideas and feelings, (4) communication is a symbolic process, (5) communication is a "real-life" process, (6) the receiver's response, or lack of response, is the best test of communication, and (7) communication is complex.

The responsibility and seriousness of communication are so great that communicators must be of the highest ethical character. This means that they should know the subject, respect the intelligence of their listeners, treat their content in an honest manner, and realize that they are changing behavior—both theirs and the receivers'.

In preparing early speeches, the student should remember to determine the purpose of the speech, choose and limit the topic, analyze the audience and the speaking occasion, gather material, organize and arrange the material, and practice aloud.

In delivering speeches it is essential that you have a good mental attitude, that you be direct, that you be physically animated, and that you use vocal variety.

Suggested Readings

Andersen, Kenneth E. *Introduction to Communication Theory and Practice.* Menlo Park: Cummings Publishing Co., 1972. Chapters 1 and 16.

Berlo, David K. *The Process of Communication.* New York: Holt, Rinehart and Winston, 1960. Chapters 1–2.

Brooks, William O. *Speech Communication.* 2d ed. Dubuque, Ia.: Wm. C. Brown Company Publishers, 1974. Introduction.

Monroe, Alan H., and Ehninger, Douglas. *Principles and Types of Speech Communication*. 7th ed. Glenview, Ill.: Scott, Foresman and Co., 1974. Chapters 1 and 4.

Nilsen, Thomas R. *Ethics of Speech Communication*. Indianapolis: Bobbs-Merrill Co., 1966.

Smith, Donald. *Man Speaking: A Rhetoric of Public Speaking*. New York: Dodd, Mead and Co., 1969. Chapter 1.

Verdeber, Rudolph F. *Communicate!* Belmot, Calif.: Wadsworth Publishing Co., 1975. Chapter 1.

Webb, Ralph, Jr. *Interpersonal Speech Communication: Principles and Practices*. Englewood Cliffs, N.J.: Prentice-Hall, 1975. Chapter 1.

Your First Speeches
Getting Started

2

In chapter 1 we noted that most communication acts are initiated because an individual seeks to accomplish a purpose or fulfill a goal. In public speaking, which is simply a specialized form of human communication, the speaker wants a specific response from the audience and communicates in order to secure that response. However, there is one major characteristic of public speaking that often sets it apart from some other types of interaction. In public speaking, the speaker has a *preconceived* purpose—a purpose that has been decided upon *before* the talk begins. Although many interpersonal situations also contain this element, it is not nearly as manifest as it is in public speaking. Imagine, if you will, trying to talk to an audience without having a clear idea of what you wanted them to know. By the time you concluded your remarks, they, as well as you, would be frustrated and confused as you drifted from point to point. What is needed is a unifying thread that weaves all the pieces together. That thread is the preconceived purpose. Therefore, to be a successful speaker you must decide upon and clarify your purpose before you send your message. By deciding upon the response you want from your audience, you can better select the ideas, the organizational patterns, the language, and the delivery methods that will enable you to reach your goal. Salespersons who come to your door may present an interesting talk with countless pieces of practical information, but their ultimate purpose is to persuade. Unless the materials contained within their speeches are aimed at securing their purpose, they will not make the sale.

FORMULATING A GENERAL PURPOSE

The classification of speech purposes has long been a subject of controversy among rhetoricians and teachers of communication. Since ancient times disagreements have arisen over the number and the nature of these purposes. However, critical study of the historical arguments leads us to conclude that there are three general speech purposes—to **inform,** to **persuade,** and to **entertain.** These three purposes apply equally to public or private communication.

We should remember as we discuss these speech purposes that we are in reality talking about responses we *desire* from our audience. Any discourse concerning this topic must take into account the obvious fact that all individuals are different, and therefore what is intended by the speaker as a speech to *inform* may well *persuade* or *entertain* certain members of the audience. Although all three types of speeches will be treated in greater detail later in the book, they are introduced now as a means of offering you some working principles early in your speech training.

INFORMATIVE SPEECHES

The purpose of informative communication is to increase the receiver's knowledge and understanding of a subject. Informative speeches may also entertain or change beliefs. A speaker whose immediate purpose is to impart information often uses amusing or dramatic illustrations to entertain his or her audience, thus holding their attention. Moreover, information, even if it consists only of "facts," may lead to changes of belief and eventually to physical action, although such results may not be a part of the speaker's purpose.

In informative speaking, your main concern is having the audience learn and remember the information you present. The teacher talking to a class or the manager of a department store explaining the duties of a job to staff members are both engaged in informative speaking. How much the listener knows at the conclusion of a talk is indeed the real test of the speech to inform.

Some examples of informative subjects would be:

1. The procedures to be followed for adding new courses to the college curriculum.
2. How to grow vegetables in an organic garden.
3. The workings of a pollution-free engine.
4. An explanation of California's marijuana laws.
5. A review of the life of Martin Luther King.

PERSUASIVE SPEECHES

The major function of the persuasive speech is to induce the audience to think, feel, or act in a manner selected by the speaker. You may want your listeners to discard old beliefs or form new ones, or you may want merely to strengthen opinions that they already hold. You may even want them to take some action. The salesperson uses the speech to persuade as a means of getting the customer to buy a coat. The person asking for a raise, the young college student asking for a date, the wife trying to get her husband to mow the lawn, the Red Cross volunteer pleading for funds, the teacher trying to get his or her class to study—all are trying to persuade someone to do something. An analysis of your own daily life will disclose the frequent need for effective persuasion.

The following are examples of persuasive subjects:

1. Final examinations in our colleges should be abolished.
2. Students should be given college credit for campaigning in behalf of political candidates.

3. Birth control pills should be distributed by the college Health Services Department.
4. All college courses on this campus should be on an elective basis.
5. The United States should condemn the actions of Rhodesia's government.

ENTERTAINING SPEECHES

The third major type of speech has the purpose of entertaining the audience. We are using the word *entertainment* in its broadest sense to include anything that stimulates a pleasurable response, whether it be humorous or dramatic.

The speaker wants the people present to have an enjoyable time listening to the speech. There is no concern that they learn a great deal or that they change their mind in one direction or another. Entertainment is the purpose of many after-dinner speeches and a favorite type of speech for the comedian.

Some subjects that lend themselves to humorous treatment are:

1. My first day as a college student.
2. My favorite method for securing a blind date.
3. The gourmet food served in the college cafeteria.
4. How to "see" San Francisco on fifty cents a day.
5. How to write a political speech.

These, then, are the three major speech purposes. If you know exactly what the purpose of your speech is, you will have a guide for your preparation —a reminder that each bit of material contained in your speech should contribute something to the accomplishment of your purpose. We shall examine each of these general purposes in greater detail later in the text.

FORMULATING THE SPECIFIC PURPOSE

We have already decided that the general reaction you want to secure from your audience may be stated in terms of informing, persuading, or entertaining. But the particular and immediate reaction that you seek must be precisely formulated into a *specific purpose*. **The specific purpose describes the exact nature of the response you want from your audience.** It states specifically what you want your audience to know, feel, believe, or do.

There are three requirements a good specific purpose should meet. It should contain but one central idea. It should be clear and concise. And most important, it should be worded in terms of the audience response desired.

When your general purpose is to *inform*, your specific purpose might be:

1. To have the audience understand the important aspects of student government.
2. To have the audience understand the basic fundamentals of boating safety.

3. To have the audience understand the history of the modern Women's Rights movement.

   If your general purpose is to *persuade,* your specific purpose might be:

1. To get the audience to give money to a college fund to beautify the campus.
2. To get the audience to agree that the United States should withdraw all its troops from Germany.
3. To get the audience to agree that we should have a Department of Black Studies on campus.

   If your general purpose is to *entertain,* your specific purpose might be:

1. To hear the audience laugh at the "clear" statements of some political leaders.
2. To have the audience enjoy hearing about the best ways to stay out of college.
3. To have the audience enjoy, vicariously, my trip to the Jazz Music Festival.

You might find it helpful to write down your specific purpose on a sheet of paper. This will give you a constant target at which to aim. It allows you, at a glance, to see if the material you have gathered, and the organization of that material, directly relates to your specific purpose.

CHOOSING THE METHOD
OF SPEAKING

Regardless of your background, knowledge, or skill, each time you speak it is a different and unique experience. An effective communicator will recognize these differences and prepare specifically for each particular occasion. Included in his or her thought and preparation will be an analysis of the type of delivery best suited for the subject, audience, and occasion.

There are four fundamental ways of presenting a speech: (1) by reading it from a manuscript, (2) by delivering it from memory, (3) by delivering it in an impromptu manner, and (4) by delivering it extemporaneously. It should be pointed out that there are many speaking situations that may call for a combination of two or three of these types.

SPEAKING FROM A
MANUSCRIPT

In this form of delivery you read your speech directly from a manuscript. In some instances this type of delivery is essential and appropriate. For example, on radio and television many speakers have to be accountable for their remarks and must be extremely accurate in what they say and in the amount of time they take to say it. Indeed, all speakers should be accountable and accurate, but the mass-media speaker has to be able to make instant referrals to sources and materials. At conventions and business meetings the manuscript is helpful for the speaker who would like a speech to be circulated.

There are certain advantages to manuscript speaking in addition to those cited above. The obvious advantage is that it puts no strain on your memory. Your speech is before you and you need only read it. A second advantage is that the manuscript, having been written well in advance of the speech situation, enables you to be very selective and meticulous in your style and choice of materials. The manuscript speech should be free from vague phrases, rambling sentences, and inappropriate colloquialism.

There are also serious disadvantages to this type of delivery. One marked disadvantage is that you often lose sight of the importance of communication. You read your remarks and many times fail to establish rapport with your listeners. The manuscript becomes more significant than the audience. When this happens all eye contact and all sense of spontaneity are forgotten.

For the beginning speech student trying to acquire the ability of sharing personal ideas and feelings, the manuscript type of delivery is not nearly as helpful—nor is it likely to be as effective—as the impromptu and extemporaneous methods. But if you find occasions for the manuscript, remember to (1) write your speech for listeners and not for readers, (2) practice reading aloud, (3) remember eye contact and other techniques of effective delivery, and (4) concentrate on getting your *ideas* across, not just the *words*. (We will have more to say about the manuscript speech in chapter 10.)

SPEAKING FROM MEMORY

The memorized speech, much like the manuscript, allows you the advantage of a carefully worked out and worded speech. Every single word is committed to memory and this, of course, frees you from the manuscript. One problem of the memorized speech is that this "freedom" often leads to mechanical delivery and the presentation of what often appears as a "canned" speech.

The memorized speech is also dangerous because one is apt to forget the entire speech. It is often difficult to recall the exact wording; and if you forget one word, you may forget the entire speech.

Even though the memorized speech permits a careful ordering of your thoughts and materials, it should nevertheless be avoided by the beginning speaker. Training in the other methods will offer the beginning student practice in speech situations that more closely resemble "real-life" occasions.

IMPROMPTU DELIVERY

When you are asked to speak on the spur of the moment, without advance notice or time for specific preparation, you are engaging in impromptu speaking. It has been remarked that much of our conversation is nothing more than a series of short, impromptu talks.

In facing an impromptu situation you must quickly tie together all of your thoughts in a few seconds or minutes. The best preparation for impromptu speaking is being well informed and having practice in the prepared speaking situations. The speaker who knows how to prepare a speech when time is *not* a factor in preparation will have little trouble in making the transition to the spur-of-the-moment occasion. Elsewhere in this volume we will examine the problems, principles, and skills of impromptu speaking in an individualized manner.

EXTEMPORANEOUS DELIVERY

The extemporaneous delivery is often referred to as the "middle course." This particular speech form is by far the most desirable of the four we have listed. Therefore, we will examine it in some detail.

Extemporaneous speaking has a number of characteristics that help explain both its uniqueness and its attractiveness. To be more specific, extemporaneous speaking calls for the speech to be (1) researched, (2) outlined, (3) practiced, and (4) delivered in a conversational manner.

When you choose the extemporaneous method you are also making a decision concerning *research* and *preparation*. Because you know about your speaking assignment beforehand, you have time to gather the necessary information. For example, if you were going to give an extemporaneous speech on the various methods of birth control, you would have to begin by finding out all you could about that particular subject. This investigation should be complete and thorough.

Once the data is gathered, the extemporaneous speaker must *organize* and *outline* the material into a clear and systematic pattern. A major advantage of the extemporaneous speech is that it is prepared in advance, and is therefore well organized. You are not asked to speak off the "top-of-your-head," but rather are granted the luxury of time to prepare.

This time factor not only affords you an opportunity for research and organization, it also means you can practice the speech and clarify your thinking. The exact language for delivery is not memorized; instead, the *speaker learns the organizational pattern,* main points and subpoints. The focus, during practice, is on ideas, not specific words. Too much practice can give your speech the appearance of a formal stage performance rather than a conversation. "Canned" or artificial speeches usually seem to lack sincerity, and often the artificiality calls attention away from the content of the speech. Learning your outline does not mean memorizing your speech.

Extemporaneous delivery usually means that notes will be employed. When using notes you should follow a few guidelines. First, your notes should be on small stiff cards rather than on long sheets of paper. Because a card is small, it should not impede any of your gestures. In addition, a small note card allows you to maintain your eye contact with the audience. When using a sheet of paper, some speakers find themselves reading, and in so doing they break the crucial link between sender and receiver.

Second, you should not write the entire speech on your note cards. A good general rule of thumb says that you should only write down what it takes to remind you of your main points and subpoints. For example, if your topic is water pollution, your note card on the causes of the problem might say:

WATER POLLUTION—CAUSES

1. OVERPOPULATION
2. POOR WASTE DISPOSAL METHODS
3. LACK OF CONCERN
   a. INDUSTRY
   b. PUBLIC
   c. GOVERNMENT

Third, there will be many occasions when you might want to write long quotations and statistics on your note cards. We have all heard speakers present false or misleading information because they tried to remember a long quotation or a series of numbers and failed.

The shortcomings of the extemporaneous method are probably obvious to you now that we have discussed three other styles. Admittedly, the extemporaneous method takes time. As we indicated, research, outlining, and practice cannot be done in haste. A second possible disadvantage of the extemporaneous form is in the area of language. Because the speech is not written out word for word or memorized, the beginning speaker often becomes careless in his choice of language. In so doing, there is a tendency to rely completely on inspiration for one's vocabulary. This particular indictment is really directed more at the misapplication of the method than at an inherent weakness in the method itself. For there is nothing in the explanation of this form of speaking that should allow you to believe that language is unimportant. In fact, the notion of preparation and practice implies that all phases of the communication process are of equal significance.

ANALYZING THE AUDIENCE

Most of us can remember when we first received our driver's license. "The family car" became an issue of great importance. Reflect on the intrigue and plotting that went into your securing permission to use the car. You had a multitude of methods and devices you could use on your father as a means of gaining your desired end—the keys to the car. Arguments ranging from "Dad, I'll wash the car" to "All my friends are driving" were used on those occasions. But when it came time for you to plead your case before your mother, you most likely brought forth an entire new set of techniques. You discovered at an early age that what accomplished your purpose with Dad often failed with Mom. When talking to your parents on topics ranging from the car to staying out late at night you had to adjust your position, and hence your message, from person to person.

While you were considering your parents' attitude toward cars, driving, responsibility, etc., you were conducting an **audience analysis.** And as you changed your message on each occasion you were using the material you gained from your analysis. **Audience analysis** means, in a very practical sense, *finding out all you can about the people you are talking to or will be talking to*. You discover what your receivers are like so that you can adapt your material directly to their needs, wants, experiences, and attitudes. Only by seeing things from their viewpoint can you deal directly with their predispositions. Remember that communication is a two-way process involving sender and receiver, and that the heart of communication is behavior change. In order to change people's behavior we must, obviously, deal directly with them. The insurance agent knows about a potential client before preparing a "sales pitch." The agent must make direct contact in order to be a successful communicator and accomplish his or her purpose.

As a public speaker you must also make an analysis of your audience if your speech is to be meaningful and not merely a verbal exercise. The speaker who presents a speech without considering the audience has very little chance of gaining support or being understood. Audience analysis enables you to establish rapport with your listeners and to promote rapport amongst listeners. This you do by discovering some common denominators that exist in spite of individual and group differences. By understanding your audience you can adapt your materials—and yourself—to the people with whom you want to communicate. Central to this idea, and to the entire process of communication, is the concept of identification. In his *Rhetoric of Motives,* Kenneth Burke suggests, "you persuade a man only insofar as you can talk his language by speech, gesture, tonality, order, image, attitude, idea, identifying your ways with his." What Burke is proposing is that successful communication must necessarily ask the speaker to "talk the language" of those he or she hopes to influence. Audience analysis allows you an opportunity to learn the language of your receivers so that you will be able to fuse your goals and purposes with theirs.

YOUR LISTENERS—
WHAT DO THEY BRING TO
COMMUNICATION?

Thus far we have been discussing your potential receivers in rather abstract terms. You may even have asked yourself whether or not audience analysis is even possible. In chapter 1 we noted that each individual was different from every other individual—that a person's uniqueness was his or her most universal trait. Placed in this context your question regarding the possibility of audience analysis is indeed a valid one.

Admittedly the concept of "the audience" is an abstraction. No such creature exists. In reality what you are faced with is a group of individual auditors—who in combination make what we call an audience. Your task, if you are to be a successful speaker, is to locate their commonalities and formulate your message accordingly.

To predict audience responses to what you possibly will say demands that you ask the crucial question: To what extent are the members of the audience

What we bring to communication has
an influence.

likely to be *similar?* It is in this area of *similarities* where you must focus your energy and attention.

Perhaps the best way to begin our analysis of "similarities" is by asking you to return to chapter 1. Briefly examine the communication model we set forth in that chapter, and you shall see why any discussion of audience analysis must include a section on "What We Bring to Communication." Simply stated, what an individual *brings* to an encounter influences how that individual behaves *during* and *after* that encounter. You know from your own experiences that you and a friend can leave a classroom or a movie theatre together and reach different conclusions concerning the worth and merit of the event. You found the communication dull and hard to pay attention to. Your companion, receiving "the same messages," was greatly entertained and completely captivated for the entire period. Or think of those occasions when you heard a speaker discussing "race relations" and decided he or she was a bigot. Yet when you shared the speaker's remarks with another member of the audience, you were surprised to hear the speaker branded a "flaming liberal." These examples, and the countless others we face each day, give credence to the notion that our backgrounds determine how we receive and respond to the remarks of others.

As you might well imagine, it is quite difficult to investigate the impact and influence of what each of us brings to a communication experience. What is manifested might be as current as what the receiver was doing *one minute before* you sent your message (for example, persons receiving bad news as they were about to walk into the room to listen to you). This "mood of the moment" could affect their response to you and your message. On the other hand, what happened to them *ten years earlier* could also have an effect on how they responded to you. We are once again left with trying to locate the essential similarities existing among the members of our audience. It is the isolating of these personality and cultural parallels that will be the main concern of this section. Once we have examined the role of our backgrounds in communication we will discuss some areas of audience analysis that must be dealt with before each specific speaking situation.

GENERAL CONCEPTS

This section will examine, in a general way, those factors that we bring to a communication situation that are apt to affect our behavior both during and after the experience. In essence, what we are doing is constructing a human model. We are suggesting some ways of viewing humanity so that we will be able to predict how it will behave in a communication situation. Most scholars of human behavior hold to the belief that people, and many of their actions, can be understood if they are viewed as both biological and social animals. Each of us is a product of heredity and culture. This orientation helps explain both our individuality and our commonality. An understanding of these two points will help you to comprehend what your communication counterpart is bringing to the communication situation. And, in turn, this information should help you formulate your messages.

Our Biological Link

Many ethologists believe that the best way to understand and predict human behavior is to compare it with the behavior of animals. In recent years such books as *On Aggression, The Territorial Imperative, The Naked Ape,* and *Love and Hate* have stressed the premise that much of humanity's behavior, like that of other animals, is fashioned by its evolutionary history. This approach contends that our reaction to violence, touching, aggression, and territory can be linked to our past. Therefore, to understand how people will respond, we must understand this link. What is being suggested is that our genetic bond is more complex than what is transmitted from our parents. More specifically, genetic transmission helps determine specific forms of detailed social interaction. This particular explanation of human behavior maintains that our heredity pack (46 chromosomes and 30,000 genes) not only transmits characteristics from our parents, but also qualities that are hard to isolate and document. In short, our mothers and fathers give us potentials for intelligence and personality, but a much older history, one going back millions of years, may also help define our actions. Realizing the full impact of this notion will aid you in understanding yourself and the people with whom you will be asked to communicate.

The Influence of Culture

The role culture plays in determining our behavior is a more manageable position to explain than was heredity. Not only is its explanation less complicated, but its specific influence is easier to document. Culture is best described as humanity's cultivated behavior. More specifically, it is the totality of learned and accumulated experience which is socially transmitted from generation to generation. What this means is that our culture gives each of us, in both conscious and subconscious ways, modes of behavior, patterns of thought, ideas and values, and even many of our habits. For the communicator, the ramifications of this definition should be obvious. To understand our coparticipants in the encounter we must know something about the culture that has acted upon them during their lifetime. For as this section has stressed, where we come from, our backgrounds and experiences, helps determine how we will respond to a communication situation. Reflection and common sense will tell you that the Englishman has had different experiences than has the Russian or the Italian, and these experiences are apt to be quite different from yours.

There are also many subcultures that have influenced us in the past, and hence will affect our thoughts and actions in the present and the future. Homosexuals, people who have been in prison, the poor, motorcycle gangs, some drug users, and many other subcultures have developed their own codes of conduct and value systems.

Most cultures and subcultures work in combination on our personal and private histories. Figure 2–2 graphically shows the relationship between culture, subculture, and our individual biographies.

As we have said throughout this chapter, the successful communicator must have some idea of how culture will manifest itself during a communication situation. Most researchers in the area of intercultural communication be-

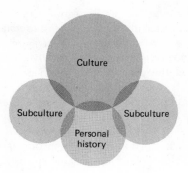

Figure 2–2

lieve that cultures and subcultures influence values and attitudes, patterns of thought, perception, language, and nonverbal behavior. Each of these areas is important enough to warrant further consideration. Therefore, let us offer a few brief examples in each category as a means of clarification.

The influence of cultural *attitudes* and *values* on communication should be quite apparent. As we said earlier, a culture gives one a world view that is often unique to that culture. The Chinese, for example, have an attitude toward life that relies on humanity rather than God to solve problems or other difficulties. For the Japanese, group loyalty and responsibility to the group are of prime importance. Different cultures even have varying views regarding women. Women's liberation, for instance, has not yet found its way to Mexico or Japan. These and countless other examples should demonstrate how our cultural backgrounds can affect our responses to a message.

The way we think, our *patterns of thought,* also shifts from culture to culture. The Western thought pattern is rather rigid and structured. This Aristotelian mode of reasoning is based on logic and the syllogism. The non-Aristotelian orientation, which is common in the Orient, depends on chance, fate, and often irrational sources for many conclusions.

Our *perception* of a communication act is often dominated by our culture. The judgment of beauty, for instance, is culturally based. In the United States thin women tend to represent the cultural stereotype of attractiveness. However, in much of Europe a heavy female is more desirable than a slim one. Even what constitutes a violent act has its roots in our culture.

The *language* that is employed in communication is also a reflection of culture. Many subcultures evolve language codes that are part of their cultural experience. Blacks, for example, have an entire glossary of terms that are unique to their culture. "To jive" may mean a way of dancing to the person raised in the fifties, but to the black of today it has a very different meaning.

The *nonverbal* behaviors of a culture, which are brought to an encounter, are often displayed during that meeting. Each culture, in obvious and subtle ways, teaches its members various uses and responses to such things as space, time, movement, eye contact, facial expressions, and touch. As we attempt to communicate with a variety of people, coming from a host of cultures and subcultures, it is imperative that we know something about cultural variations that are apt to influence communication. Realizing that the English do not appreciate close physical contact with strangers may seem like an unimportant and trivial matter, but to the speaker trying to decide how close to stand to the audience, this little fact could be useful.

SPECIFIC CONCEPTS

Having examined in rather broad terms some of the general influences on what we bring to a communication situation, we are now ready to narrow our focus and explore some specific areas that must be analyzed by the speaker before he or she begins preparation in earnest.

1. *Discover the age of your listeners.* You know from past experience that you talk differently to a group of junior high school students than to a class of college students. Even what you talk about is influenced by the age differences. It is important for you as a speaker to be sensitive to the problems that arise from age variations. Many times insight into age may also give insight into the past experiences of the audience. The depression, for example, may be a meaningful memory to an older person but only secondhand information to a younger individual. There are countless experimental studies that have revealed the effect age plays on interests, learning, opinion change, and the like. These research projects have tried to document the influence of age on communication. Their findings reveal a number of interesting conclusions. For example, because older people have had a larger variety of experiences, they are inclined to become more entrenched in their opinions and hence much harder to persuade. At the same time, studies suggest that younger children are very susceptible to persuasion. Research also seems to indicate that as we get older, social sensitivity and empathy tend to increase.

Considerations of age also make it imperative for the speaker to review language similarities and differences. Words such as *grass, stoned,* and *busted* are clearly related to age.

Admittedly, generalizations about different age groups are subject to many exceptions. Yet, by and large, a group of old people will differ in attitude and experiences from a group of young people. This simple realization will greatly aid the speaker in selecting materials to accomplish his or her purpose.

2. *Discover the sex of your listeners.* Is it a mixed audience? The answer to this question may govern everything from your choice of subject to the examples you decide to place in your speech. Even though women have been "emancipated" in many areas, the two sexes often live in different worlds. To explore the impact of our sex roles on communication would be a never-ending task, for our particular gender propels us, in both subtle and manifest ways, to behave according to certain cultural patterns. A few communication examples will give emphasis to this idea. Women tend to learn faster than men. On

certain topics women appear to be easier to persuade. Women are believed to be superior in verbal skills and more effective in developing empathy. You also know from your own experience that there are countless other differences that our culture has imposed on each sex. The public speaker must be aware of these differences and try to ascertain their effect on the message.

3. *Try to find out the occupation of your listeners.* What people do for a living is often a guide to their values, attitudes, and even their sense of humor. You know that a farmer may see things differently than a school teacher or a small shopowner. Ask yourself, is the occupation of my audience relevant to my topic?

4. *Discover the intelligence and educational level of your listeners.* In order for communication to take place it is necessary that the audience be able to understand what you say. You must be very careful not to overestimate or underestimate the intelligence of your listeners. In either case the cycle of communication can be broken if there is a lack of understanding. You should remember that formal education as well as education acquired through practical experience will help determine what your audience thinks about and how they react.

5. *Try to discover to what social, professional, and religious groups your listeners belong.* We see ourselves and others in terms of the roles we play, and the groups to which we belong contribute to the making of these roles. Group membership suggests, in a general way, types of people, their points of view, interests, and attitudes. It is apparent that such things as religious affiliation will influence our thinking on many topics. When you can learn the group membership of a large part of your audience, you have gained a valuable clue to listeners' attitudes and wants.

6. *Try to understand the influence of your listeners' geographical experiences.* Where we have been raised and where we live help determine what we believe and how we act. The small rural high school, with its 4-H programs and agricultural classes, offers experiences that are quite different from the situations faced by the student attending a large high school in the city. Interests and attitudes are partly shaped by these geographic experiences. For example, someone from an industrial section of the country, who earns a living working in a factory, might well have a view of conservation that is in conflict with the person from Montana.

There are even vocabulary shifts as we move from one geographical region to another. Someone from a surfboard-riding area would most likely know words like *hang-ten, tubes,* and *soup,* while the person from a horse region would have specific meanings for *bot eggs, tapaderos,* and *curb chain.*

In addition to exploring the backgrounds of your listeners, you will find a number of other questions useful once you have established a profile of your audience. (1) What does the audience already know about me? (2) What is the audience's attitude toward me? (3) What does the audience know about the subject? (4) What is the audience's opinion of my subject? (5) What brings the audience together? The answer to each of these questions will make possible a more complete understanding of the entire speaking situation.

YOUR SPEAKING OCCASION

We have already established the importance of knowing your audience as a means of selecting, preparing, adapting, and adjusting your speech so that it will accomplish your preconceived purpose. The speaking occasion also demands a careful analysis. Indeed, where you deliver your speech plays a prominent role in the entire communication process. A famous American humorist once observed that he could never speak in jest in a church chapel.

A speaker's analysis of the occasion should involve the following considerations:

1. *What kind of occasion will it be?*   This question is relevant because it affects the tone and purpose of the meeting, and hence the speech itself. Your initial concern should therefore be to discover why the meeting is being held. Have the people gathered only to hear your speech or do they meet on a regular basis? The speaker should also know whether the procedure will be ritualistic, parliamentary, formal, or informal. Finally, questions pertaining to the location of the meeting and the time of day should be investigated. All of these factors will have an influence on the speech.

2. *What will the physical surroundings be like?*   The physical setting in which the speech is delivered often contributes considerably to the success or failure of the speaker's attempt to get a message across. The speaker should consider factors related to whether or not the speech is delivered indoors or outside, the acoustics of the room or hall, the presence or absence of a public address system, the seating arrangements, lighting arrangements, and any outside distractions and noises. All of these factors will govern, to some degree, the mood and attention span of the audience.

3. *What will precede and follow the speech?*   Your message is never sent to a passive, inactive mind. Instead you must always remember, whether on or off the speaker's platform, that your listeners had a "state of mind" before you sent your first sound. They were thinking about something before you entered their life spaces and asked for attention—what they *were* doing is important. You should know whether or not your speech comes before or after dinner, whether other speakers will precede you, and other factors related to the mental state of the listeners.

4. *Are there any rules, rituals, and customs associated with the gathering?* The customs of the meeting might well have a control over the speaker's dress, delivery, language, and choice of subject.

EMPATHY

During the last section of this chapter we have endeavored to substantiate the concept that to be an effective communicator one must take into account the person or persons who are to receive the message. The speaker is but one half of the communication process; the audience is the second half. Being able to understand the audience is, in a real sense, being able to see things as the audience sees them. Once you are able to see and to feel as the audience does, you are in a position to put into words those ideas that will elicit maximum agreement and understanding.

All human communication, to one degree or another, demands that the sender of a message make some predictions about how people will respond to that message. We can say that all of us carry around in our minds images of other people, and take these images into account whenever we speak. We noted earlier that your image of your mother and father influenced what you said and how you said it. The successful communicator is one who is accurate in his or her prediction and fully understands the receiver. When we make predictions we are assuming we have skill in what the psychologist calls **empathy**—the process of projecting ourselves into other people's personalities. By trying to place ourselves in the shoes of the receiver we are developing empathy. Audience analysis is but one means of developing empathy. By analyzing your audience, finding out their attitudes, desires, backgrounds, interests, and goals, you are constructing a picture of them that will enable you to make predictions. It is only by empathy—the sharing of another's personality—that one can hope to send messages that are meaningful and real.

GATHERING DATA FOR EMPATHY

To project ourselves into another's personality, so that we can make predictions about how an individual will respond to us and our message, demands that we have a picture or an image of the other person. *Who is he or she?* How do I gather the data to answer that question? Basically we gather the data for our image of the other person in four closely related phases.

The first pieces of information that help form our images often come to us *before the communication encounter.* How often have you had someone tell you about Professor Jones before you met Jones? They tell you "he is a good guy, likes students, but is strict regarding attendance." This information, supplied *before you ever communicate* with Jones, helps you construct your image and, hence, helps you predict what messages and behavior will be appropriate. In addition, before the actual communication act, you may find out that the other person is a doctor, teacher, plumber, student, or bus driver. This information, once again preencounter, gives you possible data for your prediction.

One should be cautious of the danger of responding to the preencounter image as if, in some way, it represented the entire person. Empathy can be hindered by responding to only part of the image.

The second source of information regarding the other person often comes to us quickly and before any words pass between the two parties. This *nonverbal (preverbal)* information comes to us in a variety of forms. For example, there is some research that suggests that some of our images and impressions come from our first eye contact with another person. How many times have you looked someone in the eye, before a word was ever spoken, and felt you liked this person and knew something about him or her? The term *charisma* is often used to describe the "feeling" we have about another person—a feeling that is hard to isolate and label.

We get other nonverbal information about a person before we start to exchange words. Our image of the other person is shaped by such nonverbal areas as dress, manner, stature, and the like. In all instances we use this information to construct a profile of the person with whom we are to communicate.

The third body of information we gather comes from the *verbal messages* we get from other people. What we hear people say gives us a great deal of insight into what they are like. If someone tells you "I always vote the straight Democratic ticket because the Republicans have never done a thing for the working person," you use this sentence to decide many other factors about the person who said it. What people talk about and what they say about the subjects they select can offer us data for our image of those people.

A fourth area of image building comes to us by means of what we might call *extraneous messages*. By extraneous we mean that information that is often apart from the person. For example, do we not make judgments and generalizations about people when we discover what kind of cars they drive, what cigarettes they smoke (if any), and what restaurants they frequent? Even where people live and the clubs they belong to offer us insight into their personalities. This extraneous data often offers us a more complete picture of other people.

What we have been suggesting the last few pages is that we gather information about other people in basically four ways, and we use this data as a means of constructing an image or profile of them. That image often tells us what these people are like, and hence we can better empathize with them. We can better make predictions about how they will respond to us and our message.

INTERFERENCE WITH EMPATHY

It might be useful for us to pause here and look briefly at those factors that might interfere with our being able to see things from another individual's point of view.

If one is going to think constantly about oneself, it is going to be difficult to concentrate on cues being given off by other people—cues which might offer insight into their personality. A successful communicator is one who cares about people, one who is able to be aware of them, and not be preoccupied with thoughts about himself or herself. In short, constant *self-focus* often hinders empathy.

Another interference is our common tendency *to note only some features of behavior* to the exclusion of others. We notice when someone doesn't smile and at once draw a conclusion about that person—a conclusion that is based on only one bit of information. People are complex, and it is an error in communication to let one isolated act represent the entire person.

Although there are many other hindrances to empathy let us conclude by mentioning but one more, and it is perhaps the most common. We refer to our tendency to react to stereotyped notions about the meaning of physical features, race, religion, and nationality. In committing this error we assume that *all* people of the same group or class are automatically alike. We forget the uniqueness of the individual.

It is hard work to empathize. It demands a commitment on the part of both parties—a commitment that says you are willing to expend the energy to discover all that you can about the other person. Research in the area of empathy indicates that high motivation (the commitment we talked about) could help one in understanding the other person's personality.

THE AUDIENCE AND EMPATHY

The audience also experiences a kind of empathy during the speaking situation. As you deliver your talk, the audience is "feeling" (sharing) the experiences along with you. For example, when you appear nervous and tense, the audience also feels uncomfortable and strained. When you can manifest sincere enthusiasm, the audience will also experience a similar sensation. You should therefore be aware of this mutual rapport, and your appearance and actions should attempt to make the audience feel at ease.

CHOOSING THE TITLE OF THE SPEECH

You may face a few occasions when you are asked to furnish a title for your speech. For example, when you are to be introduced by a chairman it would be helpful to have a "handle" for your remarks.

A good title should be brief, should suggest the nature of your purpose, should be appropriate to the occasion and the topic, and should be interesting.

Recently one of our students gave a speech, entitled "Credit Cards: Bankruptcy Made Easy," in which she reviewed the growth of credit card buying and high interest rates in the United States. Her title stimulated interest in her talk prior to the actual presentation.

SUMMARY

Communication normally takes place because the speaker wants to achieve some preconceived purpose. Thus the purpose must be clear in his or her mind. The public speaker will usually be preparing and giving speeches that fall into three general speech purposes—to **inform,** to **persuade,** and to **entertain.** In addition to selecting a general purpose, the speaker must formulate a specific purpose which describes the immediate and exact nature of the response wanted from the audience.

In deciding on a method of preparation and delivery, the speaker can utilize any one of the following procedures: (1) speaking from a manuscript, (2) speaking from memory, (3) impromptu speaking, and (4) extemporaneous speaking. The extemporaneous method is the one most recommended for the beginning speaker.

In order to adapt his or her purpose to a specific audience, the speaker should analyze the audience. Valuable insight into the listeners' needs, wants, attitudes, and experiences can be gained by discovering their age, sex, occupation, intelligence and education, and social, professional, religious affiliations, and geographical experiences.

By implementing the material gathered through an analysis of the audience and occasion, the speaker can use empathy—the projecting of oneself into the personalities of one's listeners. Knowing what the listeners are like enables the communicator "to speak their language."

Speakers may encounter situations that make it necessary for them to furnish titles for their speeches. In those cases it is important to remember that a good title is brief, appropriate, interesting, and one that suggests the nature of the purpose.

Suggested Readings

Andersen, Martin P.; Nichols, E. Nay, Jr.; and Booth, Herbert W. *The Speaker and His Audience: Dynamic Interpersonal Communication.* 2d ed. New York: Harper and Row, Publishers, 1974, Chapter 9.

Andersen, Kenneth E. *Introduction to Communication Theory and Practice.* Menlo Park: Cummings Publishing Co., 1972. Chapter 4.

Blankenship, Jane. *Public Speaking: A Rhetorical Perspective.* Englewood Cliffs, N.J.: Prentice-Hall, 1966. Chapter 3.

Carson, Herbert L. *Steps in Successful Speaking.* Princeton, N.J.: D. Van Nostrand Co., 1967. Part 2.

Clevenger, Theodore Jr. *Audience Analysis.* Indianapolis: The Bobbs-Merrill Co., 1966.

Dickens, Milton. *Speech: Dynamic Communication.* 3d ed. New York: Harcourt Brace Jovanovich, 1974. Chapter 11.

Hasling, John. *The Message, The Speaker, The Audience.* New York: McGraw-Hill Book, 1971. Chapter 10.

Oliver, Robert T., and Cortright, R.L. *Effective Speech.* 5th ed. New York: Holt, Rinehart and Winston, 1970. Chapter 10.

Weaver, Carl H. *Speaking in Public.* New York: American Book Co., 1966. Chapter 17.

3

Sound and Action
Presenting the Message

Peggy was asked to prepare a six-minute speech to inform for presentation to her speech class the following week. She followed carefully the advice she had been given on preparing speech content. She analyzed her listeners carefully and, with a view to their needs, selected a topic that would have value for them. She formulated a specific purpose and set about to find the materials that would enable her to achieve her purpose. After she had gathered her materials she fashioned them into a well-organized, understandable, and interesting message. She presented her speech as scheduled and awaited the evaluation of her classmates and instructor. By their comments it was apparent that they had paid less attention to her ideas than to her manner of presenting those ideas. One listener remarked, "Peggy, you didn't seem to be interested in what you were saying. I had a hard time forcing myself to listen."

Unfortunately, Peggy's experience is all too common. Countless worthwhile ideas go unheeded because they are ineptly presented, and countless other ideas are misinterpreted because of misleading cues in speakers' nonverbal behavior. Imperfections in communication may result when the nonverbal elements are not supportive of the verbal elements—senders' words tell you one thing while the sound of their voices and their actions tell you something else. Which set of elements are you going to believe?

The importance of nonverbal elements was underlined by Dean C. Barnlund when he wrote:

> Many, and sometimes most, of the critical meanings generated in
> human encounters are elicited by touch, glance, vocal nuance, gestures,
> or facial expression with or without the aid of words. From the moment
> of recognition until the moment of separation, people observe each
> other with all their senses, hearing pause and intonation, attending to
> dress and carriage, observing glance and facial tension, as well as noting
> word choice syntax. Every harmony or disharmony of signals guides
> the interpretation of passing mood or enduring attribute. Out of the
> evaluation of kinetic, vocal, and verbal clues decisions are made to argue
> or agree, to laugh or blush, to relax or resist, to continue or cut off
> conversation.

The nonverbal elements of your communication behavior may tell your audience more about you than you realize. For example, your attitude toward others may be inferred from your movements toward or away from them or by other actions which seem symbolically to express intimacy, submission-dominance, and the like. Your attitude toward your verbal message is suggested by the presence of nonverbal cues which either support or belie the verbalization. And your attitude toward yourself is often expressed through nonverbal behavior. Self-confidence, or the lack thereof, frequently shows in our body language.

Almost fifty years ago Sigmund Freud pointed out, "No mortal can keep a secret. If his lips are silent, he talks with his finger tips; betrayal oozes out of him at every pore." If Freud is correct, then it is harder to censor or distort nonverbal than verbal communication. Given conflicting verbal and nonverbal cues by a speaker, an audience probably places greater credence in the nonverbal. However, it would be dangerous to generalize that our nonverbal cues are more valid than our verbal cues. The sound of the voice, the facial expression, the movements of the hand can tell lies about the speaker's internal state.

The purpose of this chapter will be to suggest principles which may assist you in bringing the nonverbal elements into alignment with the verbal. We shall be concerned with two main groups of nonverbal elements—those which the audience sees and those which it hears.

VISUAL DIMENSIONS OF PRESENTATION

Of those nonverbal elements of communication perceived visually by the audience, the three with which we shall be most concerned are the speaker's general appearance, movements, and spatial relationship to the audience. An awareness of the role each plays in influencing listener reaction to the speaker's verbal message may enable you to make constructive use of it and avoid placing barriers in your path to communication effectiveness.

YOUR GENERAL APPEARANCE

Your posture, your apparel, your facial demeanor—all send signals to the listener. We shall examine a few of the ways in which they exert an influence.

Posture

The influence of posture may be better understood if we refer to some of the more common stances adopted by speakers. One such stance, variously referred to as the "slouch" or "slump" in books on public speaking, is characterized by having most of the weight resting on one leg, while the other relaxes in a casual position, bent at the knee. This stance tends to convey an impression of speaker apathy or lethargy. If the verbal message is forceful and moving, this posture will probably be perceived as contradictory. On the other hand, if the verbal message is intentionally depicting something as devoid of excitement or vigor, this posture might be an entirely appropriate one for reinforcing the verbal message. But it is unlikely that this posture would prove to be appropriate for the entirety of a speech.

Another stance, sometimes called the "drill sergeant," finds the feet planted widely apart as though the speaker were preparing to issue orders to subordinates. This posture suggests that the speaker's attitude is domineering, officious, and intractable. Imagine trying to present a conciliatory message while standing in a posture that shouts defiance! There are, of course, occasions when one might adopt this posture with impunity because it happens to fit most comfortably with the ideas being expressed at the moment.

A third stance finds the speaker standing ramrod-straight, with feet very close together in the manner of a soldier at attention. Because the muscles are tensed, a swaying motion often occurs which can prove to be quite distracting to the viewer. The posture suggests that the speaker is very tense and nervous.

A fourth stance has these characteristics: the weight is evenly distributed on both legs, the feet are placed a comfortable distance apart, the shoulders are held straight (but not rigidly so), and the arms are allowed to hang comfortably at the sides. Such a posture tends to suggest that the speaker is comfortable but alert. For most speakers this posture will be an appropriate one to utilize during the greater part of a speech. However, one cannot prescribe a universally acceptable posture for all speakers on all occasions. The real test of a posture is its compatibility with the verbal message being uttered.

The foregoing postures have found the speaker in a standing position. We have all observed occasions when a speaker, at some point in the speech, sat on the edge of a desk or chair or perhaps sat on the apron of a stage. The seated position often communicates a feeling of informality and relaxation. Such things as the physical surroundings, the distance between speaker and audience, the social conventions operative in the communication situation, and, most importantly, the governing purpose of the communicative act will usually dictate whether the message—or any portion thereof—is delivered from a standing position, a seated position, or even a reclining position!

We shall have more to say of the postures just discussed when we turn our attention to the speaker's movements and how they are affected by the posture one adopts.

Apparel and Grooming

As listeners we tend to make generalizations about speakers from the clothes they wear, the objects they keep on their person, and their grooming generally. Before a speaker opens his mouth we "size him up" and place a tentative label on him: "He's wearing a business suit, so he must be pretty conservative." "She wearing a miniskirt. I'll bet she isn't one of those militant feminists." "He has long hair and a bushy beard. He's probably a radical freak." "Look at the size of that diamond she's wearing! Bet her old man is loaded." Then the speaker commences to talk and we reexamine that tentative label we have imposed. Perhaps we discover that the speaker's appearance has been deceiving. "Well, I'll be darned! She doesn't *look* like an engineer." "He's a college president? You've got to be kidding. He's wearing a T-shirt, denims, and tennis shoes."

We are not so much concerned with the validity of generalizations drawn by listeners on the basis of the speaker's apparel and grooming as we are in stressing the point that generalizations *are drawn,* and the speaker should be ready to accept the consequences.

It is impossible to define "appropriate dress" or "appropriate grooming" except in terms of the individual speaking situation. So it is most important for the speaker to become familiar with the audience's standards and expectations. Your grooming and apparel, like your posture, should be compatible with your subject, your purpose, your audience, and the occasion.

Facial Expression

One of the most revealing visual signals that the speaker sends comes from the face. From facial expression we form impressions of the speaker's attitude toward us, toward himself or herself, and toward the subject matter. It is possible that the expression may tell us "I like you people," "I'm really enthusiastic about my topic," "I believe what I'm saying," or it may tell us just the opposite. It may depict a wide range of emotions from fear to confidence, from joy to sadness. Tiny subtleties of expression of which we may not be consciously aware are telling us that one speaker's animation is sincerely motivated, that another speaker's animation is feigned. It is probably no coincidence that the speaker who lacks facial expression generally lacks all animation, visual and vocal. If this lack of animation stems from apathy toward the ideas being expressed, the solution would seem to be to abandon the speech rather than to affect a display of animation. While the affected animation might gain attention, it would probably result in the listener being conscious of the affectation rather than the ideas of the speech. On the other hand, if the lack of animation results from inhibition rather than from apathy, then the answer lies essentially in placing oneself in the proper psychological attitude.

YOUR MOVEMENTS

In order to appreciate the role and importance of bodily action in communication, we should be aware of these two facts about the nature of movement: (1) movement is a conveyor of meaning and (2) movement is a factor of attention.

Movement and Meaning

To watch a television program with the audio turned down is to witness the power of movement to communicate meaning. We can see at times that no dialogue is taking place—that the meaning is being communicated primarily through actions. The heroine stamps her foot in anger over a broken dish, the hero raises an amused eyebrow. No dialogue is necessary to complete the message. At other times the movement suggests only the speaker's attitude or emotional state. We need the dialogue to complete the meaning. We know the speaker is angry, but we don't know what he is angry about. So we turn up the sound to learn that he is grousing about an impending visit from his mother-in-law. Or perhaps the speaker's movements are not directly related to what he is saying at the moment. Finally, the speaker's movements may actually transmit a meaning which is contradictory to the meaning being transmitted by his words. The obviously tired and bored announcer mouthing extravagant words of praise for a product is a common case in point. He is going through the motions of enthusiasm but there is a flaccidity about his actions that tells us he is pretending.

We should note that the absence of movement—the static state—is also a conveyor of meaning. Segments of the verbal message may actually be intensified in meaning by the suspension of bodily action. All too often, however, the static state results from psychlogical factors (the inhibiting influence of a strange situation, for example) or from the adoption of a bodily position which makes movement uncomfortable or impossible.

Movement and Attention

If you were to glance up from this page for a few moments, the chances are that your eyes would rove idly around the room, not resting on anything in particular, until there was movement of some sort. Perhaps an automobile would go past your window or a curtain would stir in the breeze. Instantly your eyes would fasten on the moving object and would linger there until some more powerful stimulus drew them away. *Movement draws attention.*

There are many applications of this factor of attention in various media of communication. A motion picture will attract our attention more quickly than a still picture. A still picture that *depicts action* will attract our attention more quickly than one which depicts a static situation. Similarly, a flashing neon sign attracts us more quickly than a steadily glowing sign. The movement causes us to keep our eyes, and thus our attention, on the object.

Given this power to intensify listener attention through the appropriate use of bodily action, we are unwise not to employ it. In fact, our natural impulse *is* to use it. Bodily movement during the communicative act is a natural, spontaneous response to the stimuli of our own uttered thoughts, the reactions of the listener, and the impact of the occasion. In most informal, unstructured communication situations we use movement freely, without inhibition. We aren't even conscious of using it, because it accompanies so naturally our utterances. The public speaking situation, on the other hand, will frequently impose restraints that inhibit us from our natural impulse to move. We will root ourselves in one spot (usually behind a lectern) and remain there for the duration of the speech. We will grip the lectern or thrust our hands in our pockets or otherwise immobilize them so that they can't be used for meaningful, spontaneous gestures. Thus we are deprived of the use of an important means of reinforcing our verbal message and of successfully competing with the other stimuli that are fighting to gain the listeners' attention.

Unfortunately there is no sure "cure" for the paralysis that often besets us when we find ourselves in the formal, structured communication situation. Perhaps the adoption of a healthy mental attitude, a genuine desire to share ideas with others, is the best course to follow. The more we concentrate on our ideas and our listeners' responses to those ideas, the less we will be concerned with the inhibiting "formalities" of the public speaking occasion.

Now let us add an important qualification to our observations about the power of movement to gain and hold attention. Movements, both graceful and awkward, appropriate and inappropriate, helpful and distracting, draw our attention. So movement can be an asset or a liability. It will be an asset only if it directs the listener's attention ultimately to the verbal message being communicated.

If the role of movement is to enhance or augment the verbal message, then its effect should be essentially subliminal. Once we begin to notice the communicator's actions instead of the verbal message, then his or her purpose for communicating suffers.

Facilitating Movement

When circumstances suggest that meaningful bodily action will improve message transmission, then the communicator should adopt a bodily position which encourages (or at least does not inhibit) easy, spontaneous action. What that position should be depends upon the kind and amount of movement called for by the particular communication situation. If the occasion does not call for a formal "stand-up speech," then the movements of the speaker are likely to be largely gestural in character. When speaker and listener are in very close proximity, changing facial expressions may be the only manifestations of movement. In such cases the speaker would do well to place himself or herself in a position that does not immobilize the muscles necessary for easy use of hands, arms, and facial expression.

Perhaps we can determine the characteristics of an appropriate stance for the "stand-up speech" if we reexamine the postures which we discussed earlier. The "slouch" or "slump" tends to inhibit movement of the entire body from one location to another within the speaking area because you must first return to a position of equilibrium before you can move easily to the right or left, toward the listener, or away from the listener. So you take the path of least resistance and remain in the "slouch."

The "drill sergeant" posture tends to inhibit movement because, like the slouch, it requires you to bring your feet closer together before you initiate movement to another spot on the platform.

As we observed earlier, the "soldier at attention" posture encourages movement, but movement of the wrong kind. It produces a nervous, rocking motion that can call so much attention to itself that it overrides the verbal message.

The last posture we discussed, the "alert" posture, probably provides the best starting point for meaningful movement. From that posture many speakers find it easier to move when they feel so compelled. However, no one should prescribe such matters for another. So the best advice is to experiment with a variety of positions and make an honest appraisal of each.

Movement of the Entire Body

Movement of the entire body from one place to another within the confines of the communication situation is often motivated by a transition in ideas or by a desire to make an idea more emphatic. Lateral movements (to the speaker's left or right) frequently signal a change from one point in the message to the following point. Picture how such a lateral movement would readily accompany this statement: "Now, if you think that was a flimsy excuse, listen to the one I heard today."

A movement toward the listener is often associated with our desire to make an idea emphatic. "Now listen to this," says one person, *leaning toward* a listener in a conversation. The same principle operates in the public speaking situation except that the movement may be more pronounced; instead of leaning toward the listeners, we may actually take a step or two toward them.

We have earlier observed that the wrong kind of movement can measurably reduce the effectiveness of the verbal message. The pencil tapper, the sleeve tugger, and the nose rubber come to mind. It is probably better to have no movement at all than to have such distracting movements. They are, after all, manifestations of nervous tension seeking release. It would appear that the best way to avoid the buildup of this tension is to employ the meaningful movements we have discussed, thus affording the tension a constructive outlet.

Movement of the Hands and Arms

"Tie his hands behind his back and he can't talk!" How often we have heard this pointed reminder of the importance of gestures to the communicative attempts of some persons. Indeed, many persons are able to use gestures as substitutes for the spoken word. While we have no wish to propound a theory of communication based on gesture alone, we do wish to remind you of the power of gestural activity to heighten attention and to intensify the meaning conveyed by the spoken word.

"But it doesn't feel natural!" is a lament that every speech teacher hears when he or she suggests that a student try to employ gestural activity in a public speaking situation. Yet that same student, in a conversation out in the hall, probably utilizes scores of gestures and isn't even aware of doing so. Why does the student "freeze up" in front of an audience? Why does the act of gesturing feel "unnatural"?

Most of us acquire a number of inhibitions when we have to appear before an audience. These inhibitions are simply the manifestation of a response to a strange situation. We become tense, as we do in any fearful situation. Those same hands that moved about so freely and effortlessly when we were conversing with a friend suddenly are bound by some invisible force. Our first impulse is to get them out of sight. So we thrust them into our pockets (where they will probably begin to jingle coins and keys), we lock them behind our backs, we hide them in our armpits, we clasp them together in front of us in the so-called figleaf position, or, if a lectern is handy, we grip it until our knuckles whiten. This may well be one reason why it doesn't "feel natural" to gesture at such times; we have placed our hands and ourselves in a position which inhibits free, spontaneous movement.

Just as we have to assume a stance which will not inhibit movement of the entire body from one point to another on the platform, we have to assume a starting position for the hands and arms which does not inhibit their movement. Probably the best advice is to keep the hands and arms unencumbered.

Then when we feel the subconscious urge to gesture, they can move naturally into action.

Limitations Upon Use of Movement

Now that we have suggested ways in which bodily action can be utilized to reinforce the verbal elements of the message, we should make note of several limitations upon its use.

1. *Bodily action should be sincerely motivated.* To gesture effectively we must *feel* like gesturing. If we force ourselves to employ action when we don't feel like it, the listener can usually detect the artifice. They equate this artificiality with insincerity. If we use planned actions, we run the risk of concentrating upon the actions rather than the ideas we are uttering. Conscious use of movements, gestures, and facial expressions probably should be reserved for practice sessions.

2. *Bodily action should not be overused.* Most of us habitually utilize certain actions for emphasis, but if we're not careful, we over-work those actions to the point that the listener begins to notice the actions rather than the ideas they are supposed to emphasize. By cultivating a greater variety of actions during practice sessions, we will be less likely to overwork any one spontaneous action.

3. *Bodily action should be appropriate to the occasion.* The same speech can often be delivered in several ways, depending upon the circumstances under which it is delivered. For example, if we are speaking in a large room where there may be some distance between the speaker and the most remote section of the audience, we will have to make our actions more pronounced so that they can be clearly seen. If we have a small, intimate room, our actions will be subtler (and probably fewer in number). Careful analysis of the audience and occasion will reveal the extent to which use should be made of the visible aspects of delivery.

YOUR SPATIAL RELATIONSHIP TO THE AUDIENCE

The physical distance between you and your listeners can affect the quality of the communication encounter. It affects you as a speaker in several ways. First of all, it has an impact on your use of movement, gesture, and facial expression. If these nonverbal elements are to serve you properly, they must be seen. Therefore, the greater the distance between you and your listener, the more exaggerated these visual factors must be. Secondly, it affects your use of the voice. If there is no public address system available, you will probably have to talk louder and enunciate more distinctly as distance increases between you and your audience. Thirdly, physical distance may affect your feeling of *mental* proximity to the audience. Some speakers are disturbed when a large space separates them from their listeners. In order to "get close" to the listener mentally, they have to "get close" physically as well. The listener may well experience this same feeling. Distance may produce a feeling of estrangement from the speaker. Rapport can be affected by spatial relationships.

The most extensive studies of spatial cues have been conducted within the last fifteen years. Edward T. Hall, for example, attempted to develop a system for the classification of proxemic or spatial behavior. His schema, which should be of interest to the student of communication, is divided into various zones or proxemic distances.

Public distance—close phase—is that proxemic distance which extends from twelve to twenty-five feet. It is the distance at which a person's voice is loud and clear. Public distance is, moreover, the distance at which many interactions are first initiated.

Social distance—far phase—seems to be seven to twelve feet. This is the distance at which (1) business and social discourse of a more formal nature are conducted, (2) desks in offices are placed to hold off visitors, (3) fine details of the face and body cannot be perceived, and (4) the whole face and body of the person, with space around it, may be taken in without shifting the eyes.

Social distance—close phase—is that distance which extends from four to seven feet. At this distance the eye can take in an ever-increasing amout of the person. Close-phase social distance is the proxemic distance at which most casual social gatherings take place and which people who work together employ when interacting.

Personal distance—far phase—is the proxemic distance between two individuals extending from two and one-half to four feet. It is the distance at which one is kept at arm's length. Far-phase personal distance is the distance just outside the range of easy touching; it is also the range at which the fine details of a person's facial makeup are clearly visible. Skin texture, the presence of prematurely gray hair, wrinkles, and other features of the face can easily be seen at this distance.

Personal distance—close phase—is the proxemic distance between one and one-half to two and one-half feet. It is the distance at which one can hold or grasp the other person and where visual feedback is very noticeable.

Intimate distance—far phase—is the proxemic distance from six to eighteen inches. Detailed features of the face are clearly visible. The voice at this distance is normally held at a very low level or even a whisper.

Intimate distance—close phase—is the proxemic distance in humans extending from maximum contact to six inches. It is the distance of lovemaking, wrestling, comforting, protecting, or the distance at which physical contact or the high possibility of physical involvement is uppermost in the awareness of both persons.

It is apparent that some of the distances just described may have greater application to interpersonal encounters than to public speaking situations. Nonetheless, the speaker is well advised to remember that distance has an influence on the outcome of communication attempts of any kind. Spatial cues should be used in a manner consistent with the speaker's reason for communicating.

The space between communicating
partners tells a great deal about
the encounter.

AURAL DIMENSIONS OF PRESENTATION

While part of the speaker's message may be conveyed by visual means, it is by sound—vocalized sound—that the linguistic elements of the message are carried. But the voice does more than simply render a word-symbol into audible form; it enables us to impart various shades of meaning to that spoken word. Moreover our voice, like our posture, movements, gestures, and facial expressions, tells things about us quite apart from the verbal message we are uttering. For these reasons, then, we need to sharpen our awareness of the capabilities of the voice to help or hinder our attempts at oral communication.

VOICE AND WORD MEANING

Let us examine first how our vocal behavior affects the *sense* of what we utter. If we were to take the sentence, "Trevino is the winner," and shift the point of emphasis from one word to another, we could come up with a variety of meanings:

TREVINO is the winner (not someone else).

Trevino IS the winner (my hunch was right).

Trevino is the WINNER (not the loser).

Or note how inflectional variations modify the meaning of the simple word *"oh."*

"Oh?" (Really?)

"Oh." (I get the point.)

"Oh!" (How exciting!)

"Ohhhh!" (How revolting!)

These examples illustrate the importance of vocal behavior in adding dimension to the meaning of spoken words. The rate that we utter words, the degree of intensity we impart to each one, the variations in pitch we employ, the harshness or mellowness of the sound of each word—all add shades of meaning to the spoken word, just as punctuation marks, special type faces, and indentations modify the meaning of the written word.

VOICE AND PERSONALITY

Not only does the voice affect the meaning of the message, it also affects the listener's impression of the speaker as a person. In fact, it may very well evoke a misleading impression of the speaker as a person. A thin, weak voice may hide a person of vigor and courage. A monotonous voice may hide a person with great inner enthusiasm. The great Greek orator, Demothenes, undoubtedly realized that his speech impediment communicated a false impression of his true worth; so he labored hard to overcome the impediment. It may also be

pointed out that a voice ringing with sincerity and enthusiasm may conceal
the most unscrupulous sophist.

A word of caution to both speaker and listener is in order at this point.
The listener must not be hasty in equating tone of voice with character and
personality; the voice may be part of a mask hiding the real identity of the
speaker. The speaker, in turn, must realize that he or she is judged not only
by words spoken but by meanings that listeners attach to the sound of the voice
that carries those words.

VOICE AND ATTENTION

Earlier in this chapter we observed that movement is a factor of attention, and
we noted how movement of the body as a whole, movement of the hands
and arms, and movement of the facial muscles all served to keep the audience
attentive. This attention factor of movement or activity is applicable to vocal
behavior as well. The voice that moves—or more accurately, the voice that is
varied—holds attention. The speaker who fails to vary pitch level, volume,
speed, or tone quality may have difficulty sustaining audience attention for any
appreciable length of time unless the verbal message is especially compelling.
Of course, vocal variations should always be properly motivated. It would be
ludicrous, for example, to alter your rate of speaking just for the sake of gaining
attention. That would only call attention to your use of the device. No delivery
technique should call attention to itself; it should direct attention to the
message.

CONTROLLABLE ELEMENTS OF
VOICE

If our vocal behavior fails to gain and hold attention, fails to enhance word
meaning, or projects an inaccurate impression of personality, we tend to place
the blame upon Nature. The popular lament is, "I just wasn't born with a good
voice!" Undeniably, Nature does impose limitations upon us. Perhaps the
vocal equipment we were born with is inferior to that of our neighbors. But
it is in the use of the equipment that we are more apt to find the cause of
success or failure. Much of our vocal effectiveness depends upon the way in
which we control the loudness, pitch, quality, rate, distinctness, and correctness of the sounds we produce.

Loudness

One of the first requisites of vocal sound is that it be loud enough for comfortable hearing. The listeners may be willing to exert extra effort in order to
hear a person with a weak voice, if that person has something compelling to
say. Even so, it is likely that the sheer physical exertion of straining to hear the
speaker will ultimately cause the listener to abandon further effort. If, on the
other hand, a speaker talks at a painfully loud intensity level, the listener

will be more concerned with the discomfort of the sound than the meaning of the sound.

While attaining a comfortable loudness level should be our first concern, we must not overlook the need for *changes* in loudness level. It is by varying our loudness that we enhance word meaning and sustain attention. A speech delivered without variations in loudness is analogous to a symphony played without *crescendo* or *diminuendo*.

Changes in loudness are particularly helpful in providing emphasis to words or phrases. Uttering a word at an intensity level different from that used with the other words in a sentence will direct audience attention to its importance. While such emphasis may be attained by making the sound suddenly louder or softer, recent research suggests that a sudden change to a softer level is apt to be the more effective means of emphasis.

Pitch

The rate of vibration of the vocal folds determines the pitch of the voice. The slower the vibration, the lower the "key." The faster the vibrations, the higher the "key." The length and thickness of your vocal cords will determine the extremes of pitch which your voice is capable of producing. Persons with vocal folds of relatively great length and thickness, for example, will probably have bass voices. Whether our natural pitch range may be classified as bass, tenor, or soprano, we have a great flexibility of pitch levels within that range. When we wish to produce a higher note, a series of muscles causes our vocal folds to stretch, much in the same manner as we might stretch a rubber band. A lower note is produced by relaxing these same muscles.

Changes in pitch level within our normal range provide us with one of the most effective means of gaining attention and imparting meaning to utterance. Yet, under the duress of a formal speaking situation, some people may inhibit their natural tendency to vary the pitch level. The resultant effect, which we call monotony, robs their words of much meaning and exerts a sedative effect upon the listeners' attention. There are other people whose voices are monotonous even in informal conversation. Very likely their monotone is the product of long conditioning. For example, a person raised in a family which was opposed to any display of emotion probably learned by example to inhibit animation in delivery, both in its visual aspects and its vocal aspects. (Note how often a "poker face" and a monotonous voice go together.)

Quality

Quality is usually expressed in such terms as *strident, rasping, aspirate, mellow, harsh, orotund,* and a variety of other descriptive labels. The speaker's vocal quality can be one of the most obvious signs of emotional attitude at the moment of speaking. The speaker who is nervous usually tenses throat muscles inadvertently, and the resulting voice quality is apt to be thin and strident. As the speaker relaxes, the throat cavity enlarges, and voice quality becomes much more pleasant. When we grow angry, our voice quality becomes harsh and aspirate; when we grow nostalgic and indulge in reverie, the voice takes on an almost whispery quality.

If we truly *feel* the meaning of what we are saying, our voice quality will usually take on those characteristics which the audience associates with the sentiment we are expressing.

Rate

Intelligibility, meaning, and attention are all affected by the speaker's rate of utterance. If the rate is too fast, intelligibility may suffer. If the rate is slow when it should be fast or fast when it should be slow, meaning may suffer. Or if the rate is not varied, attention may wane.

We measure rate in terms of the number of words we utter per minute. It is generally agreed that 125 to 150 words per minute constitutes a satisfactory rate for public speaking, but modifications must be made to adapt to room acoustics, audience reactions, the atmosphere of the occasion, and most importantly, to the material of the speech.

Two factors which influence our rate of speaking are *pause* and *duration of sound*. The pause can be one of our most effective oral "punctuation marks." It does for the spoken word what the comma, colon, parenthesis, and dash do for the written word. The misplaced pause, the vocalized pause, or the pause which signals a mental blank can mar a speech that is otherwise effective. *Duration* refers to the time consumed in uttering vowel and consonant sounds. The duration of vowel sounds in particular affects word meaning. To illustrate, utter the word *long,* holding the vowel sound but briefly; now, utter the word again, prolonging the vowel sound. The emotional coloration of words is thus modified by changes in duration.

The number of words you utter per minute is, then, dependent upon how much time you spend in pausing (or hesitating) as well as in actually producing the individual sounds of each word. If you are accused of talking too fast or too slow, try to ascertain whether the problem is faulty management of duration or of pause. It is not unusual for a person, when asked to slow down his or her rate of speaking, to maintain the usual duration while pausing more often or pausing for longer periods. The real culprit in such cases is often faulty management of duration rather than an excessive number of words per minute. Eighty words per minute may seem excessive if each word is given inadequate duration.

Variety of rate is as important as variety of pitch or loudness. The speaker who seems to be following a metronome in his or her rate of utterance can cloud meaning and diminish attention almost as quickly as a person with a monotone. Emphasis and mood changes can be effectively expressed by variations in rate. For example, when we wish to emphasize one particular statement of a paragraph, we tend to utter it more slowly than the sentences which precede or follow it. A mood of excitement is usually accompanied by an acceleration in rate; a mood of sobriety, with a slowing down in rate.

Distinctness

The clarity of the sounds we produce, though determined in part by our pitch, loudness, and rate, is determined principally by the way we manage the organs of articulation. Some sounds depend upon precise lip movements, others upon critical placement of the tongue, and still others upon full use of the jaw.

Lip laziness results in the blurred enunciation of such consonants as *p, b, v,* and *f.* Tongue placement must be precise for clear production of consonants like *t, d, k,* and *g* as well as all of the vowel sounds. The importance of jaw action to clear enunciation can be seen if you try reciting the alphabet through clenched teeth.

In striving for greater precision we must avoid going to the extreme of overpreciseness, which the audience interprets as a sign of affectation. Your speech teacher may offer suggestions for the improvement of your enunciation. If so, get in the habit of implementing these improvements in your everyday conversation; then the demands of other speaking situations will be much easier to fulfill.

Correctness

While enunciation has to do with the distinctness of a spoken word, pronunciation has to do with its correctness. It is possible to enunciate a word with the greatest clarity while grossly mispronouncing it. Faults of pronunciation are apt to be less easily forgiven by the listener than faults of enunciation, because they seem to reflect the speaker's intelligence rather than just his muscular dexterity.

Probably the most practical method of determining acceptable pronunciation is to listen to the educated speakers in your particular geographic area. What might be considered as acceptable in Atlanta might not be so in Duluth, owing to differences in dialect. With the growing mobility of our society and the spread of mass media of communication, regional differences in pronunciation are becoming less evident.

For the pronunciation of little-used words, names of places, and foreign expressions, a good pronouncing dictionary is your most reliable guide. But try to use only the very latest edition, because usage may well change within a few years' time.

TAKING STOCK OF NEEDS

With these general guidelines for using bodily action and vocal variety now before you, take a careful inventory of our current delivery practices in various communication situations. Enlist the aid of friends who will offer candid views of your assets and liabilities in informal conversation, discussions, and conferences. Ask your speech instructor for an analysis of your needs in public speaking situations. Try to find answers to questions such as these: To what *degree* do I employ bodily action and effective vocal variety in each of the various communication situations? To an insufficient degree in public speaking, a sufficient degree in conversation? To a distracting degree in some cases? What is the *quality* of the action which I do employ? Does it help or hinder the communication of my ideas? Is it meaningful action? Does it call attention itself? If so, why? Does my posture communicate a positive impression? Does it combine

ease with alertness? Are my movements and gestures graceful and decisive, or
are they hesitant, tentative, lacking in vigor and enthusiasm? Do I have any
annoying mannerisms that should be curbed? Does my use of my voice add
to or detract from the communication situation? Securing answers to these
and other pertinent questions will enable you to chart your course toward
greater effectiveness in the use of visible and audible aspects of communication.

As you approach the task of improving your use of voice and bodily action
in speaking, bear in mind these words from Dr. Hugh Blair, one of the great
speech critics of the eighteenth century:

> If one has naturally any gross defect in his voice or gestures, he begins
> at the wrong end, if he attempts at reforming them only when he is to
> speak in public. He should begin with rectifying them in his private
> manner of speaking; and then carry to the public the right habit he has
> formed. For when a speaker is engaged in a public discourse, he should
> not be then employing his attention about his manner, or thinking of
> his tones and gestures. If he be so employed, study and affectation will
> appear. He ought to be then quite in earnest; wholly occupied with his
> subject and his sentiments; leaving nature, and previously formed
> habits, to prompt and suggest his manner of delivery.

SUMMARY

For effective oral communication it is essential that the verbal and nonverbal
elements of the message work in harmony. The nonverbal elements of the
message are visual and vocal. The visual constituents include the speaker's
general appearance (posture, apparel, grooming, and facial expression), movements, and spatial relationship to the audience. One's appearance should provide nonverbal cues that are compatible with the verbal message being uttered.
Movements convey meaning and help sustain attention. The speaker should
adopt a bodily position that does not inhibit spontaneous movement. Movement on the platform is generally motivated by a desire to make an idea
emphatic or to suggest a transition from one idea to another. The speaker's
action should be sincerely motivated, should be appropriate to the subject,
to the audience, and to the occasion, and should not be overused. The amount
of space between the speaker and hearer can affect the quality of the communication encounter. The speaker should employ spatial cues in a manner
consistent with the speech purpose.

The voice does more than simply render a word symbol into audible form.
It enables the speaker to impart various shades of meaning to the spoken word,
it transmits an impression of the speaker as a person, and it acts as a factor
of attention. The controllable elements of the voice are pitch, loudness, rate,
and quality. These elements should be varied in a manner consistent with the
"sense" of the verbal element of the message. Faults in distinctness of vocal
sounds are more readily forgiven than faults in the correctness of the sounds.

Acceptability of pronunciation varies from region to region. You are advised to emulate the pronunciation of the best-educated speakers in your geographical area.

Suggested Readings

Anderson, Martin; Nichols, E. R., Jr.; and Booth, Herbert. *The Speaker and His Audience*. 2d ed. New York: Harper and Row, Publishers, 1974. Chapter 13.

Bormann, Ernest G., and Bormann, Nancy C. *Speech Communication: An Interpersonal Approach*. New York: Harper and Row, Publishers, 1972. Chapters 4–5.

Brooks, William D. *Speech Communication*. 2d ed. Dubuque, Ia.: Wm. C. Brown Company Publishers, 1974. Chapter 6.

Eisenberg, Abne M., and Smith, Ralph R. *Nonverbal Communication*. Indianapolis: Bobbs-Merrill Co., 1971.

Knapp, Mark L. *Nonverbal Communication in Human Interaction*. New York: Holt, Rinehart and Winston, 1972.

McCabe, Bernard and Bender, Coleman. *Speaking Is a Practical Matter*. 2d ed. Boston: Holbrook Press, 1974. Pp. 35–47; 62–67.

Mortensen, C. David. *Communication: The Study of Human Interaction*. New York: McGraw-Hill Book Co., 1972. Chapter 6.

Mudd, Charles S., and Sillars, Malcolm O. *Speech: Content and Communication*. 3d ed. New York: Thomas Y. Crowell Co., 1975. Chapter 13.

Reid, Loren. *Speaking Well*. 2d ed. New York: McGraw-Hill Book Co., 1972. Chapters 10–12.

Scheidel, Thomas M. *Speech Communication and Human Interaction*. Glenview, Ill.: Scott, Foresman and Co., 1972. Pp. 324–31.

Listening
Evaluation and Criticism

4

During the initial planning stages of this book, we could easily have made a case for discussing listening in chapter 1. In our Introduction we suggested that these early chapters should contain the materials needed at the beginning of your training experience. Listening is such a topic. It plays a vital and essential role in our individual lives and, indeed, in our civilization. Much of what we know about the past has come to us through listening. Small children learn much about their new world through listening, for it is their first means of acquiring information and ideas about their environment. As adults we use listening more than any other communication skill. The time we spend in listening far exceeds the time we spend in reading, writing, or speaking. It has been estimated that we spend 40 to 50 percent of our total communication time engaged in listening. One of the authors of this text conducted a research project which led to the conclusion that we may be spending more than one-third of our waking hours listening. Stop in the middle of what you are doing a few times during the day, and you will soon discover that the statistics concerning listening are quite valid. We listen at home, on the job, at school, and at play.

Inherent in our definition and explanation of communication is the concept that speech is a two-way process. Speaking and listening are the two indispensable ingredients of communication; there can be no effective speech without someone to listen. If our discussion of oral communication is to have real meaning, then, we must give a proper share of attention to listening.

But what kind of listeners are we? There is sufficient evidence to support the generalization that people, as a whole, are poor listeners. Two separate studies concluded that a large percentage of those tested could not locate a central idea after listening to exposition which had been designed for clarity and simplicity. Other results point to the generalization that listeners are able to comprehend only a small percentage of what they hear. Perhaps the best proof for the assertion that people are poor listeners can be found by some serious self-introspection on the part of all of us. Many of the most common communication breakdowns can indeed be assigned to faulty listening. Too many of us have been conditioned to believe that if we don't understand something, it is the fault of the speaker.

Research into the listening habits of students also reveals some alarming results. Ask yourself how well you rank in regard to the six common weaknesses uncovered by researchers.

1. People tend to stop listening when the material is uninteresting. The findings show that most of us pay attention only to that material we "like" listening to.

2. People tend to be influenced more by the dramatic elements of a message than by logical elements.

3. Most people have a short listening span.

4. Most listeners have a difficult time separating the essential from the non-essential.

5. Listeners are influenced more by the speaker's voice than by the "truth" of the message.

6. People tend to believe what they hear in broadcast speeches. Their assumption seems to be that if speakers are on radio or television, they must be important and their ideas therefore merit belief.

Substituting these common faults with good listening habits can produce important benefits. Good listening enables you to add to your storehouse of information, to update and revise your collection of facts, skills, attitudes, and beliefs. It adds depth and dimension to even the simplest daily experiences. You will find yourself noticing and appreciating things of which you had previously been unaware. This sharpened awareness is also good protection against the devices and techniques of the unethical and sophistic speaker. It should also be noted that good listening is not the same thing as paying attention. It is far more complicated and involved. Finally, good listening helps to improve your speaking. By listening carefully to the speeches of others, you will be able to select those characteristics of content and delivery which ought to be emulated and those which should be avoided.

You will discover that most of the time spent in speech class is spent in listening to student speeches and to remarks of the instructor. In fact, you will probably listen to over one hundred speeches in your class, while you deliver only five or six. Take full advantage of this listening time to sharpen your perception, and you will be a better speaker as well as a better listener for the experience.

PURPOSES OF LISTENING

The purposes of listening are as diversified as the reasons we have for speaking. Yet we can generalize that there are basically two major purposes for listening—social and informational.

Social listening is often used when our purpose is either therapeutic or for enjoyment. By therapeutic we mean those countless communication contacts that have us sharing feelings and building and maintaining supporting relationships. For example, imagine that a close friend has just smashed his new car and tells you how frustrated and upset he is. In this circumstance there is really nothing you can do, yet your friend feels better because you have listened and offered moral support.

The enjoyable aspects of listening are rather obvious. We listen to music, watch television, go to movies and plays, and engage in a great deal of social conversation.

Listening is hearing sounds and deciding
what the sounds mean.

Although most listening involves *information,* there are many occasions when that information has some specialized purpose. We may need it so that we can perform a specific act—for example, someone telling us how to saddle a horse. The information we are listening to may also be used as part of our decision-making processes—listening to a political speaker asking for our vote.

BARRIERS TO
EFFECTIVE LISTENING

Listening is a complex activity. It consists of two component activities—the physical operation of a sense organ and an accompanying mental process. Some authorities distinguish *hearing* from *listening,* maintaining that when we hear, we perceive sounds only, but when we listen, this hearing is accompanied by a deliberate and purposeful act of the mind. To listen means to get meaning from that which is heard. This distinction has merit in that it cautions us that attention to a speaker's voice is no guarantee of efficient listening. There are so many other reasons why our listening behavior is often impeded. Some of these barriers are worth examining in detail, for they can keep us from participating in an enjoyable and enlightening experience.

PHYSICAL CONDITIONS AS
A BARRIER

As a listener you will experience physical barriers over which you have no control and those over which you will be able to exercise some regulation. Distracting sounds, poor acoustics, and uncomfortable seating arrangements may usually be classified as distractions which you can't manipulate, although there are times when you can move your seat or close a window. The most effective device for surmounting most physical barriers is *concentration,* the core of all good listening.

The real danger of physical barriers is that the listener may use the barrier (distraction) as an excuse for "tuning the speaker out." We all know from experience that we can yield to any distraction quite easily, and thus make this distraction the main focus of our attention. The conscientious listener and the sincere speaker are aware of the problems caused by physical barriers, and both work diligently to overcome these obstructions to listening.

A CASUAL ATTITUDE AS
A BARRIER

Too often we approach the communication situation without the right frame of mind. We all seem to have a tendency to believe that because we hear noises and sounds, we are listening. As already mentioned, one can hear and yet not listen. Because hearing is relatively easy, we assume that listening can also be somewhat casual and something we can do without much concentration and effort. Yet, it is this very attitude that forms one of the major barriers to listening.

It has been suggested that this casual attitude toward listening develops in a very subtle way and over a long period of time. What appears to happen is that all day long we move in and out of listening situations that have different purposes. We listen to music or talk to friends and then quickly go to our history class. In short, without even realizing it, we slide from situations that demand very little concentration to informational encounters that call for higher levels of emotional commitment. While a casual listening attitude is permissible in a pleasurable encounter, it represents a serious barrier when one is attempting to listen for information.

SPEAKING-THINKING RATE AS
A BARRIER

It is estimated that we speak an average of 125 to 150 words per minute. Our mind, however, is able to cope with approximately 400 words per minute. This means that the mind has a great deal of "idle" time. This excess time forms one of the major barriers to proficient listening. In most instances the time is spent in wandering away from the task of critical and careful listening. It is during this "free time" that many listeners surrender to external distractions. The listening-thinking gap is often used for mental excursions ranging from daydreaming to thinking about the speaker's hairstyle. It would be far more beneficial to both sender and receiver if this time were spent analyzing the message.

STATUS AND ROLE AS
A BARRIER

Experimental evidence indicates that your impression of a person's status will determine, to a large degree, what you learn from that person and what influence he or she will have over your attitudes. From your own experience you have seen how your regard for the speaker influences what you actually hear. Status relationships between speaker and listener, as well as the various roles they both play, frequently determine the success or failure of the communication act.

We also know from research that when we respect someone, we tend to listen more attentively. Unfortunately, we may become overly concerned with the speaker as a person and neglect to think critically about what is being said. This barrier applies both to speakers for whom we have a high regard as well as to those for whom we have a lower regard. The good listener must recognize prestige, role, and status as factors present in all communication and must not let them prevent maximum comprehension and evaluation of what is being said.

POOR LISTENING HABITS AS
A BARRIER

Like so much of human behavior, listening tends to follow consistent patterns. Most of us fall into listening patterns that tend to become so habitual that we fail to fully realize we are creating a listening barrier. Although all of the barriers discussed in this section can become habitualized, Nichols and Stevens have suggested the six most common bad habits. At the risk of some duplication, they are listed here.

1. *Faking attention.*   Perhaps most of us have learned to fake attention so as not to appear discourteous. Or maybe we wanted a teacher to think we were interested and learning. The danger of such fakery is that it tends to become habitual. It is easy for us to fall into the habit of faking listening and forget to sincerely pay attention.

2. *Listening only for facts.*   Many times we listen only for the facts and forget to locate the main ideas. Try to listen for the ideas first and then facts that support or explain the ideas.

3. *Avoiding difficult material.*   Most of us feel comfortable with what we know and tend to avoid what is unfamiliar or difficult. We turn off those listening situations that require too much energy. Such avoidance becomes a habitualized pattern: whenever the material becomes slightly difficult, such a listener will drift away mentally, if not physically.

4. *Avoiding the uninteresting.*   Perhaps this habit is only a corollary of an earlier barrier (Premature Evaluation), but avoiding the uninteresting can hurt communication. We often make the mistake of equating "interesting" with "valuable" and, hence, stop listening too soon.

5. *Criticizing delivery.*   We often become overly concerned with *how* someone says something and forget to listen to *what* he or she said. A speaker is rejected and not listened to because of delivery rather than ideas.

6. *Yielding to distractions.*   We have already discussed how physical conditions can be a barrier to listening. But there are mental and semantic distractions as well. *Mental* distractions occur in the situations where we talk silently to our favorite companion—ourselves. When our daydreams and fantasies take over and we forget about the speaker, we have a mental distraction. Ask yourself how many times a day you are supposed to be listening but, instead, find yourself planning about tomorrow or evaluating what you did yesterday.

We also frequently yield to *semantic* distractions. These normally occur over the use of a word or phrase. People often have different meanings for the same word, and if these differences are too great, a semantic distraction can occur. For example, if the speaker and listener were from different generations and cultures, a phrase such as "My, what a foxy chick" could cause a semantic distraction. What usually happens is that the listener must stop and think about specific meanings while the speaker continues his presentation.

LACK OF COMMON EXPERIENCES AS A BARRIER

A barrier in listening can occur when speaker and listener are far apart in their backgrounds and in their current living environments. It is difficult to understand what is being said if you have not experienced, either directly or indirectly, the concepts being discussed. A college graduate, born and raised in a large eastern city, may well have a difficult time understanding and experiencing the messages and ideas of a farmer who has always lived in a small rural community. A true meeting of the minds is hampered when speaker and listener have lived in two separate worlds.

PRECONCEIVED ATTITUDES AS
A BARRIER

When we listen we also make abundant use of our prejudices and our personal beliefs. These attitudes are usually deep-seated and developed over a long period of time, and it is therefore not always easy to create a posture of open-mindedness. A Democrat listening to a Republican speaker will be less likely to give the speaker a fair hearing because of preconceived attitudes about the characteristics of Republicanism. To break down the barrier of preconceived attitudes we must try to exert some command over our emotions and initial responses. We must try to hold off judgment until we have *listened*—completely and objectively—to what was said.

CONSTANT SELF-FOCUS AS
A BARRIER

We have talked about being overly concerned with self in connection with a number of the other barriers; yet this particular problem is important enough to warrant special consideration. There are usually three reasons why we allow personal concerns to dominate our listening behavior. First, listening is often obstructed when we adopt the "I must defend my position" attitude. In these instances we stop listening and engage in a mental debate. If someone says to us, "Gun laws in this country are too rigid," and to ourselves we say, "What is he talking about? Last year there were over ten thousand people killed with hand guns," then clearly a barrier to continued listening has arisen.

Second, many of us adopt the "I already know what you have to say" attitude. This barrier usually begins to form when we say to ourselves, "Oh no, not another speech on drug addiction." We would suggest that the person who assumes this position may be missing a great deal from life. Think of what a narrow view we have when we are so dogmatic as to believe we know all there is to know on any subject. Much of what we have learned has been acquired by listening, and we would be foolish to ever stop listening.

Our last self-focus barrier finds us wondering, "How am I coming through?" In such a situation our concern is not with the listening, but rather with what we are going to say and how we appear. We can all grant that most people are slightly egocentric and vain; however, when this preoccupation with self dominates our thoughts, we have trouble deciding where to focus our attention. Listening is suspended when we pause to ask ourselves, "I wonder if she thought my remark was clever?"

It is important to remember that these barriers can destroy the critical link between speaker and listener. In communication we receive word-symbols representing someone else's message, and we attempt to extract from them the meaning intended by the sender. In speaking we cannot go back and re-listen as we can go back and reread; so the word-symbol relationship must be free from barriers whenever possible.

IMPROVING YOUR LISTENING

Listening is one of the communication skills that can be improved with serious practice and training. A large number of research projects, in particular those conducted by Ralph Nichols of the University of Minnesota, demonstrate that listening ability can be enriched if the individual desires such enrichment. Your speech class offers an arena for just such practice and training.

BE MOTIVATED TO LISTEN

Probably the most important step you can take in becoming a better listener is to resolve that *you will listen* more efficiently. This simple commitment will give you a sound new attitude about listening, and improvement will be noticeable at once. What we suggest is quite transparent—*want to listen.*

Efficient listening begins with motivation. Researchers in the area of listening have concluded that if one is motivated to listen, that person will be a more alert and active receiver. The material will be more meaningful if you believe it affects you personally. What prompts you to listen might be something as pragmatic as making a sale if you listen carefully to what your customer is saying or as abstract as listening because you "owe it to the speaker." In either case, if you are motivated, you will discover that you cannot be easily distracted.

Although motivation, in itself, is not enough to overcome all problems in listening, it is the first prerequisite to becoming a good listener. In short, to be a good listener you should bring the following attitudes to the listening situation: (1) you want to listen, (2) you find a personal reason for listening, and (3) you are willing to do your part in the listening situation.

BE PREPARED TO LISTEN

Think about listening even before the speaker sends the first message by keeping yourself informed on topics that you may have occasion to judge and evaluate.

For specific listening experiences prepare yourself in four ways:

1. Try to learn all you can about the subject, speaker, and situation. This knowledge, much like an audience analysis, will help you understand and appraise what the speaker will say. It will also aid you in comprehending and overcoming the problems of word-symbol relationships.
2. Try to minimize physical barriers by placing yourself in a position where you can easily see and hear the speaker.

3. Try to eliminate all those distractions in your environment which might call attention away from the speaker. For example, leave the school newspaper outside the classroom; it might later become a distraction.
4. Be ready to take notes when appropriate. Having to stop and look for paper and pencil during the talk may force you to miss key points.

BE OBJECTIVE

You can improve your listening immeasurably by maintaining an attitude of objectivity as you listen to what is being discussed. You should approach a communication situation with an open mind and a spirit of inquiry.

Attend critically to each of the speaker's words, but do not make judgments until points are fully developed. Be alert for items that are implausible and misleading; but be aware of the larger principle the speaker is developing. Let the speaker explain and summarize all the main points before you draw final conclusions.

We cease to be objective listeners when we allow our emotions and our prejudices to control our understanding. As we listen to speakers who profess views alien to our own, we sometimes fail to hear them out because our feelings are so deeply involved. Our natural tendency is to start composing a rebuttal of the opposing ideas and thinking of further arguments. Our emotions are getting in the way of what is actually being said. Admittedly, it is difficult to control our emotions and our preconceived attitudes, but conscious effort to declare a truce with bias will aid our overall comprehension of what is being expressed.

BE ALERT TO ALL CLUES

In listening it is important to look for the speaker's *main* ideas. This must be a conscious and diligent search, for we cannot expect every speaker to underline the main point or stop and say, "What follows is my central thesis."

Be watchful for all specific clues to meaning as contained in the elements of the speaking situation. The setting, the staging of the event, and the program notes can give insight into what will be said. The speaker's inflection, rate, emphasis, voice quality, and bodily actions can often offer clues to the meaning of what is being said and what the speaker feels is most important.

Clues naturally abound in the content and arrangement of the material. The vigilant listener makes note of the speaker's use of partitions, enumerations, transitions, topic sentences, and internal and final summaries. Clues common to writing, such as bold type, italics, and quotation marks, are replaced with clues of voice, body, material, and arrangement.

MAKE USE OF THINKING-
SPEAKING TIME DIFFERENCE

As noted earlier, evidence indicates that we normally think at a pace about three times faster than our speaking pace. As good listeners we can use this time to think about what the speaker is saying. We can ask ourselves, "How does this item relate to the speaker's main purpose? How does this main point support that purpose?" As alert listeners we can make this time gap work for us instead of against us. By concentrating on what is being said, instead of worrying or mentally arguing with the speaker, we can put the time difference to efficient use. This extra time can also be used to take notes when the situation warrants such action. Finally, the free time can always be used to summarize mentally and review what the speaker has said.

AVOID THE "MYSTERY OF WORDS" FALLACY

A good listener is always aware of the fact that the words being used by the speaker may not accurately represent what the speaker thinks or feels. The person talking is using words to represent an idea or a feeling; *the word is not the idea or feeling but rather an abstract symbol standing for what the speaker really means.* As a trained listener try to go beyond the words you hear. Be concerned with the speaker's motives and purposes. Finding out *why* someone is talking can often yield information far more valuable than that gained from the words themselves.

Empathy provides another way of avoiding the "mystery of words" fallacy. If you can see the problem (issue) the way the speaker sees it, the chances of reaching a mutual frame of reference will be greatly enhanced. In essence, you must ask yourself if the words being used by the speaker really represent his or her *true* feelings and ideas.

USE FEEDBACK

Making abundant use of feedback is yet another way we can gain more from our communication encounters. As listeners we can use the opportunity feedback affords us to talk back to the sender of the message. In its most undisguised form this feedback can be as simple as telling the speaker you don't understand. This form of feedback lets you hear the message again, either repeated in the same words or explained in a different manner.

There are a number of ideas for the listener to keep in mind when utilizing feedback. First, the speaker must perceive the feedback you are sending. Requests for clarification are lost if they are not received. Second, the feedback must not be ambiguous. It doesn't aid a speaker if he or she must stop and try to decide what emotion your facial expression is trying to convey. Are you smiling to say you understand what is being talked about, or is the grin you wear a reflection of sarcasm? Third, the feedback you give the speaker should directly relate to what is going on. It is of little benefit to either party if we delay our response to the point when it is no longer germane.

PRACTICE LISTENING

Proficiency in any skill is the result of a great deal of conscientious effort. *You should therefore practice listening.* The poor listener avoids difficult listening situations and evades dull material. A case in point might be a college

lecture on some highly abstract concept which defies the application of interest devices by even the most skillful speaker. In such cases the listener has
to work along with the speaker at gaining meaning. It is a great temptation to
stop listening when listening requires effort. Because of this the weak listener
never improves. Force yourself to practice; make yourself listen to music,
speeches, and conversations that seem to hold no *obvious* interest value.

LISTENING TO SPEECHES

The act of receiving oral language involves three things: (1) the recall or deduction of meanings from each spoken word-symbol, (2) the comprehension
of ideas presented by different combinations of these word-symbols, and (3)
the use of the ideas presented to build understanding by adding to, modifying,
or rejecting previous learning. We must perceive, comprehend, and finally use
or reject what the speaker says.

We are constantly being besieged with requests to vote, give, buy, feel,
and think in one way or another. A poor listener is easy prey for the sophist,
huckster, shyster, and propagandist. Our major defenses against those who
choose to influence and control our behavior are critical thinking and captious
evaluation. Both of these skills can be learned, and your speech class, by allowing you an opportunity to hear over a hundred speeches, is an excellent place
to cultivate your listening ability.

As a listener you have a responsibility to listen attentively if you are to
judge and evaluate, and possibly accept or reject what is being said. What
we are suggesting is that the ethical responsibility in the speech act is not
borne by the speaker alone. The listener as well as the speaker shares in the
moral issues of the speech act. We might say that a listener's first obligation is
to offer full attention to the speaker. Admittedly this is much easier to write
about than to carry out. Each communication act is characterized by countless
distractions, but these must be overcome if we are to fairly analyze what we
hear.

Once you have paid attention, you are better able to locate the techniques
and devices of the unethical speaker. You will also be able to make valid decisions on what is being proposed.

As a responsible listener you must be alert to the ethical character of
those who address you. It is useful to be aware of the propaganda devices that
are daily employed. The Institute of Propaganda Analysis has defined the following forms as a partial list of the most common techniques.

1. *Name-calling.* This device, which is often employed by unethical
speakers, attempts to give a person or an idea a bad label. It is used to make
us reject and condemn the idea or person without examining the evidence.
For example, you have heard people say, "This clearly shows that Ms. Smith,
by her immoral actions, is un-American and disloyal to the principles of our
great country." "The proposal recommended by the school board is undemo-
cratic, dishonest, and riddled with graft and corruption." Or how often we

have heard, "Senator Jones should not be elected to the U.S. Senate because he is a 'radical liberal.' "

Name-calling has played an immense and powerful role in the history of our civilization. Bad names have ruined reputations, caused wars, and sent people to prison cells. Be wary of the individual who uses name-calling instead of concrete evidence and logical reasoning.

2. *Glittering generality.* In this case a "virtue word" is used to make the hearer accept and approve the thing or idea without examining the evidence. We believe in, fight for, live by "virtue words" about which we have deep-seated feelings. Such words are *Christianity, freedom, right, democracy, motherhood,* and *liberty.* If a proposition is "for the good of the people," or "will maintain the Constitution," the speaker suggests it cannot be bad.

3. *Testimonial.* This technique consists of having some respected person say that a given idea, program, product, or individual is good or bad without furnishing any basis for the value judgment. In many instances the "expert" is not even competent to evaluate the issue under discussion. Be on the watch for phrases such as, "My doctor said . . . ," or "The President said . . . ," for these, in many instances, may be an indication that the speaker is appealing to you through testimonial. *Remember the issue, not just the person.*

4. *Plain Folks.* This method is used by the speaker who is attempting to convince an audience that he or she and the ideas presented are good and honest because they are "of the people," the "plain folks." This is often the technique of military dictatorships. How often have we heard new regimes say, "We have overthrown the government because it was cruel to the poor and simple peasants." In our own country we hear politicians say they want the vote "of the common person." Speakers even use the jargon of a particular group to demonstrate they are the "plain folks."

5. *Card Stacking.* This method involves the selection and use of facts or falsehoods, illustrations or distractions, and logical or illogical statements in order to give the best or the worst possible case for an idea, program, person, or product. The sender selects only those items that support his or her position, regardless of the distortion they may produce. Listing a few of the accomplishments of one's administration while leaving out all of the failures would be an example of this technique. A speaker, of course, may not always have to offer all sides of a question; therefore the listener must be alert.

6. *Bandwagon.* This device implies that since everyone else has accepted a given proposal, the listener should likewise do so. "Jump on the bandwagon," "Be on the winning side," "Everyone is doing it,"—all are examples of the bandwagon technique.

It would be foolish to say that these techniques cannot on occasion be used legitimately, but their unethical use should not be condoned.

SPEECH CRITICISM
One of the major themes of this book has been the notion that through communication we influence other people. In most instances this influence alters

another person's behavior in the direction of predetermined goals. Because of the impact we have on each other, it behooves us as listeners to question much of what we hear. Being critical does not mean that we offer blanket rejections to all we encounter, nor does it imply that we accept all we hear at face value. Instead, criticism enables us to question, evaluate, and eventually make logical judgments concerning the messages with which we are confronted.

Perhaps the first issue facing any critic is the one concerning the speaker's purpose. Although all communication induces a change on the part of the listener, there are some specific changes that the critical listener should be aware of. In discussing these changes we should remember that *each person*, by the response he or she makes, represents the most accurate gauge of the speaker's purpose. One person may well laugh at material that brings a companion to the brink of sorrow. This is why any analysis of purpose must begin with the assumption that speech purpose is the domain of the *creator* of the message. Therefore, the listener asks this important question: "What does the speaker want from the audience?" Many critics find it useful to answer this question by placing the speaker's intent under one of the General Ends of Speech (informing, persuading, and entertaining). Others use the setting of the speech to analyze the speaker's purpose (courtroom speeches, ceremonial speeches, and so forth).

The critical listener who seeks to analyze speech purposes in even more detail can attempt to investigate the speaker's specific purpose. You will recall that this was the specific response being sought by the speaker ("By the end of my speech I want my audience to . . .").

The critical listener seeks to distinguish the issue from the person. We can sometimes become so impressed with a speaker's personality, voice, and "image" that we neglect to evaluate what he or she is saying. The critical listener separates what the speaker says from what the speaker is.

The critical listener is aware of the problems inherent in our language and our use of words. Words are only symbols standing for things—they are not the things themselves. The critical listener recognizes the loaded word and the ambiguous word and learns to be careful of words such as *un-American, freedom, liberalism, socialism,* or *extremism.* Words have real meaning only if they represent something in reality. One word may have many uses, and the critical listener tries to interpret the speaker's meaning in light of this variety of uses.

The critical listener applies the tests of evidence and reasoning. He or she is familiar with the propaganda techniques we have discussed and is able to isolate the half-truth, name-calling, and the other devices.

The critical listener detects the substitution of generalities for specifics—of glibness for sincerity. He or she demands dates, names, numbers, and places. The speaker who omits key information is often the same person who relies on innuendos and who exaggerates some points out of proportion to their importance while understating other more fundamental points (a favorite device of Adolf Hitler).

The critical listener applies the tests of evidence and reasoning (to be discussed in chapter 5) to the material presented by the speaker. He or she is concerned with the validity and reliability of illustrations, examples, statistics, testimony, and analogies. By checking the authenticity of the facts presented and the probability that the facts mean what they are said to mean, he is able to make more accurate judgments.

The critical listener questions the relevance of the material offered by the speaker. He or she knows that material may meet all the tests of reliability and validity and yet be irrelevant to the point under discussion. "So what?" or "What is the point?" are the critical listener's inevitable questions.

EVALUATING SPEECHES

At the end of most classroom speeches you will have an opportunity to present an informal critique, either oral or written. As you evaluate the speeches of others, try to implement the broad principles discussed by your instructor and by this text. The following items are designed to serve as a guide for your assignments in speech evaluation:

1. Did the speaker have a worthwhile purpose? Whenever we speak we are occupying both the life space and the time of another individual. Therefore, all listeners have a right to ask whether or not the purpose of the speech justified the amount of time they gave it (or were asked to give it). Was the purpose clear or was the speaker and the audience part of an ambiguous encounter? Aimless ramblings, touching on topics from pets to pollution, serve no real purpose and only contribute to confusion.

2. Closely related to the first question is the issue of the speaker's level of commitment. Has the speaker made an attempt to be objective and fair to himself or herself, to the audience, and to the subject? Did the speaker seem to care about communicating, or was he or she simply going through the motions of fulfilling an assignment? For example, did the speaker appear to have practiced the speech?

3. Did the speaker know the subject? Listeners have a right to ask that the sender of any message be prepared. More specifically, we can inquire as to the amount of research that was manifested in the speech. We have all listened to speakers who sounded as if they had prepared their remarks as they walked from their chair to the rostrum. This may be appropriate for an impromptu speech, but it should not be tolerated when the topic calls for in-depth analysis and research.

4. Was there evidence that the speaker had analyzed the audience? Were such factors as the audience's age, sex, education, and attitudes taken into consideration? Did the speaker indicate that the speech was being directed at the classroom audience or at some hypothetical audience?

5. Was the speech structurally sound? Did the subdivisions, both major and minor, relate to and support the main ideas? Were the transitions between ideas clear?

6. Did the speaker utilize language meaningfully? Did he or she employ

words or phrases that were clear and adequately defined? Were imagery and word pictures used effectively? Did he or she avoid clichés, slang, poor grammar? Was the speaker's usage appropriate to the audience, the occasion, the subject?

7. Did the speaker utilize factors of attention and interest in both the content and delivery of the speech? Too many of us are guilty of assuming that all we have to do is talk and people will listen. The folly of this view is made evident when as listeners we are asked to consider a speech that not only lacks interest, but also is presented by someone who makes no attempt at arousing and focusing our attention.

8. Did the speaker's illustrations, examples, statistics, testimony, and analogies meet the tests of evidence? Was enough evidence employed to support each point?

9. How effectively did the speaker employ visual aspects of delivery? Did he or she maintain good eye contact? Did he or she have good posture? Were gestures and movements skillfully executed? Were animated facial expressions used?

10. How effectively did the speaker employ his or her voice? Was there sufficient variety of rate, pitch, loudness? Was enunciation clear and pronunciation correct?

11. Was the speaker a credible spokesperson on the subject? Did words, actions, and dress contribute to the speech's believability? Or did the speaker behave in ways that detracted from his or her credibility?

12. What was the total impression left by the speech? As listeners, we should evaluate the main idea as well as the subpoints. The end of the speech is a good place to ask ourselves, "What is the overall effect of the speech?"

These are by no means the only categories for evaluation. Doubtless you will discover others as you gain experience in listening to various types of speeches.

Two other important suggestions are worth noting before we conclude this section. First, speech evaluation, in the classroom or out, should include much more than negative critical comments. We should point out praiseworthy qualities so that the speaker will be aware of those things he or she is doing well. For example, praise should be offered if the speaker employs concrete evidence for all of the assertions in a speech. In addition, our evaluations should tender suggestions for improvement. Constructive criticism allows both the speaker and the listener to learn from the communication experience. How helpful it would be if you could tell certain members of your class that their speaking would be improved if they provided transitions as they moved from main point to main point.

Our final bit of advice. Listen carefully to your classmates as they evaluate other speeches and speakers. You may very well find that your own speaking profits from remarks directed to other speakers. For instance, if a speaker is told that he talks too fast, you may want to pause and reflect on your own rate of speech.

LISTENER RESPONSIBILITY

One of the central themes of this book is that communication is a two-way process—that speaker and listener are interrelated and need each other for a variety of reasons. To be effective listeners we must therefore do more than listen; we must assume some of the responsibility for the total communication act. Not only should we evaluate what we have gained from the speaker but also should be aware of what we have *given* the speaker. Did we make the speaker feel comfortable? Did we encourage or discourage communication?

We all know from personal experience that we not only feel better about ourselves and other people, but we communicate more effectively when we are receiving positive feedback from our listeners. Ask yourself how much incentive you would have to continue speaking if the people before you were frowning or reading a newspaper. In short, our behavior, as listeners, affects the speaker.

A "listener response" that adds to the communication encounter can be a very brief comment or action of some kind which conveys to the sender the idea that the receiver is interested, attentive, and wishes the sender to continue. It is made quietly and briefly so as not to interfere with the sender's train of thought. We are, of course, talking about the receiver's role—the giving of information back to the sender so that the sender may know something of his or her effectiveness and that someone is listening and caring.

There are a number of specific actions the listener can take that will aid the speaker in communicating. Some of the acts listed below apply to platform speaking, while others are useful in discussion, interviewing, or even everyday conversation.

1. *Eye contact* has the effect of establishing rapport between sender and receiver and also tends to encourage communication. Research indicates that we seem to look at people more when we feel comfortable around them. This bit of information should be used by the communicator who is sincere in his or her effort.
2. *Nodding the head slightly* also tells the speaker that you (the listener) are part of the communication process.
3. An act as simple as *smiling* can offer warmth and support to the speaker. It may be just what he or she needs to get over the nervous feeling that often confronts speakers.
4. *Casual remarks* such as "I see," "uh-huh," and "is that so" involve the listener with the speaker.
5. There will be times when you can help the speaker by *remaining silent*. Too often we contaminate a communication encounter by talking.

The important thing to remember is that listening also means helping and aiding the speaker. Creating an atmosphere that will bring out the best in the speaker should be a goal of every listener. It is to the advantage of both parties that the communication act be a pleasurable one.

One additional point should be made concerning the listener's responsibility. The five suggestions above should not be carried out in an artificial or deceptive manner. Remember, faking attention is a poor listening habit. Therefore, actions that offer support should be genuine and sincere.

SPEAKER RESPONSIBILITY

It is the sender who initiates the communication act in order to have an influence over the subsequent behavior of other people. The sender is the one who has the need and the desire to communicate. As speakers, then, we must constantly strive to meet our communication responsibilities. We must see to it that the listener is attentive to what we are saying. In this way we can better meet our specific communication needs.

It might be helpful if we were to briefly explore some of the more common techniques the sender can use to encourage more effective listening.

TRY TO EMPATHIZE

It is important that you speak to your listeners. To do this you must understand them—understand how they will react to you and your message. This is best accomplished by trying to hear your ideas and words as the listener will. For example, if you have not thought about your listeners, you might well talk on a subject that holds little or no interest for them. By employing empathy, you will be able to view the content as the listeners will and will not be asking them to listen to material that is inappropriate and uninteresting.

ADJUST YOUR DELIVERY

In chapter 3 we talked about how our voice and body can aid the listener in understanding our verbal message. We should always make sure we can be heard. It is very frustrating for a listener to have to strain in order to know what is being said. Moreover, our delivery should be animated enough to arouse and maintain interest. We have all been witnesses to the speaker who communicates in a boring and dull manner.

UTILIZE FEEDBACK

We told the listener to use feedback to improve his or her listening, and now we suggest that the same principle applies to the speaker. As senders we should be sensitive to what our messages are doing to the people who receive them. Are they paying attention? Do they look interested? Do they look confused? Are they seeking more information? These are but a few of the questions feedback can help answer. Once we secure this information, via feedback, we are in a better position to make the necessary adjustments. If we sense apathy, we can try to arouse attention and point the material directly to the needs of the audience.

BE CLEAR

There is nothing harder to listen to than a speech that rambles aimlessly. As speakers, we can meet part of our responsibilities by being well organized. We will have much more to say about clarity and organization later in the book, but for now, remember that it is unfair of us to ask a listener to try to make sense out of our disconnected and disjointed wanderings.

BE INTERESTING

The obvious implications of this point hardly warrant discussion. If material lacks interest for us, it is difficult to listen. Hence, as speakers we must strive to have our content lively, stimulating, and relevant.

SUMMARY

Listening is one of our most important communication skills. Effective listening is an active process that demands conscientious effort on the part of the listener. Virtually everyone can improve his listening ability by simply becoming aware of some of the problems of listening and their remedies.

The listener who is sincere about improvement should be alert to the major barriers to effective listening: physical conditions, a casual attitude, speaking-thinking rate, status and role, poor listening habits, lack of common experience, preconceived attitudes, and a constant self-focus.

We noted in this chapter that listening could be improved by our being motivated, prepared, objective, and alert to all the communication cues (verbal and nonverbal) contained within the speaking situation. In addition, making use of spare time, avoiding the "mystery of words" fallacy, using feedback, and practicing can also be useful for improving our listening behavior.

Speech criticism and evaluation were also explored in this chapter. We recommended that the listener question much of what he or she hears, and whenever possible offer constructive criticism to the speaker.

Finally, we pointed out that both the listener and the speaker have certain communication responsibilities built into each encounter. The listener should create a mood by a listening attitude and posture that will encourage the speaker to reach his or her full potential—the listener should try to put the speaker at ease. The speaker can meet some of his or her obligations by (1) trying to empathize with the listener, (2) making adjustments to the delivery, (3) utilizing feedback, and (4) being sure that the message is clear and well organized.

Suggested Readings

Barker, Larry L. *Listening Behavior*. Englewood Cliffs, N. J.: Prentice-Hall, 1971.
Black, Edwin. *Rhetorical Criticism: A Study in Method*. New York: Macmillan Co., 1965.

Brooks, William D. *Speech Communication,* 2d ed. Dubuque, Ia.: Wm. C. Brown Company Publishers, 1974. Chapter 4.

Cathcart, Robert S. *Post Communication: Critical Analysis and Evaluation.* New York: Bobbs-Merrill Co., 1966.

Dominick, Barbara A. *The Art of Listening.* Springfield, Ill.: Charles C Thomas, Publisher, 1958.

Duker, Sam. *Listening: Readings, Vol. 2.* Metuchen, N. J.: Scarecrow Press, 1971.

Nichols, Ralph G., and Stevens, Leonard A. *Are You Listening.* New York: McGraw-Hill Book Co., 1957.

Oliver, Robert T., and Cartright, Rupert L. *Effective Speech.* 5th ed. New York: Holt, Rinehart and Winston, 1970. Chapter 4.

Reid, Loren. *Speaking Well.* 2d ed. New York: McGraw-Hill Book Co., 1972. Chapter 8.

Weaver, Carl H. *Human Listening: Processes and Behavior.* New York: The Bobbs-Merrill Co., 1972.

Your Ideas

Evidence
*The Foundation of
Your Ideas*

5

As members of a society that uses communication as a means of sharing experiences, thoughts, and feelings, we are constantly telling others about our ideas and beliefs. When we have an idea we wish to share with another party, we endeavor to express that idea clearly and effectively so that the listener will "see what we are talking about." If we desire to change someone's mind, we also strive to clarify, amplify, and defend our position. It is, indeed, an exhilarating sensation to know that what we asserted is interesting, understandable, and believable because we explained, illustrated, and demonstrated its merits and usefulness.

What is true with respect to explaining and supporting your ideas in everyday conversation is just as true in public speaking, but more demanding. Just as the builder uses certain materials to construct a house, so you, as a speaker, have to supply the materials for developing main ideas, primary and secondary headings. We all know that simply stating a point does not necessarily render it believable or true. There may be some assertions that listeners will accept at face value because the assertions are consistent with their existing beliefs and prejudices. But more frequently listeners require that assertions be backed up with proof. Recently a speaker on a college campus was advocating that the football team be disbanded on the grounds that it was a financial burden to the student body. Because this charge was merely asserted, and not supported with proof, the speaker's pleas were never heeded. The efficient communicator seeks to support his or her observations and positions and does not depend on chance or fate to win a point. The communicator furnishes the listener with the materials that prove the assertion to be credible and reliable.

VERBAL SUPPORT

Among the things we say about a particular subject, some are incidental while others are fundamental. The incidental are often used to get and hold attention; while the fundamental are vital to the accomplishment of our purpose. Therefore, one of our basic tasks as speakers is to study our subjects until we can recognize those elements in them that are closely pertinent and essential to the accomplishment of our purpose. Those essential components, which help render our ideas understandable and believable, are called *forms of support*. The word "support" furnishes an accurate description of their function, for the materials selected offer sustenance for the central theme of the speech.

Let us consider some of the forms of support that are available when we find it necessary and beneficial to clarify and/or prove an important and fundamental assertion.

Evidence offers support for our ideas.

ILLUSTRATION (EXAMPLE)

From the earliest days of the history of the human race, the storyteller has commanded and held attention. Use of the narrative as a device for proving, clarifying, and maintaining interest has been discussed by writers of communication from Aristotle to the present. The very fact that a story or an example holds our attention renders it an excellent tool in many communication situations.

An illustration is the narration of a happening or incident which amplifies, proves, or clarifies the point under consideration. It is, in a sense, the speaker saying to the audience, "Here is an example of what I mean." In addition, it often aids memory in that it makes the important features more noteworthy.

The illustration usually takes one of three forms—**the detailed factual illustration, the undeveloped factual illustration (specific instance), and the hypothetical illustration.** Some overlapping may occur as the speaker limits, or extends his details.

The detailed, factual illustration usually takes the form of a narrative (story) which answers the questions who? what? where? when? and how? Because of the detail in the story, and because the story is true, the illustration is both vivid and meaningful to the audience. The knowledge that something actually occurred is a source of interest. Notice how interest is stirred when we hear someone say, "Let me tell you of a case that actually happened."

A student in a speech class recently made use of a detailed, factual illustration in a talk dealing with LSD. Trying to convince the audience that LSD is dangerous, he said:

> A friend of mine had heard so much about lysergic acid diethylamide, more commonly called LSD, that he decided to try some. He and a few friends went to the home of his girlfriend. He took the LSD and waited for the "trip." He had one! He had a vision of police—you know cops. On his "trip" the police were always after him. Wherever he went the police were there. They were always trying to catch him, but in his vision they never could reach him. When he came "down" (off his "trip") he had paranoia tendency towards the police. He had the feeling for weeks after that the police were trying to catch him. It became so bad that he had to leave school and go to a hospital for treatment. For my friend LSD was indeed dangerous and a very bad "trip."

Still another speaker used a factual illustration in an attempt to establish the premise that teaching by television is often more effective than the traditional methods. She told, in detail, of the success of a college class in anthropology that was taught by television, and how the students in this class learned more than those students enrolled in the classes taught in the usual manner.

Through such illustrations the speaker is able to have the audience see and experience the point he or she is trying to make. Because it is limited to but one example, the illustration often serves as the springboard for the presentation of additional and more specific examples.

In utilizing the detailed, factual illustration, you will find it worthwhile to keep a few criteria in mind. First, see to it that your example relates directly to your point. It is often a temptation to use an illustration simply because it is a "good story." If the audience has a difficult time seeing the connection between your assertion and your illustration, confusion may result. Second, use sufficient detail, clothed in image-evoking language, so that your illustration holds the interest of the audience. Third, be accurate. Avoid making your narrative a mixture of truth and fiction. Fourth, use the factors of attention discussed in chapter 8 as a means of making your illustrations appealing to the audience.

The undeveloped factual illustration is an example that omits much of the detail and development which characterize the extended factual illustration. Several such brief, condensed examples may be advanced by the speaker as a means of indicating the widespread nature of the situation or suggesting the frequency of an occurrence. The main advantage of the undetailed example is that since it is short and takes little time to present, it allows the speaker an opportunity to present a great deal of proof material in a minimum amount of time. For instance, if you are asserting that college graduates are having problems locating positions of employment, you might establish your point by stating: "San Diego State University was only able to place 65 percent of its graduates last year. UCLA reported that positions were hard to find, and San Francisco State College could only place 55 percent of its graduating class last year."

Still another example of this form of evidence would be the speaker talking about the value of the honor system. The case could be aided by saying, "The University of Indiana has found the honor system successful. Purdue University and the University of California at Davis have also reported satisfactory results from the honor system." By using actual people, places, events, and things, you are making the material both meaningful and persuasive.

Some examples may require only one word, like the name of a town or a person, while other may call for a sentence or two. In any case, the use of undeveloped illustrations adds strength and understanding to an idea. They provide excellent proof and are often most effective when they directly follow a detailed factual illustration. For example, a student who wanted to prove that a recent automobile strike had adversely affected the workers supported the position by relating the true story of an actual worker and his family. The speaker then bolstered the case by citing a number of undeveloped factual illustrations involving other workers.

The hypothetical illustration is a detailed fictional illustration which seeks to let the audience see "what could be" or what they might "suppose." It is most often used as a method of depicting future events or of making the future seem graphically clear.

If you were discussing the dangers of invading Cuba, you might use a hypothetical illustration by asking the audience to imagine a raging battle on a Cuban beach. In a speech dealing with a proposal to raise school taxes you might offer a hypothetical illustration of how the proposal would affect the audience. Or, you might offer a detailed illustration to convince the listeners that high school dropouts have a difficult time securing employment:

Suppose a friend of yours in high school decides that he has had enough school. He is doing poorly in math and English and therefore feels there is no real need to finish the semester. On Saturday he asks the owner of a local market to give him a job. The market owner can pay only eighty dollars a week. But your friend, having never made that much money, decides to take the job instead of reporting back to school on Monday.

After about two weeks on the job he is dismissed. Business is off at the store and the owner can't afford any extra help. Your friend then goes from store to store and from factory to factory looking for some sort of employment. But he soon discovers that employers are not interested in hiring someone without at least a high school education. Your friend, in essence, is unable to find work because he left school.

Depicting the future with the illustration can place the listener in a situation that affects him or her personally and emotionally. A statement such as "What happens if you reject this plan?" affords the speaker an opportunity to place the listener in the center of a hypothetical picture.

In using the hypothetical illustration you should keep a few key points in mind. First, you can select any story you want when you use a hypothetical illustration, but you should never present an imaginary story as being true-to-fact. Employing phrases such as "imagine a situation such as this," or "suppose you discover . . ." will allow the listener to separate fact from fiction. Second, if the hypothetical illustration is going to be effective, it should be reasonable and capable of happening. An illustration that is an obvious exaggeration might well offend the watchful listener. Third, always remember that an imaginary story proves very little. Therefore, as a student of communication you should try to locate a factual example if you are trying to prove a point, and rely on the hypothetical illustration if you are trying to clarify a point or arouse the emotions. Fourth, in using the hypothetical example, like the factual, make certain that it is appropriate and related directly to the point in question. The story must not be in the speech for its own sake, but rather for the purpose of supporting and/or clarifying some idea.

Testing Examples and Illustrations

If we are going to be confronted with examples, both as speakers and as listeners, we must be sure that the examples meet certain requirements. When we employ an example or an illustration, we may be asking the listener to draw a conclusion from the specific illustration. For instance, someone might try to condemn all New York drivers because of a bad experience while driving on Broadway. In drawing the generalization from the specific example, the speaker is suggesting that the example supports the assertion. Therefore, the following precautions should be observed whenever you use or listen to examples and illustrations that are presented as a justification for a specific hypothesis.

1. *Are there enough examples to justify the generalization?* There can be, of course, no absolute measure of "enough" in applying this test. The answer depends on many factors, but largely upon the phenomena being discussed. If the conclusion being drawn is somewhat controversial and

primarily a value judgment, one should expect more than one or two illustrations. Someone telling you a friend was beaten and robbed in downtown Burbank would not be in a position to establish the premise that Burbank streets are dangerous with that single example.

2. *Is the example or illustration a typical case?*   Too often people try to change our beliefs and opinions by offering as proof an example that is, under closer examination, an isolated case. It would be unfair, for example, to judge the entire membership of a fraternity by the experience of one person.

3. *Is the example clearly relevant to the idea?*   When we talked about critical listening in chapter 4, we suggested that the careful listener learns to ask "So what?" to certain information. Checking the relevancy of examples is merely an extension of that idea. If you were talking about the dangers of *night driving* and cited only an illustration of someone whose *brakes failed,* you would be guilty of offering an irrelevant case.

4. *Is the illustration properly detailed and explained?*   There are times when the illustration used lacks sufficent detail, and therefore may not contain the essential material. If you were talking of smoking and lung cancer, you might hurt your cause if you were to tell of a man who died of cancer, while at the same time forgetting to tell us anything about his smoking habits.

5. *Is there other evidence to support the conclusion being made by the generalization?*   This test should be applied to any evidence, whether it is presented in the form of an illustration, statistics, testimony, or analogy. Before we are satisfied that the example proves the specific point, we should ask for other facts and authoritative opinions which might suggest the falsity or validity of the generalization. Suppose, for example, that you are urging reforms in college registration procedures and have offered a single illustration to substantiate the need for reforms. Your position will be enhanced if you offer additional support—such as citing remarks of the dean of admissions which add believability to your thesis.

STATISTICS

In a sense, statistics are examples. Instead of talking about one or two cases or instances, we attempt to measure and define quantitatively. Statistics are facts represented numerically; they compare or show proportions as a means of helping a speaker develop and prove a point. Used in this way statistics help compress, summarize, and simplify the facts that relate to the issue in question. The essential characteristic of statistics is that they are simply generalizations derived from comparisons of individual instances.

Statistics, like illustrations, may be brief or quite detailed. The mere citation of a figure, such as the statement, "Medical authorities estimate that there are approximately 30,000 hemophiliacs of all types in the United States," would be considered statistics. There are also occasions when the statistics take a much longer form. Discussing the fact that in the 70s the utilities are depending on the atom to supply electric power, a speaker used the following statistics:

The trend toward atomic power is clearly illustrated by the information that tells us that in 1969 the major utilities bought 7 power plants with 7,200,000 kilowatts, and in 1973 the number jumped to 15 more plants with 16,400,000 kilowatts.

Since statistics are a strong form of proof, they should be gathered and presented in the most effective manner possible. The following few rules may increase your efficiency.

1. Whenever possible, present your statistics as round numbers, especially when several are offered. It is much easier to remember the population of a city if we hear "one and a half million," instead of "1,512,653." There are, of course, certain instances where exactness is essential. The purpose for which the statistics are being used should be the main factor in making your selection.

2. Give specific and complete source citations for your statistics. Saying "these statistics prove that . . ." or "quoting from a reliable source . . ." does not tell your audience where you located your information. If the material is controversial, it is useful to cite the magazine or book, specific pages and the date. In most cases, however, the date and the name of the magazine will be sufficient—for example, "According to the June 14, 1974, issue of *Time* magazine . . ." The act of documentation adds to the credibility and acceptability of your arguments.

3. Avoid presenting too many statistics at one time. A speech crammed with numbers can often create confusion and boredom. Imagine a speaker who says:

Let us look at what happened in 1974. On January 14 the profits for IMT went up 3%, a rise of 1% over 1973. This is a dollar increase of $2,474,743.32. When compared to April of 1973, which also had a 4% increase, we can see a net gain of over $3,499,812.79.

4. Make certain that your statistics directly relate to the point you are making. The relationship between your statistics and your assertion would be hard to discern if you were to say, "Last year the sale of riding horses increased by 100%, so we can see that most people are tired of paying for gasoline."

Testing Statistics

Statistics can have a telling effect on an audience as they listen to the comprehensiveness inherent in most statistical data. When used with factual examples, this comprehensiveness is combined with concreteness. Unfortunately, however, statistics are highly liable to error and abuse. The conscientious speaker, as well as the critical and careful listener, must therefore be willing to apply certain criteria to the statistics he or she confronts.

1. *Are the units being compared actually comparable?* It may be said that city X has twenty-five more crimes than does city Y, but if city X counts all crime and city Y counts only crimes against people and not those against property, the statistics are unreliable. In addition, city X may have a population of one-hundred thousand, while city Y has only thirty-five thousand residents. In both of these cases the units compared are not comparable.

2. *Do the statistics cover a sufficient number of cases?*   A statement that fifty percent of the voters polled favored Proposition II would be quite misleading if only ten people out of forty-thousand were asked their opinion.

3. *Do the statistics cover a sufficient period of time?*   There are really two considerations in applying this test. First, if one is going to talk about the high cost of foreign aid, current statistics must be given. The foreign aid bill changes each year, and what was valid five years ago is likely to be outdated today. In short, use current references whenever possible. Second, if you wish to draw conclusions from your data, you must be sure that the period covered is not exceptional. The flow of mail in December, unemployment figures in summer and winter, earnings of some companies during war time, and traffic after a football game are obviously exceptional cases.

4. *Are the statistics presented in a logical form?*   Often a speaker will jump from percentages to raw scores without any explanation. When talking about the political makeup of New York City a speaker noted:

> City census figures show 15% of New Yorkers are Negro, 8%
> Puerto Rican, 11% Italian, 4% Irish. There are an estimated 1,800,000
> Jews, 3,400,000 Roman Catholics, and 1,700,000 Protestants. And
> there are 3½ times as many registered Democrats as Republicans.

Notice that the speaker offers three different sets of numbers in one passage, and each set is presented in a manner different from the other sets.

5. *Were the gatherers of the statistics strongly interested in the outcome?*   Whenever you gather and analyze evidence it is crucial that you examine the bias and attitudes found within the special groups that originally compiled the data. For example, if you were considering the cost of living and union membership in states with the "Right to Work Law," you might find different results as you approached the Bureau of Labor Statistics, the AFL-CIO, the Democratic National Committee, and the National Association of Manufacturers. In these instances the speaker should consider as many different sources as possible and try to locate a neutral source.

TESTIMONY

In the complex world we live in it has become impossible for someone to be an authority on all topics. We have become increasingly dependent upon the expert testimony of others as a way of helping us find the relevant facts on an issue or a concept. The public speaker must also, on many occasions, turn to an expert. The testimony of an authority, as a form of support for a specific point, is often the most important type of evidence a speaker can use. It can show that the opinions of persons of authority, or experts in the field, corroborate the speaker's own views. For example, if you were trying to convince an audience that periodic chest X rays could save lives, you might quote the testimony of the surgeon general of the United States: "Our office has long held to the belief that systematic and regular chest X rays could help save the lives of many cancer and TB victims." A speaker giving a talk for the purpose of convincing an audience that the ex-convict has a difficult time reentering society used expert testimony in the following manner:

Lester N. Smith, who served as Head Warden of Sing Sing prison
for eleven years, indicated the scope of the problem faced by the
ex-convict when he stated that society rejects the convict right down the
line. It is hard for him to locate a job, almost impossible to own a
home, and difficult to lead a normal life. The labor unions often bar him
and big companies fear him. In a very real sense, he finds most roads
back to a normal life filled with social and economic blocs.

Your use of testimony can be made more effective by observing some
simple guidelines.

1.   Cite complete sources when using testimony. Let the listeners know
where you found your evidence, whether it be magazine, book, newspaper,
television program, or personal interview. You increase your personal credibility as well as the believability of your sources when you say "In the Sunday,
November 17 issue of the *New York Times*, Chief Justice Burger noted . . ."

2.   In selecting experts you will find it helpful to select those individuals
who will carry considerable weight with your audience. You should in all
circumstances establish the person's credibility and explain to your audience
why he or she is an expert. That is, make it clear to your listeners that this
particular person should be respected. The audience's acceptance of the
person will go a long way toward proving your point.

There is a common tendency for many speakers to equate expert testimony
with testimonial. Flip Wilson may be a good comedian, but that does not
qualify him as an expert on tooth decay.

3.   Don't try to memorize your quotations. By reading your quotations
directly you can assure accuracy and also avoid forgetting. In addition, reading
small portions of your speech, such as some of your evidence, will offer your
audience a change of pace. Furthermore, the act of reading a particular quotation will enhance its credibility. A small card will not detract from your speech
if you handle it correctly.

4.   The testimony should be relevant to the point being discussed. Speakers will often cite an authority to prove a position, but on closer examination
it is discovered that the expert is talking about another problem. Try to imagine
how ineffective it would be if you were talking about mental health and quoted
this testimony: "There are a great many people in hospitals today who would
not be there if they were not rushing to keep an appointment."

On some occasions you might find it helpful to explain the relevancy of
a piece of testimony in your own words. You could say, "What Police Chief
Jones is telling us is that . . ."

5.   Whenever possible use quotations that are brief. Quotations that
are long are often quite difficult to follow and on occasion hinder the audience's ability to concentrate. Even when paraphrasing you should aim at
brevity.

6.   Attend carefully to the means of introducing quotations. Lead-ins such
as "In a speech last week the Secretary of State noted . . ." and "So we see, as
Professor Jones pointed out, overpopulation and food shortage present serious

problems . . ." will help hold the audience's attention at the same time that they tell the source of the quotation and the time that it was delivered.

7. Indicate the beginning and the end of any quotation so that the audience will be able to distinguish your opinions from those of the expert you are quoting. However, try to avoid the all-too-common practice of "quote" and "unquote." A change of voice, a pause, a move, or a certain phrase can indicate the beginning and end of a quotation.

Testing Testimony

In using and listening to testimony, you should always remember that an expert's opinion may not be based on any concrete and comprehensive data. There are some safeguards we should observe whenever expert testimony is being used.

1. *Is the authority being quoted recognized as an expert in his field?* A common error today is to judge people as experts in many areas because they happen to be particularly qualified in one field. A college professor may teach eighteenth-century English literature, but this does not qualify him as an expert in economic affairs. The person's training, background, and degrees are one indication, but common sense and critical judgment are additional tests of expert testimony and qualification.

2. *Is the person an unbiased observer?* Objectivity is essential if we are to respect and believe the testimony of the expert. The chairman of the Republican National Committee would hardly be qualified to give an objective and accurate account of a Democratic president's term in office.

3. *Is the reference to authority specific?* Quotations such as "according to an eminent authority" or "an expert in the field concluded" are vague and misleading. We should know exactly *who* is being quoted.

4. *Are the opinions and feelings being expressed supported by other authorities and other evidence?* If you look hard enough and long enough, you can find testimony on all sides of a question and on all subjects, but careful and thorough investigation will reveal whether or not the expert is all alone in his or her views.

5. *When and where was the opinion expressed?* We live in such a changing and dynamic society that statistics, theories, and findings are soon outdated. What an expert said in 1969 may not express his views today. In addition, the place a statement is made may well influence what is said. The secretary of labor might well state one view at the Teamster's convention and yet expound another position, on the same theme, before the Chamber of Commerce.

ANALOGY OR COMPARISON

We are constantly asking someone to compare one idea or item with another. In trying to make our ideas clear, interesting, and impelling, we suggest that item A "resembles," "is similar to," or "is not as good as" item B. By using comparison we try to support our main thesis and explain our principal ideas.

Comparison usually takes the form of an **analogy.** In using an analogy, similarities are pointed out in regard to people, ideas, experiences, projects, institutions, or data, and conclusions are drawn on the basis of those similarities. The main function of the analogy is to point out the similarities between that which is already known and that which is not. In using this technique as support or proof, you should show the listener that what he already believes or knows is similar to what you are trying to prove or explain. For example, if you are suggesting that it is dangerous to drive while intoxicated, you might offer the following analogy:

> We all know that driving a car at a high rate of speed during a foggy
> night is dangerous because of our impaired vision (known). The same
> can be said of those who try to drive after consuming a number
> of alcoholic beverages, for their vision is also obscured, and their life
> is in peril (unknown).

Ordinarily, analogies are divided into two types: **figurative** and **literal.** The **figurative** compares things of different classes, such as the United States Banking System with a human being's circulatory system, or an airplane with a bird. To say that writing a term paper is like learning to swim, because both have certain basic rules that are difficult at first and get easier with time, would be an example of a figurative analogy. This type of analogy is generally vivid, full of imagery, but has limited value as proof, since the dissimilarities of things in different classes are usually obvious and can be readily attacked—often to the disadvantage of the creator of the analogy.

Much more useful and valid is the **literal** analogy, whereby you compare items, ideas, institutions, people, projects, data, or experiences of the same class. You might point out similarities between one instructor and another, one political creed and another, or one city and another. On the basis of the similarities, you build up a theorem. We reason that if two or more things of the same class contain identical or nearly identical characteristics, certain conclusions that are true in one case may also be true in the other(s). For example, Winston Churchill employed a literal analogy when he compared the turning point of the Civil War with what he believed to be the turning point in World War II. Still another example can be found in the speaker who was trying to persuade an audience that the United Nations Charter should be obeyed by all member nations:

> We Americans take a great deal of pride in the Constitution and
> the Bill of Rights. We know that our country would not be as great and as
> strong as it is if we were to discontinue our obedience and allegiance
> to the laws and regulations contained in these documents. The same
> can be said of the United Nations Charter. For just as each of us,
> as individuals, must comply with the Constitution and is provisions, so
> must the members of the United Nations comply with its laws and rules.
> If the individual nations do not observe, and obey the laws of the
> Charter of the United Nations, it will not be an effective instrument for
> world peace.

The comparison and similarities are obvious—we are aware of the concepts behind the Constitution (known), the speaker suggests that the same concepts are inherent to the United Nations Charter (unknown). In summary, you believe and understand one, therefore, you should believe and understand the other, for they are basically the same.

Testing Analogy

In selecting and using analogies, either figurative or literal, it is essential that your analogies meet certain requirements.

1. *Is the analogy clearly relevant to the idea?*   To argue that since Sue and Mary both belong to the same social organization they must therefore think the same way politically is an example of irrelevant use of analogy. The similarity of their organization may be interesting, but is certainly not relevant.

2. *Do the points of likeness outweigh the points of difference?*   If the differences, on the *essential* features being compared, outweigh the similarities, one can hardly establish a logical connection. If we compare a supermarket to a high school in order to make the point that each must keep its customers, we have overlooked some fundamental differences that exist in the two cases.

3. *Is the premise (generalization) upon which the analogy is based accurate?*   Saying "just as a ship sinks without a captain, so will our club be destroyed without a president" is an example of a false circumstance being used as a basis for the generalization, for a ship does not necessarily sink without a captain. The premise for the entire analogy and conclusion is therefore inaccurate and invalid.

4. *Is the analogy appropriate to the audience?*   It is important for the audience to observe clearly the likenesses and the essential characteristics of the analogy. If one-half of the comparison confuses your listeners, you may find that your analogy has hindered rather than aided your speech. It would probably be confusing to a group of high school freshmen if you were to say, "The workings of the rotary engine are much like that of the epiglottis."

5. *Is the analogy supported by other forms of support?*   Analogies alone are seldom sufficient to prove a point. You should try to examine other types of evidence to see if the relationship between the known and the unknown can be verified.

OTHER FORMS OF SUPPORT

At the beginning of this chapter we made note of the fact that the forms of support occasionally overlap—that a factual illustration might well contain statistics. Certain other forms of support are closely related to the six already discussed. Many of these are further extensions and refinements of those just mentioned. For example, the **anecdote,** in which real-life characters are usually featured, the **fable,** in which animal characters speak and act as if they were human beings, and the **parable,** which is a fictitious story from which a moral or religious lesson may be drawn— all are forms of the illustration. Long quotations, at times, may be listed as a type of testimony.

Other devices for developing, amplifying, and clarifying, such as explanation, definition, restatement, repetition, and description, will be discussed in detail in chapter 10 when we examine the principles of informing. There are also many situations in which a speaker will use a combination of these devices. For example, you may have occasion to cite an expert who is, in turn, citing statistics or using an analogy. The important concept for the student of communication to remember is that any of the techniques discussed in this book should be used if they will aid in the securing of the response you desire. The various classifications suggested throughout the volume are only a guide for specific occasions; the real communication situation must determine your final selection.

VISUAL SUPPORT

The importance and use of visual aids will be discussed in a very specific manner when we examine the speech to inform. However, visual aids are also useful as a means of supporting and providing an idea, principle, or concept. By *seeing* what is being talked about, the listener brings still another one of his or her senses into play. In trying to convince the judge that the stop sign was blocked from view by a large tree, the lawyer brought forth a photograph. On seeing the picture the judge ruled the defendant could not have seen the sign from his car. The old adage "seeing is believing" is made real by a specific chart, model, demonstration, or exhibit. In addition, statistics that are often detailed and confusing can be clarified and reinforced by a graph or table that highlights the main features.

The best advice for both the novice and the professional speaker using visual aids is to *practice!* By practicing with your visual aid, you will discover the strengths and weaknesses of the aid before the actual speaking situation occurs. In addition, the conscientious student should try to answer the following questions: (1) Can the audience see the important details contained within the visual aid? Are they large enough and clear enough? (2) Will the visual aid distract the audience? When and how shall I display it? (3) Does my visual aid directly support the point under consideration?

FINDING MATERIAL

Clarence Darrow, one of the most famous trial lawyers of all time, once noted, "Anybody who speaks should spend a thousand days on trying to get ideas and knowledge to every one day they spend on the way to tell it." What Darrow is telling us is obvious: While much of the information of our speeches will come from our personal experiences, we must remember that support and clarification are important and that they take hard work.

Once you have selected your topic and decided on your purpose, the serious task of deciding what you want to say begins. In making decisions concerning your material, you must begin by carefully thinking about the audience and your objectives. By placing the topic in its proper perspective, you will be better able to determine what you know about the central issues and what you must find out.

EXPERIENCE AND OBSERVATION

One of the best ways to gather material for speeches or for everyday conversation is to be alert to what goes on around us. If we go through life wearing blinders and not taking full advantage of all our senses, we are apt to miss much of the detail and information that life can offer. Plato once wrote, "Knowledge is but to remember." To have the experiences and observations to remember, one must develop the philosophy of "awareness." Being aware of the world around you is as simple as listening to speeches, listening to news programs, taking part in conversations, and keeping both eyes wide open as you move from environment to environment.

If being aware and alert is part of your daily philosophy, you can call forth personal experiences and firsthand observations for your speeches. These personal examples are often more vivid and lively than those examples you have read about. Therefore, as we suggested earlier, start your speech preparation by discovering your own ideas, beliefs, and feelings on the subject. *Examine your memory.*

You should be cautioned, however, about depending solely on the conclusions reached from observations. We all know that our perception of any happening is colored by our background and earlier experiences. This lack of objective perceptiveness can often influence what we *really* see and hear. Therefore, make effective and abundant use of observations and past experiences, but always remember you are dealing with a statistic of one. More proof may be needed for a valid generalization.

INTERVIEWS

The experiences and observations of other people, who might be in a better position to know more about the subject than you, are often excellent sources of information. The interview has several advantages. First, it enables you to ask specific questions that are directly related to your topic. This face-to-face situation lets you acquire quick responses to your questions. Second, the interview allows you a certain degree of selectivity. Instead of simply talking to someone who knows a little about the topic, you can gather data by going directly to an expert—someone with firsthand information.

As a college student you are in a position to make extensive use of interviews. Most professors are experts in specific fields and can offer you some valuable assistance. To illustrate, if you were going to give a speech dealing with the problems of interracial marriages, you might gain some useful information and some new ideas from interviews with professors in sociology, psychology, religion, and marriage and family relations. In addition, you might also seek an appointment with some of the campus ministers. In all of these instances you are increasing your background on the topic.

An interview of any kind requires forethought—arranging for the meeting, preparing an agenda, and thinking out the means of securing frank responses. The interviewer should also be on time, explain his or her purpose, take careful notes, and be careful not to misquote the person when the material is used.

PRINTED MATERIAL

Donald C. Bryant and Karl R. Wallace, in their text on oral communication, noted, "The library is to the speechmaker what the laboratory is to the scientist. It is a place of search and research." We would also suggest that reading in books, magazines, periodicals, newspapers, documents, and the like, constitutes the largest single source of information at the disposal of any speaker.

Before recommending some places to look for printed material, let us offer some advice for all researchers.

1. Read with a definite purpose. We wrote earlier in this section that your preparation begins after you have decided on your specific purpose and reviewed your personal fund of information. With those two tasks behind you, it is much easier to seek out only that material which is relevant. You will also be able to be more selective and avoid going off in many different directions.

2. Read more than you think you will use. Most beginning students feel compelled to read only enough to "get by." You will discover, however, that the most effective speakers have a grasp of the topic which goes beyond the material given in the speech.

3. Be critical. Examine many sources and opinions on the same topic. In this way you will be able to determine the validity of your ideas as well as the authenticity of what you read.

4. Take complete and accurate notes on what you read. It is important, for ethical as well as practical reasons, for you to keep a record of exactly where your material came from. For example, if your material is from a magazine, you should have the name of the author, title of the article, name of the magazine, volume, date, and page. This material is often cited in your speech and shown in your outline and bibliography. You should also use quotation marks when quoting directly. Plagiarism is to be avoided at all times.

5. Know your library. Although similarities exist, no two libraries are alike. Discover what catalog system your library uses, what reference books they have, their physical facilities, their special collections, their regulations, and their hours. Feel free to ask questions of those who work in the library. Timidity may well cost you access to some valuable information.

INDEXES

The library card catalog, with its subject, title, and author index, is a superb starting point for your research. In this file you will find a complete listing of the books found in your library. The *Reader's Guide to Periodical Literature*, which is published each month, is a cumulative index to articles published in more than a hundred selected periodicals. Articles are listed alphabetically as to author, title, and subject. Two newspapers, the *New York Times* and the *London Times*, are also indexed.

In addition to the common indexes cited above, the diligent student might have occasion to consult the *Bulletin of Public Affairs Information Service* and the *International Index*. The activity of the United States Senate and the House of Representatives is completely indexed in the *Congressional Record*. Some learned information can be secured by investigating the *Agricultural Index, Applied Science and Technology Index, Educational Index, Psychological Index, Psychological Abstracts, Social Science Abstracts* and *The Monthly Catalog—United States Government Publications*.

REFERENCE BOOKS

Most of us are familiar with the practice of starting our research by turning to the encyclopedia. However, the task of investigation must not stop there; the sincere communicator makes use of other reference materials.

The World Almanac, The Statesman's Year Book, Information Please Almanac, Statistical Abstract of the United States, and *Commerce Reports*—all furnish facts and figures that the speaker may find useful.

Literary references can be found in such books as *Bartlett's Familiar Quotations, Oxford Dictionary of Quotations,* and *The Home Book of Quotations*.

For information about people, it is always beneficial to look at some biographical guides. Some of the more useful guides are *Current Biography, Dictionary of American Biography, Who's Who, Who's Who in America, Webster's Biographical Dictionary,* and *International Who's Who*.

NEWSPAPERS

Information on almost any topic can be secured from newspapers. While books normally take years to be written and published, newspapers are an excellent source of current happenings and information. Some of the leading newspapers are the *New York Times, Christian Science Monitor, Washington (D.C.) Post, St. Louis Post Dispatch,* and the *Los Angeles Times*. Two highly regarded foreign newspapers are the *London Times* and the *Manchester Guardian*. Students with speech topics limited to regional problems and issues will find it helpful to consult the local newspapers.

MAGAZINES AND PAMPHLETS

There are hundreds of magazines available in the United States, and it would be impossible to list all of them. However, there are some current publications which often contain articles on a wide range of subjects: *Time, Newsweek, United States News and World Report, Business Week, Fortune, New Republic Reporter, Nation, Atlantic Monthly, Commonweal, Harper's Magazine, Current History, National Geographic, Atlas, Foreign Affairs, Yale Review,* and *Vital Speeches of the Day*.

Most libraries have a large collection of pamphlets that are hard to catalog and index because of their size and subject. These pamphlets, which are printed and circulated by various groups and organizations such as the American Medical Association and the Automobile Club, cover a wide range of topics. Normally this material can be secured from the library's "vertical file" or by asking the librarian the location of the college's pamphlet collection.

ACADEMIC JOURNALS

In addition to the countless magazines written for the general public there are also hundreds of very specialized journals written for specific audiences. There will be times when it will be helpful to consult one of these academic journals in preparing a speech. Scholarly journals are found in all areas and fields. Whether the topic be education, political science, sociology, speech, home economics, or engineering, there are academic publications available. Ask any library assistant to help you locate the specific journal related to the field you are investigating.

WHEN TO USE THE FORMS
OF SUPPORT

To determine when the various forms of support are needed is no easy task. Every audience, occasion, and topic has special demands that make each communication encounter a unique and dynamic experience. There are, however, some basic rules to remember when you are trying to decide where support should be utilized.

Are you making a statement that will be accepted as true simply because you assert it? For example, if you want to convince an audience that educational benefits for veterans should be increased, you must do more than say, "The meager grants now awarded under the GI Bill are so small that many veterans cannot attend college." Any intelligent listener would most likely respond by saying, "What do you mean?" or "How do you know this is true?" You should use forms of support when you are making a statement that needs substantiation as a means of establishing its authenticity, believability, and plausibility.

How much substantiation is needed? There is no simple formula for deciding how much support any assertion will require. In most instances you will have to depend on your own good judgment and common sense. View the assertion or statement from the perspective of your audience. If you were a listener, would you need and demand proof for the opinions being expressed? One audience might accept the contention that a college education is useful; a skeptical audience would demand support.

Are you making a statement that requires no further clarification? As we have pointed out, the forms of support are often used for clarification as well as for proof. Now we ask, "Is my idea clear?" If the answer is no, support is needed. If we were to say, "There is often a stigma attached to people who have been mentally ill," we run the risk of our audience not knowing what we mean. However, we could clarify our point by an illustration about someone who has been stigmatized because of confinement in an institution.

DETECTING FALLACIES

Thus far in this chapter we have stressed three closely related principles: good speakers include sufficient evidence to support their positions; test their evidence to see that it is valid and reliable; and do some serious research and investigation to supplement their ideas. However, simply locating and employing evidence and material are not enough, for the use the speaker makes of this material is as important as the material itself. In short, the speaker's reasoning must be clear and free from fallacies.

Since communication is concerned with the processes of sending and receiving messages, the thorough student must be alert to mistaken arguments, faulty reasoning, and irrelevant evidence. The examination of evidence, reasoning, and ideas for weaknesses is a search for fallacies. Over one hundred years ago Richard Whately, a noted logician, classified as a fallacy "any unsound mode of arguing which appears to demand our conviction, and to be decisive of the question in hand; when in fairness it is not."

The communication of the market place is often characterized by politicians who seek our vote but haven't earned it, or by salespeople who want our business but don't deserve it. By the words they use and the arguments they offer, they seek to have an influence over our actions. But we must ask ourselves if their appeals are free of fallacies. We are confronted daily by individuals who seek to change our behavior by offering us unsupported generalizations or, even worse, conclusions based on blemished evidence. Being cognizant of some of the more common fallacies will enable us to avoid their use in our own utterances, while at the same time building defenses against the sophistry of others.

Logicians, social psychologists, and rhetoricians have made repeated attempts to classify the different tyes of fallacies, but experience has shown that a satisfactory hard-and-fast division of them has not yet been found. Not only is there a problem of classification and division, but there is also the question of what to include and what to exclude. Discussions of fallacies often contain lists with as many as fifty-one specific kinds of fallacies. In the course of talking about propaganda and listening, we have mentioned some of the more common types of errors in reasoning and evidence. What is included now is a partial list of some additional fallacies with which the student of communication should be familiar.

HASTY GENERALIZATION
Snap judgments, jumping to conclusions, or generalizations based on insufficient evidence or experience are all examples of the hasty generalization fallacy. In this fallacy the error is committed because the speaker draws a uni-

versal conclusion from evidence which warrants only a restricted conclusion. If you were to meet a Norwegian and find him lazy, and from this meeting conclude that all Norwegians are lazy, you would be guilty of a hasty generalization.

This fallacy is very common in daily life. Most of us can recall instances in which travelers have experienced one or two unpleasant situations and then reached conclusions concerning the honesty and character of the people in that particular city. Or the example of the person who will not take Professor Smith for history because he knows two students who received "D's" from Smith. Still another example is the speaker who concluded that all supporters of the Peace and Freedom Party were Communists. The speaker stated, "Eric Foresman supported Peace and Freedom and he is a Communist; Scott Allen supported them and he, too, is a Communist. So, you see that all supporters of Peace and Freedom are Communists." And how often we hear people say, "Artists are immoral," "All Republicans are conservatives," "German shepherds are mean and vicious," only to discover later that these same people know very few artists, Republicans, or German shepherds.

We mentioned some ways to guard against this fallacy earlier in this chapter when we looked at ways of testing the example and the illustration. It might be wise to return to that section and notice how one can use some of those same techniques to detect the generalization that is irrelevant and based on an isolated case.

BEGGING THE QUESTION

The fallacy of begging the question occurs in several forms, but in every one of its compositions it is committed by assuming at the onset of the argument the very point which is to be established in the conclusion. That is, in this fallacy the speaker assumes the truth or falsity of a statement without proof. If someone making a speech were to state, "Cheating among our students is widespread and bad and should therefore be abolished," he or she would be begging the question. In this example the speaker is taking for granted that cheating exists, when in essence the statement can't justify such a conclusion.

Begging the question normally appears in the form of "arguing in a circle." When one proposition is used to prove another proposition, we are engaging in this fallacy. Arguing in a circle would usually appear in the following form: "Medical Plan X is best because the experts say so. How do we know who the experts are? They are the people who prefer Medical Plan X." In this case, begging the question is illustrated by taking as a premise what is true only if the conclusion has been granted to be correct.

NON SEQUITUR

In a broad sense, any argument which fails to establish its conclusion may be said to be a **non sequitur,** for the meaning of the term is simply, "It does not follow." In a more specific sense, however, the fallacy of **non sequitur** means that a conclusion is drawn from premises which provide no adequate logical ground for it, or which have no relevant connection with it. "Jones is a good husband and a fine father, so he ought to be elected mayor." It is quite obvious in this example that a logical cause-effect relationship cannot be made. Still other statements point out how speakers often reach false conclusions as they try to establish cause-effect connections. "Since only a few people have the ability to handle the complex problems of industry, the wealth and power of this country rightfully belongs in the hands of the rich." "The child is un-happy, beautiful, and a college freshman; she must therefore come from an average American family."

One of the most common and insidious forms of this fallacy is **post hoc, ergo propter hoc,** or "after this, therefore because of this." This fallacy mani-fests itself in assuming that because one occurrence *precedes another in time,* the one is the *cause* of the other. Superstitions belong here. If you walk under a ladder on your way to class and receive an "A" that same day, and then con-clude that walking under the ladder gives "A's," you are guilty of **post hoc, ergo propter hoc.** Recently a speaker noted, "Since minority groups have been given more educational opportunity we have had an increase in the crime rate throughout the United States. I would conclude, therefore, that the growth in crime is directly related to education," Here again it is just not sufficient to say there is a connection simply because one thing followed the other. In short, because two things happen in sequence does not mean that they are logically or causally connected.

NONRATIONAL AND IRRELEVANT EVIDENCE

The use of nonrational and irrelevant material is one of the greatest causes for errors in our reasoning. We have already pointed out that many of these prob-lems were discussed in chapter 4 when we mentioned the techniques and devices employed by the propagandist. However, these fallacies are so prev-alent that they warrant further examination. The most common types of non-rational evidence are (1) appeals to the emotions and prejudices, (2) appeals to tradition and authority, and (3) appeals to personalities rather than issues.

Appealing only to the emotions and prejudices of the audience, often called **argumentum ad populum,** is a common technique of the speaker who prefers to deal exclusively with the passions of his audience rather than talk about the salient issues. Instead of presenting empirical evidence and logical argument, the **ad populum** speaker attempts to win support with phrases such as, "Jewish parasites," "slaughtered women and children," "un-American trai-tor," "Catholic demagogue," and "friend of the Communists." Fortunately, appeals to passions and prejudices become less successful as we become more educated. Yet we must be alert at all times so that we will be able to separate the essential from the nonessential.

A second fallacy, often called **argumentum ad vercundiam,** shows itself when the speaker offers proof for his or her position by making an appeal to authority, to a "name," or to an institution. If the authority is legitimately con-nected to the subject, we have a valid use of expert opinion. However, the fallacy occurs if the appeal is made to justify an authority who is out of his domain or an authority who is unreliable. For example, "George Washington, the Father of our country, warned us against the danger of foreign alliances. Therefore, we should withdraw from the North Atlantic Treaty Organization." It is agreed that Washington was an influential figure during the early history of the United States, but the needs of modern foreign affairs are quiet different from the needs expressed in Washington's era. The best defense against the **ad vercundiam** fallacy is the use of the tests of authority discussed earlier in the chapter.

In the **argumentum ad hominem** fallacy the speaker attacks someone's character instead of dealing with the relevant issues at hand. That is, the arguments are transferred from principles to personalities. A speaker is engaging in an **ad hominem** argument when he or she states, "The city's new highway program should be vetoed. The highway commissioner is a notorious trouble maker and a former lobbyist." Still another case is the speaker who notes, "How can the Rockefellers help the poor? They have never been cold or hungry." Notice that in both of these instances the merits of the point at issue are disregarded while attention is focused upon the source. The best defense against this approach is to demand that the person speaking, whether yourself or someone else, stay on the topic and include only material that obviously is relevant.

SUMMARY

In this chapter we have been concerned with four factors of communication that directly affect one another—evidence, the testing of evidence, locating material, and detecting fallacies.

The forms of support treated in this chapter represent the fundamental devices used in most types of public discourse and in most private communication situations. These forms are the detailed factual illustration, the undeveloped illustration (specific instance), the hypothetical illustration, statistics, testimony, analogy, and visual aids.

Evidence must meet certain standards if it is to be clear, persuasive, and effective. In his book *Argumentation and Debate*, Austin J. Freeley sets forth an excellent summary for testing evidence. His interpretation, in addition to the specific tests discussed in this chapter, should always be considered in using forms of support.

(1) Is there sufficient evidence? (2) Is the evidence clear? (3) Is the evidence consistent with other known evidence? (4) Can the evidence be verified? (5) Does the evidence come from a competent source? (6) Does the evidence come from an unprejudiced source? (7) Does the evidence come from a reliable source? (8) Is the evidence relevant to the problem? (9) Is the evidence statistically sound? (10) Is it the most recent evidence?

In the search for material, the speaker can use personal experiences and observation, conduct interviews, consult indexes, and use newspapers, pamphlets, magazines, and academic journals.

One must, in addition to finding evidence, use the forms of support in a sound and logical manner. In thinking straight, the speaker, as well as the listener, should be alert to certain fallacies. The most common errors in reasoning and using evidence are hasty generalization, begging the question, **non sequitur,** irrational and irrelevant evidence.

Suggested Readings

Aldrich, Ella Virginia. *Using Books and Libraries.* Englewood Cliffs, N.J.: Prentice-Hall, 1960.

Baird, A. Craig; Knower, Franklin H.; and Becker, Samuel. *General Speech Communication.* New York: McGraw-Hill Book Co., 1971. Chapter 9.

Bettinghaus, Erwin P. *Message Preparation: The Nature of Proof.* New York: The Bobbs-Merrill Co., 1966.

Connolly, James E. *Public Speaking as Communication.* Minneapolis: Burgess Publishing Co., 1974. Part II.

Fearnside, W. Ward, and Holther, William B. *Fallacy: The Counterfeit of Argument.* Englewood Cliffs, N.J.: Prentice-Hall, 1959.

Monroe, Alan H., and Ehninger, Douglas. *Principles and Types of Speech.* 6th ed. Glenview, Ill.: Scott, Foresman and Co., 1967. Chapter 10.

Newman, Robert P., and Newman, Dele R. *Evidence.* Boston: Houghton Mifflin Co., 1969.

Terris, Walter. *Content and Organization of Speeches.* Dubuque, Ia.: Wm. C. Brown Company Publishers, 1968. Chapter 5.

Walter, Otis M., and Scott, Robert L. *Thinking and Speaking.* 3d ed. New York: Macmillan Co., 1973. Chapter 3.

Organization
Assembling Your Ideas

6

Preceding chapters have dealt with those aspects of message preparation which involve selecting a topic, finding and evaluating material, and determining both the general purpose and the specific purpose of the message in light of what we know about the listener. The actual starting point of message preparation will, of course, be dependent upon the situation calling forth the message. For example, if your speech instructor were to assign you the task of explaining to the class your daily job routine, you would not have to deal with the problems of selecting a subject and fixing a purpose. Very likely you would start by analyzing your knowledge of the subject with an eye to its applicability to the audience, the occasion, and other limiting factors that might be operative. But if the instructor were to say, "Speak to us next Tuesday," then the problem of subject selection would have to be resolved before any other steps could be undertaken.

Regardless of the starting point of your speech preparation, you will eventually become involved in an assessment of the pieces of evidence, the ideas, issues, and conclusions which emerge during your investigation of the subject. You will probably experience an initial feeling of frustration at seeing a mass of jumbled parts, not unlike a disassembled jigsaw puzzle. Then frustration will turn to comprehension when you manage to get several pieces together and see a design beginning to emerge. You will detect relationships of certain items to other items. You will find it easier to sort the materials and compartmentalize them. In short, you will call into play habitual patterns of organizing your perceptions so that they may have meaning for you. These initial efforts at organizing, then, serve to clarify the subject for you; they facilitate your detection of the relationships that exist among the items of accumulated material. This taking apart of the subject in order to discover its parts and the interdependency that exists among those parts is called *analysis*. Subsequently you will reassemble the materials with a view to communicating them to others in order to achieve your predetermined purpose. This process is called *synthesis*.

The organizational process benefits speakers in several ways. It helps them detect any weaknesses in the fabric of their logic and any inadequacies in the amount and quality of their evidence. It enables them to juxtapose ideas in a variety of ways and thus determine the sequence that is best fitted to their audience and to the accomplishment of their purpose. Clear organization helps them to retain ideas with greater ease during the pressure of message presentation. Finally speakers benefit in most cases from the added credibility attached to their well-organized ideas.

But it is ultimately for the listener's benefit that we attend to organizational strategies. Our message must be understood at the moment of encounter, because the listener, unlike the reader, cannot arrest the message and study it at leisure. Clear organization facilitates understanding and encourages the listener to remain attentive.

In this chapter we shall discuss the organizational principles and methods one may use in the carefully prepared speech, but many of these principles and methods will have application to informal communication acts as well. Whether the message emerges as a formal speech or as a chance remark, whether it be carefully prepared or composed on the instant, it will be more effective if it has organizational clarity.

While there are a variety of ways to approach the task of assembling the message, we shall concentrate upon the method that involves formulating a core statement which expresses the central idea of the message, phrasing main points to support the core statement (and subpoints to support the main points, if needed), and choosing appropriate patterns to show relationships among the points. We shall discuss the devising of an overall speech plan, the mechanics of outlining, and the formulation of the introduction and the conclusion.

Our approach presumes the traditional three-fold division of the message into introduction, body, and conclusion. While not all messages require this formal division, it is workable in the great majority of cases.

THE CORE STATEMENT

The simplest form of speech has essentially two ingredients: (1) a statement or point that requires clarification, amplification, or proof and (2) the materials which clarify, amplify, or prove the statement. A complex speech is simply a combination of such units revolving around an even more general statement. The most general statement of the speech we shall call the **core statement;** the less general statements we shall call the **main points;** the least general statements we shall call **subpoints.** We may visualize the levels of generality as follows:

Core Statement:		Gasoline consumption is declining in all parts of the United States.
Main point:	I.	It is declining in the South.
Subpoint:	A.	Florida is experiencing a sharp decline.
Support:	1.	Gasoline dealers in the Tampa Bay area report sales are only 65 percent of the usual volume.
Support:	2.	The Jacksonville *Journal* reports that northern Florida is witnessing twice as many station closures this year.
Subpoint:	B.	Louisiana is experiencing a decline.
Support:	1.	Refineries in the Baton Rouge area are operating at only 55 percent of their capacity because of bulging storage tanks.
Support:	2.	The Louisiana Highway Patrol reports

passenger-car travel is only 50 percent of the
normal volume expected at this time of year.

Main Point: II.   It is declining in the West.

The core statement is called by some authors the subject sentence, the theme
sentence, the thesis, or the proposition. Whatever the label used, it signifies
that element which gives unity to everything in the speech.

The core statement sometimes is phrased as a value judgment, such as,
"Legal obortion is just as immoral as illegal abortion." It may take the form of
a statement of alleged fact, such as, "President Kennedy was struck by bullets fired from two different rifles." It may be worded as a policy position,
such as, "State employees should be given the right to strike." It might suggest
the steps in a process, "Decorating a concrete surface involves etching the
surface, priming the surface, and painting the surface." It might suggest the
parts of a whole, "The vocal apparatus consists of vibrators, resonators, and
articulators." Or it might indicate the characteristics which distinguish the
subject from other closely related subjects, as in a definition of rhetoric:
"Rhetoric is that form of communication that is intentional, largely verbal, and
designed to achieve a specific objective."

Ideally, the formulation of the core statement will take place at the end
of your investigation or analysis of the subject. With the results of your research before you, you will be in a position to ask yourself, "What does all
this add up to?" Your answer to that question should provide you with your
core statement. Then you will be ready to reassemble the subject for your
hearer—to organize your speech.

The principal benefit to be derived from formulating the core statement
at the outset of the organizational process is that it will provide you with an
immediate test of the relevance of any material you expect to introduce in the
speech. If any main point, subpoint, or supporting material does not clearly
relate to the core sentence, then it should be discarded as irrelevant. *Thus the
core statement helps insure the unity of the speech.*

It is entirely possible that the core statement may not be spoken during
the speech, but it should be implicit in the way in which the speech unfolds.
If it is spoken during the speech, it may occur in the opening statement of the
introduction, at the start of the body or development of the speech, or at the
end of the speech. Whether it should be spoken and when it should be spoken
cannot be prescribed by rule. Your careful analysis of the audience should
afford you a clue. Remember, one of its functions is to keep you from introducing into the speech materials that are irrelevant and hence confusing to
the listener.

FORMULATING MAIN
POINTS AND SUBPOINTS

Since the core statement is the most general statement of the speech, we must
ask: What less-general statements does it suggest? These less-general state-

ments, as we have noted earlier, constitute the main points of the body of the speech.

Selection and phrasing of the main points should be undertaken with the following guidelines in mind: (1) each main point must grow out of the core statement; (2) each main point must be separable from the other main points; (3) main points must possess consistency; (4) collectively, the main points should develop the core statement completely. Let us examine more fully these four guidelines in operation.

1. *Kinship to the core statement.* If a statement is to be labeled a main point, it must contribute toward providing, explaining, or illustrating the core statement. In an argumentative speech, one quick test of relevance is to place such connectives as *because* and *for* between the core statement and the alleged main point. For example:

Core Statement: Aerosol spray cans are dangerous,

because

   I.   They can explode if stored indiscriminately.

  II.   They can cause serious injury if the release valve is accidentally pointed toward the user.

 III.   Some cans contain propellants that are allegedly capable of depleting the Earth's ozone layer.

In an expository speech you can test relevance by using *for example, as follows, namely,* and *in that.*

Core Statement: Nylon netting has a variety of uses.

for example,

   I.   It is useful in dressmaking.

  II.   It is useful in crafts.

 III.   It is useful in household tasks.

Can you detect which of the following main points does not meet the test of relevancy?

Core Statement: The so-called classical pattern of speech organization is *useful* today.

   I.   It can be *used* to fashion speeches on questions of fact.

  II.   It can be *applied* to speeches dealing with questions of value.

 III.   It can be *traced* to the speeches of early Sicilian rhetors.

2. *Separability from other main points.* Just as brothers and sisters are related (but separate) components of the family, so main points are related (but separate) components of the speech. The *violation* of separability of main points can be seen in this example:

Core Statement: Capital punishment should be abolished.

     I.   It is not effective.

    II.   It is not a deterrent.

    III.   It is not morally justifiable.

It is apparent that there is overlapping between I and II, inasmuch as the deterrent issue is part of the larger issue of effectiveness. Therefore, II is really a subpoint of I. Or viewed in another light, if effectiveness can be measured only in terms of deterrency, then II is really a restatement of I.

Unless the characteristic of separability is observed in the selection and phrasing of main points, the listener is likely to become confused.

3. *Consistency of main points.*   Maine, California, and Georgia form a consistent grouping if we are discussing statehood. City, county, state, and nation form another consistent grouping if we are discussing levels of government. Trains, buses, and planes may be regarded as consistent with one another if we are discussing public transportation.

Where do you detect *inconsistency* in the following?

Core Statement: Transcendental meditation is practiced nationwide.

     I.   It is practiced in the West.

    II.   It is practiced in the East.

    III.   It is practiced in New York.

    IV.   It is practiced in the South.

The foregoing represents not only a violation of consistency of pattern but also a violation of separability. "New York" breaks the pattern of direction and is not separable from "the East."

We shall have more to say of consistency of main points when we turn to the next section of this chapter.

4. *Collective completeness of main points.*   We have not discovered all of the main points of a speech if there is a facet of the core statement that has not been developed. We don't think of a family as being complete unless we have all the children and both parents. The mainland visitor to Hawaii often makes the mistake of alluding to matters "back in the States," only to be reminded by the islander that "you *are* in the States." A person who makes a generalization about the United States without taking Hawaii into account is quickly corrected.

Determining all of the essential constituents is not always easy. The salesperson who wants to convince the customer that a particular automobile is the best one to buy has to determine the essential constituents of "best," not from a personal vantage point, but from the predicted vantage point of the customer. To the customer the "best" car might be the most stylish, or the most economical to operate, or the most powerful. So it is necessary for you to look at your core statement from the vantage point of the listener and ask, "What points will the speaker have to cover before winning my agreement?" or "What points will the speaker have to clarify before I understand fully?"

Although our discussion in this section has centered around the selection and phrasing of main points, all of the principles brought out are equally applicable to the selection and phrasing of subpoints, since the subpoint bears the same relationship to the main point as the main point bears to the core statement.

PATTERNS OF RELATIONSHIP

Psychologists tell us that things perceived in isolation tend to lack meaning until we see them in relationship to other things. All of us employ habitual patterns of organizing our perceptions into meaningful relationships. Some things we perceive within a temporal frame; others in terms of spatial placement; still others in terms of logical parts, components, or divisions. We have patterns for perceiving relationships that are argumentative in character, others that are nonargumentative. The number of possible patterns of organization is probably incalculable, but we wish to call your attention to some that have proved to be particularly serviceable to speakers over the years.

GENERAL PURPOSE PATTERNS

TIME RELATIONSHIPS

Certain subjects lend themselves ideally to development in terms of a time sequence. For example, if we wished to discuss the growth of the fast-food industry, we would start with the earliest signs of growth and then move forward in time to the present or move in reverse from the present to the past. Our main points might appear as follows:

Core Statement: The fast-food industry has enjoyed phenomenal growth in the past twenty years.

     I.   Drive-through hamburger stands sparked the trend in the mid-fifties.

    II.   Chains of fast-food restaurants spread throughout the U.S. in the early sixties.

    III. Western Europe and Japan are currently witnessing an invasion of fast-food franchises from the U.S.

The step-by-step method used in describing a process or in offering instructions is a kind of time pattern. In discussing what happens to a letter from the time it is mailed until it is received, we might arrange our points accordingly:

Core Statement: Mail handling involves collection, sorting, and distribution.

    I.   The first step is mail collection.

    II.   The second step is primary sorting.

   III.   The third step is final sorting.

   IV.   The fourth step is primary distribution.

   V.   The fifth step is final distribution.

Instructions in changing a tire might include these steps: (1) laying out the proper tools, (2) jacking up the car, (3) removing the flat tire, (4) putting on the spare tire, and (5) letting the jack down.

It is generally advisable to keep the number of main points in a time pattern as few as possible—ideally, between three and five—so that they can be easily retained by the speaker and easily followed by the hearer. This necessitates placing a number of chronolgical details under such general groupings as "The first era was . . . ," "The first decade was characterized by . . . ," or "The ancient Greeks were the first to systematize the study of public speaking."

SPATIAL RELATIONSHIPS

The way in which a series of items relate to one another in terms of their placement in space affords the speaker an effective organizational device. In describing a building, you might arrange the details from basement to attic, from north wing to south wing, from entrance to exit, from front to rear. For example:

Core Statement: The new Audiovisual Center has three equipment areas.

   I.   The ground floor houses film equipment.

   II.   The second level houses videotaping equipment.

   III.   The third level houses audiotaping equipment.

Fairgrounds might be visualized by employing the spatial pattern:

Core Statement: Each quadrant of the fairgrounds features a special exhibit.

   I.   The northwest quadrant features the livestock exhibit.

   II.   The northeast quadrant features the flower exhibit.

   III.   The southeast quadrant features hobbies and crafts.

   IV.   The southwest quadrant features the homemaking exhibit.

Other topics can best be discussed in terms of a geographical distribution. In discussing population growth, you could arrange your materials as follows:

Core Statement: Birthrates vary widely in the Western Hemisphere.

   I.   Mexico, Central America, and South America are experiencing a steady increase in the birthrate.

   II.   The United States and the western provinces of Canada are experiencing a steady decline in the birthrate.

III.   The eastern and maritime provinces of Canada are experiencing little change in the birthrate.

It is possible to combine a spatial pattern with a time pattern in discussing certain topics.

Core Statement: The Brazilian "killer bee" is spreading northward at an alarming rate.

I.   It was introduced into Brazil shortly after the close of World War II.
II.   It has now reached Central America.
III.   Scientists predict it will invade the southern United States by 1985.

TOPICAL RELATIONSHIPS

The constituent parts of certain subjects seem to show relationships that are neither temporal nor spatial in character. Instead, the relationships seem to be in the form of natural divisions, such as component parts, qualities, features, functions, roles, levels of hierarchy, to name but a fraction of the variations that are possible. A few examples may illustrate the wide array of speech subjects that can be treated topically.

Core Statement: The good leader combines four basic qualities.

I.   He is intelligent.
II.   He is decisive.
III.   He is emotionally mature.
IV.   He is compassionate.

Core Statement: Governmental reforms are badly needed.

I.   The executive branch has too much power.
II.   The legislative branch has too little power.
III.   The judicial branch does not use its power.

Core Statement: The School of Communications will have three departments.

I.   It will have a Department of Journalism.
II.   It will have a Department of Telecommunication and Film.
III.   It will have a Department of Speech Communication.

Core Statement: The car of the future must meet certain criteria.

I.   It must be safe.
II.   It must be pollution-free.
III.   It must operate efficiently.

Core Statement: There are important ramifications to our new policy.

  I. There are economic ramifications.

  II. There are social ramifications.

  III. There are military ramifications.

The foregoing patterns of time, space, and topical division are particularly useful in presenting nonargumentative thought relationships. Speeches of exposition, description, and narration provide many opportunities for the employment of these patterns.

LOGICAL PATTERNS

When ideas are so arranged as to prove a point, as in the case of speeches involving questions of fact, value, and policy, then the speaker is probably making use of some of the following logical patterns.

DEDUCTIVE ORDER

This familiar pattern involves a generalization or "rule" which is applied to a particular situation. The main point to be proven is the conclusion of the deductive inference. For example,

> John T. is running from the pressures of civilization.
> Everyone who goes to Tahiti is running from the pressures of civilization. (stated)
> John T. has gone to Tahiti. (implied)

CAUSAL ORDER

Patterns of causal relationship may be shown as movement from cause to effect or from effect to cause. For example, if you argue that a given policy will have dire consequences, you will be proceeding from what you feel in a known "cause" (the policy) to predicted effects. On the other hand, if you want to assign causes for some present condition, you are proceeding from a known effect (the present condition) to alleged causes. For example,

> John killed Mary (John caused this effect, Mary's demise).
> He had a motive. (cause)
> He had a weapon. (cause)
> He had an opportunity. (cause)

INDUCTIVE ORDER

If the announcement of the proposition at the outset would erect barriers to belief, then the speaker might begin by presenting a number of examples, illustrations, instances, or other supporting data which lead inevitably to the establishment of the main points which in turn lead to the establishment of the proposition.

PROBLEM-SOLUTION ORDER

A very popular pattern in espousing propositions of policy, the problem-solution format, is built around (1) presentation of the problem area, (2) presentation of the solution, (3) defense of the solution. An example of this mode of arrangement follows:

Core Statement: The United States should convert to solar energy.

    I.   Present energy sources are unsatisfactory.
       A. They are in diminishing supply.
          (support)
       B. They are costly.
          (support)
       C. They are hazardous to the environment.
          (support)

   II.   Solar energy would represent a solution to our energy problems.
       A. It would be inexhaustible in supply.
          (support)
       B. It would be inexpensive.
          (support)
       C. It would present no hazard to our environment.
          (support)

 III.   Conversion to solar energy would be feasible.
       A. It would be technically feasible.
          (support)
       B. It would be economically feasible.
          (support)

 IV.   Disadvantages of conversion would be minor.
       A. Workers in affected industries such as coal and petroleum could be absorbed into other industries.
          (support)
       B. The physical facilities affected could be converted to other uses.
          (support)

   V.   Conversion to solar energy would be the best solution to adopt.
       A. It would not have the limitations of geothermal energy.
          (support)

B. It would not present the dangers of nuclear
energy.
(support)

You will note that both main heads and subheads are arranged topically. The
main heads involve the topics of problem, solution, and defense of solution.
The subheads involve several groups of topics. In I and II the subheads utilize
the topics of cost, supply, and safety. In III they utilize the topics of engineering
feasibility and financial feasibility. In IV the subheads are displaced workers and
obsolete facilities. And in V the subheads are limitations and dangers.

In the course of a single speech it is possible that a number of the patterns
we have just examined can be employed. The main points, for example, might
follow a topical pattern, the subheads developing a given main point might
follow a spatial pattern, the subheads developing another main point might
utilize the time pattern. An expansion of the patterns just discussed, and some
additional patterns, will be seen in detail when we approach the processes of
informing and persuading.

MORE CONSIDERATIONS
OF DESIGN

Up to this point our focus has been upon organizational practices as they apply
to the internal structure of individual proof units. We have not looked closely
at total speech structure as it is accommodated to the needs of informing and
persuading.

Over the years speech theorists have proposed a variety of speech formats
in attempting to answer the question: What is the best order for a speech in
general to follow? The very fact that many answers have been proposed suggests how elusive the universally applicable formula is. There simply is none
because of the highly unique character of each communication situation. Perhaps some insight into the breadth of choices available to the speaker might be
gained from a brief examination of some of the formats that have been
employed.

THE MOTIVATED SEQUENCE

Professor Alan H. Monroe in his *Principles and Types of Speech* recommends
the division of the persuasive speech into five steps which constitute "The Motivated Sequence": (1) The Attention Step (the label suggests its function); (2)
The Need Step (wherein the problem area is exposed); (3) The Satisfaction Step
(wherein the solution to the problem is explained); (4) The Visualization Step
(wherein the speaker describes conditions as they will be in the future relative
to the proposal); and (5) The Action Step (wherein the speaker gives directions
for implementing the solution).

Advertisers have long recognized the utility of "The Motivated Sequence."
Witness, for example, a typical commercial message on television:

Attention Step:	Closeup of a gasoline pump dial spinning madly. Harried driver looks on aghast.
Need Step:	Voice asks, "Own a gas guzzler?"
Satisfaction Step:	Voice replies, "Why not trade it in on our new SUBCOMPACT?" There follows a verbal and visual account of salient features of the car.
Visualization Step:	Driver, no longer harried, waves to service station attendant as he drives by without stopping. Attendant looks forlornly at idle gas pump.
Action Step:	Voice says, "Come to 2320 Mesa Boulevard today. We're open till nine."

THE CLASSICAL DESIGN

The formal structure employed by orators of the Roman Empire has been found suitable for many speaking situations ever since. The classical design involves six divisions of the speech: (1) The Exordium, which is roughly analogous to the Attention Step of the Motivated Sequence; (2) The Narration, wherein the speaker furnishes background details on the subject; (3) The Partition, or "preview" of the points to be dealt with subsequently; (4) The Proof, wherein the speaker develops the argument; (5) The Refutation, wherein the speaker answers the counterarguments that have been or could be raised; (6) The Peroration, which is roughly analogous to what we have called the conclusion.

THE EXTENDED ILLUSTRATION

This speech design is applicable to both informative and persuasive speeches. A speaker who wishes to explain the duties of a police officer, for example, might build the speech around "a typical day" in the life of a real or hypothetical officer. By translating the facts into narrative form the speaker utilizes an effective ingredient for keeping audience interest high.

A persuasive speech designed to elicit contributions to the multiple sclerosis fund might be translated into a narrative involving a person who contracts multiple sclerosis and the ensuing battle for survival.

EXPOSITORY DESIGNS

The placement of ideas in terms of their increasing difficulty is as old as the history of teaching. Instruction frequently follows the sequence from the *simplest idea to the most complex*. For example, multicellular speech structure can be better comprehended if one begins by comprehending the simplest form of speech, the single cell, and then moves in increasing complexity toward the most sophisticated forms.

Another application of placement in terms of increasing difficulty is movement from *familiar ideas to unfamiliar ideas*. It has become virtually axiomatic that explanation is the process of relating the unknown to the known. *Extended comparisons or analogies* likewise epitomize this expository design.

OTHER PERSUASIVE DESIGNS

There are times when the most judicious way of gaining listener acceptance of a controversial point of view is to imply that point of view rather than espouse it openly. The use of this *implicative order* enables the speaker to present all of the steps which lead inevitably to the desired conclusion without risking the possibility of alienating those who might be offended by an open declaration of the conclusion.

When there is apt to be strong listener resistance to the point of view held by the speaker, a favorite organizational method is to start with ideas known to be acceptable to the listener and then working gradually toward less acceptable ideas until one reaches the least acceptable idea. This movement from *most acceptable to least acceptable* is often signalled by the speaker's early use of the "common ground" technique.

Glen E. Mills in his book, *Message Preparation: Analysis and Structure,* poses a question that has fascinated speech theorists and experimenters for the past four decades: "Will an idea be retained longer and exert more influence if it is the most recently perceived, or will it fare better if it is the first of its group to be perceived?" To put it another way: Should the speaker place the strongest argument at the beginning or at the end of the argumentative chain? While a variety of notable experiments have been conducted, conflicting conclusions leave the question still unresolved. The speaker would be well advised, then, to utilize such reinforcement devices as restatement and repetition when presenting the argument early in the chain.

OUTLINING THE MESSAGE

The tool for arraying the constituent parts of the message into the most orderly and dynamic sequence is the speech outline. Outlining is the process of synthesis rendered into tangible form so that the speaker can see the interrelationship of the parts, their proportions, the adequacy of their development, how well they function in the aggregate.

The person who makes optimum use of outlining will first assemble a master outline (sometimes called a *brief*) designed to promote the thorough understanding of a subject in all its ramifications. Such an outline will undoubtedly contain far more material than will ever reach the presentation stage. It will serve as the warehouse from which to draw materials for the presentation outline. The presentation outline will be drafted with the listener in mind; thus it will be much more selective than the master outline.

Although experienced speakers may employ an abbreviated form of outlining which features use of key words or key phrases, beginning speakers will profit more from use of the complete-sentence outline. It is especially important in outlining argumentative discourses that the complete-sentence form be used, since logical relationships cannot be clearly expressed through use of key words or phrases. You will discover, too, that the extra effort involved in constructing a complete-sentence outline pays off in greater ease of retention of ideas during presentation.

The following principles should be observed in the preparation of outlines:

1. *Assign but one idea or statement to each unit of the outline.* Note the difference in clarity between a and b.

(a)

I. Since it applies more easily and costs less, latex-base paint is preferable to oil-base paint; in addition, it dries faster and it is not as messy.

(b)

I. Latex-base paint is preferable to oil-base paint. (for)
   A. It dries more easily.
   B. It dries faster.
   C. It is not as messy.
   D. It costs less.

2. *Do not allow points to overlap.* The following example represents an infraction of this rule:

I. Animals are in danger of contracting the disease.
   A. Wild animals are in danger.
   B. Domesticated animals are in danger.
   C. Pets are in danger.

The inclusion of C throws the pattern into confusion since pets could be either wild or domesticated animals.

3. *Maintain consistent levels of importance among coordinate points.* Units which are labeled as main points, for example, should share common elements. The intrusion of a unit of greater or lesser magnitude will destroy the consistency of the pattern. For example:

I. The senator's political base is interracial.
   A. Blacks support him.
   B. Whites support him.
   C. Chinese support him.

Because C represents a different level of classification, an annoying element of disproportion is introduced.

4. *Maintain clear levels of subordination.* Through proper use of symbols and indentation, the hierarchy of points is indicated. Compare the examples that follow:

(a)

I. Advantages of natural gas
   A. Convenience

B. Efficiency
C. Safety
D. Sources of Gas
    1. In the Southwest
    2. In the East
    3. In the Midwest

(b)

I. Advantages of natural gas
    A. Convenience
    B. Efficiency
    C. Saftey

II. Sources of natural gas
    A. In the Southwest
    B. In the East
    C. In the Midwest

5. *Use a consistent set of symbols and indentations to indicate relationships among main headings, subheadings, and so forth.*   The usual system is:

I. Main heading ————————————————————————
    A. Subheading ————————————————————————
        1. ——————————————————————————————
            a. ——————————————————————————————
                (1) ——————————————————————————
                (2) ——————————————————————————
            b. ——————————————————————————————
        2. ——————————————————————————————————
    B. ——————————————————————————————————————
II. ——

You will note that main headings are consistently designated by Roman numerals, that subheadings which explain, illustrate or prove the main headings to which they are immediately subordinated are designated by capital letters, that the level subordinate to the subheadings is designated by Arabic numerals, and so on down the scale of importance.

An outline for an entire speech would probably be divided into four parts: introduction, core statement, body, and conclusion. In some speech classes the instructor might require a title for the speech, a statement of general and specific purpose, and, perhaps a bibliography of sources consulted. The following is a sample outline of a short informational speech:

The Landscaper's Dream

Introduction

I. Over five million words are printed in U.S. newspapers every week concerning lawn care.

II.   Today I want to tell you of a new grass that may revolutionize the week-
      end habits of the American homeowner.

Core Statement: New Hybrid R50 is an ideal grass for western homeowners.

Body

I.   It is attractive.
      A.   It has a rich green color.
           1.   Photo A shows a plot of R50 in early spring.
           2.   Photo B shows the same plot in late summer.
      B.   It has a carpetlike texture.
           1.   Photo C shows a cross section of a piece of R50 sod.
           2.   Photo D shows R50 used in a putting green.

II.   It is inexpensive.
      A.   The initial cost is low.
           1.   Seed cost is lower than that of *Dichondra*.
           2.   Turf prices are about the same as the cheapest Bermuda grass.
      B.   Maintenance cost is low.
           1.   It requires only a light application of all-purpose lawn food in
                the early spring.
           2.   At the height of the growing season it requires mowing only
                twice a month.

III. It is tough.
      A.   It resists weather extremes.
           1.   It tolerates extreme heat.
                a)   It flourishes in a test plot in Death Valley.
                b)   Landscapers have planted it on the shores of Lake Havasu
                     in Arizona.
           2.   It tolerates moderate cold.
                a)   It does well in the Sierra foothills.
                b)   It flourishes in the Southern California mountain areas.
      B.   It resists the usual enemies of grass.
           1.   It resists lawn moths.
           2.   It resists fungus.

Conclusion

I.   R50 is not yet available for you hapless lawn mower jockeys, but it should
      be in plentiful supply within five years.

II.   Meanwhile, you'd better wear glasses if you're planning to read all five
      million words printed about lawn care every week.

PREPARING THE INTRODUCTION

An examination of representative speeches to inform and persuade will reveal
that the introduction to any speech should accomplish two basic purposes: (1)

it should get the attention of the audience and (2) it should prepare the audience for what is to follow. Unless the first purpose is achieved, all of the speaker's efforts are for naught. Unless the second purpose is achieved, the speaker risks failure in the accomplishment of the desired goal.

GAINING ATTENTION

What percentage of the introduction should be devoted to getting the audience's attention? The answer must be, unfortunately, "It all depends." Perhaps the audience is waiting expectantly for the speaker. The mere act of the speaker appearing on the platform may gain attention. On the other hand, the speech may face the stiffest sort of competition for the audience's attention. Perhaps the audience is more concerned with the discomfort of sitting in a hot, stuffy room. Perhaps members of the audience are engaged in animated conversation. Perhaps the speaker faces the kind of captive audience found in required speech classes!

While it would be impossible to catalog all of the possible ways of opening a speech in an attention-compelling fashion, the following devices are among the most commonly employed. No one device can be regarded as universally applicable. Your choice will ultimately be governed by your subject, purpose, and your audience.

The Quotation

A thought-provoking or curiosity-arousing quotation can be an effective device for opening many speeches. For example, if you wished to discuss reasons why your listeners should study public speaking, you might utilize this opening:

> "If it is a disgrace to a man when he cannot defend himself in a
> bodily way, it would be odd not to think him disgraced when he
> cannot defend himself with reason." This contemporary-sounding piece
> of advice was offered by Aristotle almost 25 centuries ago when he
> wrote perhaps the most famous speech text ever, *The Rhetoric.*

A speaker who discussed the relative longevity of men and women opened a speech with this quotation:

> "The stronger sex is actually the weaker sex because of the weakness
> of the stronger sex for the weaker sex." This humorous observation
> noted in the evening newspaper just yesterday has more truth to it
> than appears at first glance.

The important criteria to use in selecting a quotation for an opening are *relevancy, provocativeness,* and *good taste.* A quotation cited simply to gain attention and nothing more is apt to create ill will when it becomes obvious to the listener that the device bears no connection to the speaker's subject. The quotation that is not provocative simply fails in its task of eliciting audience attention. Finally, the quotation which is in poor taste will certainly get the audience's attention, but it is apt to be the kind of attention that militates against the accomplishment of the speaker's purpose!

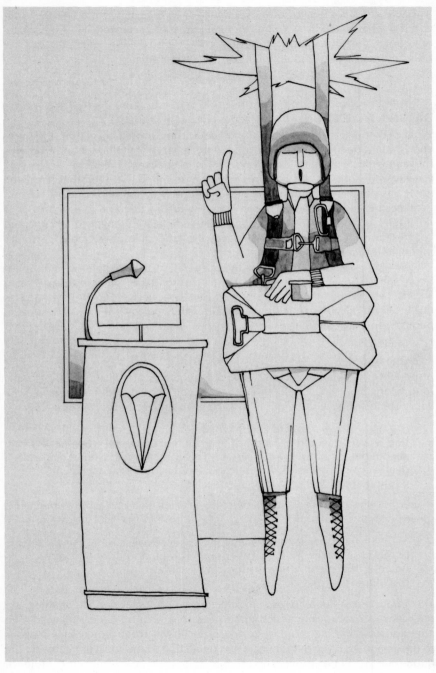

The speaker's first duty is to get the
attention of the audience.

The Illustration or Story

Among the most familiar devices for opening speeches are stories or illustrations. When properly handled they can be perhaps the most effective openings of all, because interesting narratives tend to cause the listener to attend effortlessly. On the other hand, tired stories that the audience has heard innumerable times in the past can turn off audience attention. Before using this familiar opening device the speaker should make certain (1) that the story or illustration is fresh (old stories told from a new slant are as fresh as brand-new stories), (2) that it is pertinent to the main theme of the speech, (3) that it can be effectively related by the speaker (any limitations as a storyteller should be considered), and (4) that it be in good taste. This last quality cannot be stressed too much, especially if the story is a humorous one. The speaker must be extremely thorough in audience analysis to ferret out any information that would signal issues of taste. As a general rule it is wise to avoid stories that derive their humor from ridicule of religion or racial origin. Self-directed ridicule is perhaps the safest form of humor to employ in the story or illustration. (See our treatment of illustrations in the preceding chapter for additional guidelines.)

The Reference to a Recent Event

While sitting in the waiting room at your dentist's office, have you ever discovered that the only magazine remaining in the rack is a two-year-old copy of a weekly news magazine? Even if you hadn't read it when it was published, you aren't very curious to read it now because it's "old hat." You are concerned with what is current.

Whenever possible the wise speaker will try to associate the theme of the speech with something recent. For example, a speaker who wishes to explain the principles of rocket propulsion might well allude to the recent launching of a space vehicle as reported on television or in the newspaper. Or a person wishing to discuss measures for tax reform might first of all refer to a news clipping reporting the number of millionaires who escaped payment of income taxes by utilizing loopholes in existing tax laws. This association of your theme with a recent happening usually gives a freshness and immediacy to your ideas that tends to make an audience interested in listening further.

The Rhetorical Question

We are all familiar with the interest value of suspense in drama. Even when we know the hero is going to emerge triumphant in the final scene, we can't help but feel anxiety for his welfare as he meets obstacle after obstacle along the way. Of course, when the final outcome is unpredictable, then the suspense can become even more extreme.

The speaker would do well to emulate the playwright in employing suspense as a factor of interest. Starting the speech with a rhetorical question is one application of suspense to speaking. A skillfully phrased question that puts the audience into a state of expectancy for an answer can be a very effective means of gaining attention. But let us call attention to that important qualification—*that puts the audience in a state of expectancy for an answer.*

Without this qualification, the rhetorical question is ineffectual as an attention device. Of course, what it is that puts an audience into a state of expectancy will differ from audience to audience. A group of entering freshmen would have their attention piqued by hearing the Dean of Admissions use this rhetorical question at an orientation meeting, "How many of you will be here next year to start your sophomore year?"

The question, "Where can you buy a first edition of Campbell's *A Philosophy of Rhetoric* for 29 cents?" would probably evoke this reaction from a group of chemistry majors: "I don't know and I don't care to know!" To an audience of graduate students of rhetoric or to a group of dedicated bibliophiles it might well have an electrifying effect. Here again you can see the importance of knowing your audience before you plan your strategy.

The Startling Statement

An audience that is apathetic toward the speaker's topic can often be made attentive by a statement that startles or shocks them. This is particularly true of speeches on familiar themes, such as requests for contributions to charitable organizations, to cancer drives, to heart funds, or speeches exhorting hearers to exercise their right to vote, or urging them to wear seat belts. The startling statement in such cases might be characterized by a direct reference to a person or persons in the audience. For example, a speaker might begin: "I'm sure that all of you are just as sad as I am that these three gentlemen sitting in the front row are going to have to undergo a lengthy hospitalization which will cause them to use up all their savings, sell their homes, and most of their belongings." Such a statement would certainly get the attention of the "three gentlemen" and would probably arouse the curiosity of the other members of the audience. To be effective, the startling statement, like all attention devices, should be relevant to the topic and should rest upon a thorough understanding of your audience. It is easy to see that indiscriminate use of the startling statement could have a self-defeating effect.

The Promise of Reward

A statement that promises a reward for careful listening can, like the rhetorical question, generate suspense. Thus it can serve as an effective opening device for speeches on a wide variety of topics.

Here are examples from classroom speeches that have generated suspense: "That next five minutes may be the most important five minutes of your life," said the speaker prior to giving instructions on administering heart massage. "If you follow the suggestions I'm about to cite, you'll be two hundred dollars richer by the end of this semester," was the preface to a speech on deceptive food packaging. Another speaker provoked attention by needling the listeners as follows, "Whether you realize it or not, you are a major contributor to air pollution because of some common faults in your driving habits."

The Reference to the Subject

The use of a simple reference to the subject as a means of gaining attention should be reserved for those subjects in which you are confident your audience is already interested, so that the mere mention of the subject will provoke a high level of interest. If your topic does not possess an inherent interest value for your audience, then avoid this type of opening. To illustrate, we can guess that an audience will be inherently interested in gossipy information about famous public figures. Therefore, we can, with impunity, open with, "Today I'd like to share with you some little known facts about the after-hours behavior of one of our highest ranking government officials." We can also guess that an audience will not be inherently interested in an explantion of some esoteric subject. Thus, "Today I'd like to talk about residual disjunctive enthymemes" will probably produce a yawn from the listener.

If your topic has a high curiosity potential or if it is a topic that people are talking excitedly about before your speech, then a simple reference to the subject may be your quickest way to achieve audience attention. If your topic doesn't have these built-in guarantees of audience interest, then you'd better choose another attention device.

The Reference to the Occasion

This device may be very useful on relatively formal speech occasions, such as a banquet, a graduation ceremony, a dedication, a special lecture—in short, in any case where the *occasion* is the dominant factor. In the average speech class, however, such a formal opening would seem "stuffy" and affected, unless it happened to be the first day or the last day of the semester.

PREPARING YOUR AUDIENCE FOR THE SPEECH

This function of the introduction may be accomplished in a wide variety of ways. What constitutes adequate audience preparation can never be universally prescribed. However, we can describe some of the things that are commonly done; your topic, your purpose, and your analysis of the audience will dictate which of these will be applicable in your case.

Justifying the Topic

In those instances when your listeners have not gathered for the express purpose of hearing you talk about a given topic, you need to offer them a reason for listening. "So you're going to talk about petroleum distillates. What's in it for us?" may well be the kind of reaction the audience experiences upon the announcement of your topic. Well, what *is* in it for them? How do petroleum distillates affect their lives? Will your treatment of the subject benefit them in some tangible way? Will it help them be healthier, be more productive? Will it benefit them in intangible ways? Will it satisfy their sense of curiosity? Will it satisfy their need for emotional expression?

In speeches to inform, the justification of the topic answers the question, "Why do I need this information?" In the speech to persuade it answers such questions as "How does this issue affect me?" "Why should I be concerned about this problem and its solution?"

Sometimes the device used for gaining attention can also serve to justify the topic. For example, a rhetorical question may provoke attention and instill a need for information.

It should be remembered that the justification of the topic is not always needed. In many cases the audience will arrive already motivated. For instance, it would be unnecessary to spend time justifying a discussion of proposed pay raises before an audience of college professors who would be the recipients of the salary increase.

Delimiting the Topic

It may be necessary for you to draw the boundaries of your discussion when approaching certain topics. To say "I'm going to discuss marijuana" is to lead the audience to anticipate a number of possibilities. Will you discuss the structure of the marijuana plant, where marijuana is grown, how marijuana is processed, how marijuana affects the user, the legalization of the sale of marijuana, who uses marijuana, the effects of marijuana versus the effects of alcohol? In such cases it may be well for you to point out not only what you are going to cover but also what you are going to exclude from the discussion. By providing the listeners with the boundaries of your discussion, you enable them to adjust their expectations accordingly. It helps them clear their minds of issues that are beside the point of your speech. Furthermore, it gives the audience a certain kind of security to know just how far the speaker intends to go. It will then not be so impatient for those beautiful words, "And in conclusion. . . ."

To be sure, there are occasions when it is unwise to indicate the boundaries of your discussion, especially if the creation of a feeling of suspense is essential to the accomplishment of your purpose. (But be sure this is not a rationalization resulting from confusion in your own mind as to the boundaries of your discussion!)

Presenting Your Credentials
to Speak

If your authority to speak on a subject is not known to your listeners, it may be necessary for you to establish it in the speech. Normally, this would be done for you by the person introducing you to the audience, but if the introducer is derelict in this duty (or if there is no introducer at all), the task falls upon you.

Why should your credentials be made known? Audiences tend to place greater credibility in the remarks of speakers they consider to be "expert." Furthermore, they tend to listen more attentively to the "expert." An older student in a speech class once gave a talk on how pilots landed an airplane by instrument alone. After his talk he was asked by one of his classmates where he had found his information. He replied, "I was a commercial airline pilot for five years." Suddenly his remarks became much more vital to the class, and one student said, "I wish he'd give the speech over again."

What are your credentials? Obviously you cannot always be an "expert" in the sense of being directly involved. But that does not mean you cannot speak with authority on a subject. Through reading and research you can so familiarize yourself with a subject that you are an "expert" in comparison with your listeners. Perhaps your authority derives from close association with those who are, in fact, "experts."

How shall you make your credentials known? This can usually be accomplished without creating the impression of immodesty. Here are a few examples:

> "I'd like to share with you some facts about radiation poisoning that I learned in a class in radiological medicine last semester." ·

> "As a 'Navy brat' I've had more 'hometowns' than I can remember right offhand. But my favorite hometown has always been San Diego. Today I'd like to discuss just what it is that makes San Diego unique."

> "In doing a term paper for American history last semester, I became interested in Benedict Arnold's role in the American Revolution. Just how serious were his misdeeds? Was the war effort really hampered? I shall attempt to give you my answers to these questions today."

Defining Terms

If the subject you are discussing involves special terminology, jargon, or "technical talk," it will be advisable for you to offer definitions early in the speech. Perhaps you will set aside a portion of the introduction to define all terms to be used, or perhaps you will define each term when it first appears in the speech.

Providing Background Information

There are occasions when a full appreciation or understanding of a subject cannot be gained unless one is familiar with certain background details. The background materials often are in the form of historical details. To discuss some great event without indicating the historical context in which it occurred is to deny the listener an important dimension for understanding the event.

Other background details may be physical in nature. For example, to have the audience sense the grandeur of the Lincoln Memorial one has to put it in its physical context. An architect's genius cannot be fully appreciated by simply examining the building that he has designed. One has to see how it integrates with its physical environment.

Establishing Common Ground

Not infrequently we are forced to take an unpopular stand on some controversial issue. If we wish to win audience support for our position, we must pave the way carefully. One of the measures that is often used is the establishment of a common ground of belief between speaker and listener. In essence, this means that you will take pains to stress areas of agreement before turning to those issues on which you and your audience hold divergent viewpoints. It is even conceivable that this act of establishing a common ground may occupy the major share of your speech.

PREPARING THE CONCLUSION

"Well, I guess that's about all. Are there any questions?" This is an all-too-common ending to speeches. Judge for yourself whether it accomplishes the usual functions of a speech conclusion: (1) Does it redirect the audience's attention to the central point of the speech? (2) Does it usher the listener into the frame of mind that should be dominant at the end? (3) Does it leave the listener with a sense of completeness?

We would hazard the guess that the average speech student gives less thought to preparing the conclusion than to almost any other facet of speech preparation. Yet the conclusion can be the most critical part of the speech. An ineffectual ending can undermine all that has been accomplished by the speaker in the preceding portions of the speech.

Let us examine, then, some of the possible methods of ending a speech effectively.

THE SUMMARY

A brief recapitulation of the main points of the speech is a common device used in concluding. It is particularly valuable in instructional speeches, because it reinforces the instructions which the speaker wishes the audience to recall. For example, in concluding a speech on "The Fundamentals of Tennis" a speaker would use the summary in the following manner: "Today, having learned some of the elementary techniques of tennis, you should try to remember (1) that your eye should always be kept on the ball, (2) that you should keep your arm firm, and (3) you should remember to follow through with your swing." In persuasive speeches it can serve to remind the listener that sound reasons have been advanced for the belief the speaker wishes them to hold or for the action he or she wishes them to take.

Usually the summary is employed in conjunction with other concluding devices, since by itself it may not accomplish all of the purposes of a conclusion that we have discussed.

THE QUOTATION

Just as the quotation can be effectively employed as a means of gaining attention at the beginning of a speech, it can be employed to end the speech on a graceful, stimulating note. Sometimes it is possible to use two quotations from the same person, one for a beginning and one for an ending. Or perhaps a repetition of the same quotation used in the opening will be fitting at the end of the speech. Whatever the quotation chosen, it should meet the tests of relevancy, good taste, and impact.

A good example of the effective use of a quotation can be seen in Martin Luther King's famous "I Have a Dream" speech:

From every mountainside, let freedom ring, and when this happens
. . . when we allow freedom to ring, when we let it ring from every
village and every hamlet, from every state and every city, we will
be able to speed up that day when all of God's children, black men and
white men, Jews and Gentiles, Protestants and Catholics, will be able
to join hands and sing in the words of the old Negro spiritual, "Free
at last! Free at last! Thank God Almighty, we are free at last!"

THE ILLUSTRATION OR STORY

Like the quotation, the illustration or story can be used effectively at both extremities of the speech. It is particularly useful as a method of visualizing for the listener the import of what you have been discussing in the body of the speech. It distills the essence of your message and presents it in a form that makes it memorable to the listener.

If the prevailing mood of your speech has been one of unrelieved seriousness, an illustration or story in a light vein may provide the touch needed to leave the audience in the right frame of mind.

THE CHALLENGE

Speeches which are designed to stimulate the audience to greater efforts or stronger devotion to some cause or ideal lend themselves well to this kind of ending. Occasionally an informative speech can employ this ending as well if the speaker wishes the audience to seek information in addition to that just presented in the body of the speech. In any case, the challenge should be worded in such a way as to encourage a spirit of optimism in the audience's attempt to meet the challenge. If the challenge seems impossible of fulfillment, a negative attitude is generated which runs counter to the speaker's intentions.

A good example of the use of the challenge may be seen in Henry George's famous speech, "The Crime of Poverty."

. . . . I cannot hope to convince you in talking for an hour or two, but
I shall be content if I shall put you upon inquiry. Think for yourselves;
ask yourselves whether this widespread fact of poverty is not a crime,
and a crime for which every one of us, man and woman, who does
not do what he or she can do to call attention to it and to do away with
it, is responsible.

DECLARATION OF INTENT

Speeches intended to induce action can be concluded effectively when the speaker sets an example for the audience by declaring what he or she personally plans to do. Patrick Henry's famous closing remarks in his "Liberty or Death" speech is perhaps the first example that comes to mind. A less familiar example can be seen in a speech delivered by Daniel Webster in the U.S. Senate when he and Calhoun were debating the nature of the Constitution:

> I am ready to perform my own appropriate part, whenever and wherever
> the occasion may call on me, and to take my chance among those upon
> whom blows may fall first and fall thickest. I shall exert every faculty
> I possess in aiding to prevent the Constitution from being nullified,
> destroyed, or impaired; and even should I see it fall, I will still, with a
> voice feeble, perhaps, but earnest as ever issued from human lips, and
> with fidelity and zeal which nothing shall extinguish, call on the
> People to come to its rescue.

SUMMARY

The process of assembling the speech usually begins with the formulation of a core statement that embodies the central idea of the speech. Growing out of the core statement are the main points, subpoints, and supporting materials. Coordinate points should be (1) related to the core statement, (2) related to one another yet separable from one another, and (3) collectively they should fully develop the statement under which they stand. Coordinate points should be meaningfully grouped. Among the patterns of grouping are chronological arrangement, spatial arrangement, and topical arrangement. Once grouped, they should be put into a sequence which will most effectively support the core statement. Overall strategies of arrangement include the Classical Design, the Motivated Sequence, the Extended Illustration, and various designs suitable to either exposition or persuasion.

The outline is the tool for arranging the constituent parts of the message into an orderly sequence. Good outline form features the use of a consistent set of symbols to show proper subordination of ideas. Each unit of the outline should contain only one idea; points should not be allowed to overlap; coordinate points should have consistency.

After the body of the speech has been designed, the speaker formulates an introduction and a conclusion. An introduction serves to gain attention and prepare the audience for what is to follow. Among the methods of gaining attention are the quotation, the illustration or story, the reference to a recent event, the rhetorical question, the startling statement, the promise of reward, the reference to the subject, and the reference to the occasion. Preparing the audience for what is to follow may involve justifying the topic, delimiting the topic, presenting your credentials to speak, defining terms, providing background information, and establishing a common ground.

The conclusion serves to redirect the audience's attention to the core statement, to usher the audience into the proper frame of mind consistent with the speaker's purpose, and to give the listener a sense of completeness. Some methods of concluding are the summary, the quotation, the illustration or story, the challenge, and the declaration of intent.

Suggested Readings

Anderson, Martin; Nichols, E. R., Jr.; and Booth, Herbert. *The Speaker and His Audience*. 2d ed. New York: Harper and Row, Publishers, 1974. Chapter 13.

Brooks, William D. *Speech Communication*. 2d ed. Dubuque, Ia.: Wm. C. Brown Company Publishers, 1974. Chapter 11.

Bryant, Donald C., and Wallace, Karl R. *Fundamentals of Public Speaking*. 4th ed. New York: Appleton-Century-Crofts, 1969. Chapters 9–11.

Hovland, C. I.; Janis, I. L.; and Kelly, H. H. *Communication and Persuasion*. New Haven: Yale University Press, 1953. Pp. 120–23.

McCabe, Bernard, and Bender, Coleman. *Speaking Is a Practical Matter*. 2d ed. Boston: Holbrook Press, 1974. Pp. 100–112.

Mills, Glen E. *Message Preparation: Analysis and Structure*. New York: The Bobbs-Merrill Co., 1966.

Monroe, Alan H. *Principles and Types of Speech*. Chicago: Scott, Foresman and Co., 1962. Chapters 14–16.

Reid, Loren. *Speaking Well*. 2d ed. New York: McGraw-Hill Book Co., 1972. Chapter 9.

Scheidel, Thomas M. *Speech Communication and Human Interaction*. Glenview, Ill.: Scott, Foresman and Co., 1972. Chapter 10.

7

Language
The Medium of Your Ideas

Perhaps the best way to begin this chapter would be by posing a question: During your waking hours what are some of the ways you use language? What do you ask words to do for you? If you have paused to answer these questions, you should be sufficiently motivated to continue with this chapter, for this chapter focuses on language. As we have already implied by our rhetorical questions, we employ language in a variety of ways. For example, we use words (1) to tell others something about how we feel ("The killing of coyotes in the backcountry is a very cruel act."); (2) to explain a process to a friend ("Carol, changing the oil in your car is really quite simple."); (3) to influence our environment ("We must see to it that handguns are no longer available in the United States."); (4) to gather information ("John, what do you know about solar heat?"); and (5) to have others offer us comfort ("I received a traffic ticket yesterday and I'm sure upset."). In all of these instances, and there are countless others, we have asked words to help us share our internal states.

This ability to manipulate words is one of our most unique features. Unlike most of the other animals, humans are able to use a sophisticated coding system (word-symbols) as the main means of communication. Through millions of years of evolution we have developed both the physical and social tools necessary for language to function. Because we can hear, speak, and reason we are able to use word-symbols as one way of sharing our experiences with others. We can have sounds, or marks on a paper, stand for (represent) objects, things, ideas, and feelings. As a society we have decided that when the word *dog* is spoken or written it stands for "a domesticated, carnivorous mammal." Even a word as abstract and general as *love* is a man-made symbol representing something else (often deep affection we have for another person).

What we have been suggesting is that words are a kind of shorthand. They are substitutes for the real thing. We tinker with them and manipulate them so that we can have some degree of influence over the environments in which we find ourselves. Realizing these facts about language and its influence, the student of speech communication should ask himself or herself two questions: Do my verbal accounts give the listener a true picture of reality? Does my word selection really convey to others the impressions I want to make? The answers to these two questions will serve as the basis for this chapter. First, we will examine those principles and techniques of language usage that will help your material come closer to the life-facts (reality), and second, we will examine those principles and techniques that will enable others to see and feel what you are trying to share.

LANGUAGE TO
REPRESENT REALITY

Language, in the broad sense, is usually defined as a set of symbols used in a common and uniform way by a number of people who are thus able to manipulate these symbols for the purpose of communication. We have already mentioned many of the elements of nonverbal symbols, such as facial expressions, gestures, posture, and the like. Now we are primarily concerned with that form of language in which words are the basic symbols. In this first section we will discuss those aspects of language that can, depending on their use, either help or hinder an accurate symbolic representation of reality. As we have noted, when we use verbal language we are asking words to help describe that which is inside of us, something we know or feel. If we wish to share that information (our personal reality), we must describe that reality in ways that will accurately mirror what we "have in mind." If, for example, we see a traffic accident caused by speeding and wish to tell others about the dangers of driving too fast, we must ask our vocabulary to serve as an approximation of what we are experiencng and what we saw. The discussion that follows will focus on that approximation. Specifically, we will look at those aspects of our language that are concerned with the accuracy with which our words match reality.

WORDS ARE ONLY SYMBOLS

Because words are the basic symbols of verbal language, it is important to remember that they are purely *arbitrary symbols*. We call them symbols because they are used to *represent* objects, ideas, concepts, or feelings. The word *dog* may well stand for a four-legged, domesticated animal, but the *word* "dog" is actually *not* the dog, but rather a sound that our society, and past generations, have decided upon to *stand for* that particular thing. You will also notice that we used the word *arbitrary*—there is no necessary relationship between the word and the thing it stands for. People often forget this fact and confuse a word with the thing for which it stands. They lose sight of the principle that a word exists only as a representation of a fact—a word is not the fact, thing, or occurrence to which it refers. Consequently, there is no assurance that the word selected represents or depicts reality. If Senator X calls his opponent "dishonest" and accuses him of "stealing," these symbols may not accurately represent actuality.

The conscientious communicator must always remember that the word is not the thing itself; it is a symbol. He or she should develop the habit of asking, "Do the words fit the facts?" Irving Lee, in his book *Language Habits in Human Affairs,* summarized this view when he noted that the communicator should not only be concerned with what *it* was called (symbols), but also what *was* being so called (object).

WORDS CAN HAVE MANY USES

It would indeed be convenient if we had one word for each thing or occurrence. But we are faced with the fact that a limited number of words must serve to cover an unlimited number of things. Wendell Johnson, a writer in the field of general semantics, underscored the problem when he wrote, "A rather large share of our misunderstanding and disagreement arises not so much because we are constitutionally stupid or stubborn, but simply because we have to use the same words to refer to so many different things."

We could cite an endless number of examples for those words that have many uses and meanings. Take the simple word *foot*. It can represent a part of the body, a means of measuring, or it can be used as a slang expression. Or take the word *pot*. It can represent a cooking utensil, a rather large stomach, or even something that is rolled in paper and smoked. A glance at any standard dictionary will reveal numerous words with twenty-five or more meanings.

Due to this multiple-meaning characteristic of our language we must be very careful when we use symbols that have a variety of meanings. An *awareness* that any word may have a whole list of uses is perhaps the first step in handling the problem. Another step is to realize that what is being said may not represent what the user intended or assumed. In conversation one can also develop the habit of asking directly how a person is using a particular word or phrase. In addition, as speakers, we should try to select words that lend themselves to direct translation and also define those words and phrases that have a variety of meanings.

Whenever in a speech or conversation the words or phrases being used are ambiguous or are used in an incorrect sense, they may, if unexplained, produce confusion. Frequently ambiguity stems from inadequate definitions, hasty word choice, or loaded language. In each of these instances the words and phrases involved may be interpreted and defined in two or more ways.

In speaking and listening be ever vigilant for words and phrases that are intangible and abstract. "Is a liberal arts education worthwhile?" "Is liberty worth the price?" "Economic democracy is desirable for all of us Americans." "Various races of humanity have not progressed during the last few decades." "Sports are essential for a healthy mind and body." If you look carefully, you will discover that each of these statements is meaningless as long as clear and precise definitions are lacking. Verbal disputes can also occur over a single word. Notice the lack of specific meaning for words such as *justice, religion, conservative, liberal, Communist, democracy, extremism,* and *happiness*.

WORDS OFTEN OMIT ESSENTIAL DETAILS

Whenever we think or talk about a situation, we make decisions as to what to include and what to leave out. We abstract some of the details from the total situation and ignore others. This means, in a very real sense, that when we use language we are only giving a partial picture of what happened. When we say to someone, "Let me tell you about the riot I saw last night," we are about to make certain selections as to what to talk about and what *not* to talk about. We cannot, by the very nature of our language and our processes of perception, tell our listener each detail we perceived and experienced.

Words often omit essential details.

Three problems present themselves as each of us decides and selects what to include and what to exclude from our verbal descriptions. First, what is left out—that which is not talked about—is often more important and vital than what is retained. If a speaker says, "Unemployment is not a serious problem; I drove past the shoe factory and noticed a 'help wanted' sign clearly posted," he or she has decided to tell you about the sign. However, because language forces selection and makes it impossible to tell all there is to tell, the speaker did not tell you about the long lines of people waiting to be interviewed. This fact, which was omitted, may indeed be more important than what was actually talked about.

Second, our selection of what to share is governed, in part, by our attitudes and past experiences—we personally decide what to say and what not to say. Because each of us has certain prejudices and biases, we are inclined to pick those words that have individual appeal. Our speaker's view of unemployment was a factor in the mention of the sign while omitting discussion about the large number of people looking for a job.

Finally, our vocabularies also put certain limits on the details that we can include in our verbal accounts of reality. We can't talk about what we can't label. How do we describe something in reality if we are unable to name it? For example, as speakers we would have a difficult time explaining the working of a computer if our vocabulary did not contain the words necessary to talk about its essential processes and components.

It is the awareness of the problems, and the realization that details are omitted, that must be kept uppermost in the minds of both sender and receiver as they engage in communication. Writers in the field of general semantics suggest that as communicators we should learn to wait, to stop and see if more is to be said, and then reach our conclusions; further, that we should develop the use of the **etc.,** silently or orally, to remind us of the concept that factors are left out. In short, we should remind ourselves that there is always more than can be said.

MEANINGS ARE IN PEOPLE

Words, as language symbols, have no meanings in themselves; their real meanings are in the things or events for which they stand. Each person, acting as an individual, must decide what a symbol means to him or her. Take the word *school.* To the person who likes education it is a place of learning; to the person who hates school it means a place he or she is made to go, and to still another individual, who desires an education, it means a place where he or she would like to go. What the word means depends on an individual's experience with the thing or occurrence the word is representing. No two people ever have exactly the same experiences; so consequently no single word has an identical meaning for two people. But the speaker must at least try to select words, phrases, and ideas that approach this ideal of common meaning. If understanding, and hence communication, is to take place, the sender and receiver must share a reasonably common code.

This sharing of a common code is not a simple matter. Because we come to the encounter from a variety of backgrounds, we are apt to find that agreement on the meaning of a word is often elusive. For example, to the baseball player a *bird* is a fast runner. A carnival worker uses the word *slum* to talk about cheap prizes. A *monster* in the rock music industry is a successful record. To the person in prison a *hit* means rejection for parole. And *Levi's* are a bad set of sails to the sailor. These, and countless other instances, should add credence to our initial observation that meanings are in people and not in words.

WORDS HAVE DENOTATIVE AND CONNOTATIVE MEANINGS

As we have noted throughout this section, when we use language we must remember that there is seldom a one-to-one relationship between the word and the referent. This notion is often discussed by students of language in terms of denotative and connotative meanings.

Denotative meanings normally involve those types of words we learn first (*ball, dada, cat,* and so forth). They usually refer to words that have a visible connection between the symbol and the object or thing in reality. That is to say, we can often see and/or touch those items that have denotative meanings (*tree, car,* and so forth). Because the word directly denotes, or refers to the object or thing, there is often agreement on denotative meanings.

Connotative meanings, because of their subjective nature, present a far more serious problem to the speaker who seeks to have messages accurately represent reality. Connotative meanings are more personal, emotional, and ambiguous. The referents for connotative words are much more abstract and, therefore, subject to personal nuances. In fact, a connotative meaning is often so personal and emotional that it may be difficult to ever agree on a single meaning. How, for example, do we begin to define what is meant by *democracy, freedom, hope, love, sexuality,* or *censorship?* The task that confronts the conscientious communicator is not a simple one. We must be ever vigilant in our scrutiny of language. Knowing that connotative meanings are abstract and intangible may well be the first step toward developing an attitude of linguistic awareness—an attitude that does not take communication for granted, but instead realizes the nebulous nature of words and therefore seeks to use them with caution and care.

LANGUAGE TENDS TO BE STATIC

Much of our trouble in the use of words comes from our forgetting that the world changes much faster than do words. We often use words that are somewhat out of date and may no longer represent or describe reality. Laura Lee, writing in the *General Semantics Bulletin,* once noted:

> The same word stands for a person, thing or activity day after day, although the thing it stands for may change, grow, transform. We do not name the process, the originality, the development, the flux. We speak in static terms and learn to perceive and think that way.

The successful communicator is aware of the fact that reality changes and often words don't. Phrases such as "If John said it, I know it is a lie—he lied to me before," negate the whole notion of change. The most effective word-symbols we can use are those that take the dynamic nature of life into account.

As communicators we may have noble purposes and lofty goals, but if our language does not convey our thoughts, communication is doomed to failure. Therefore, what we have been suggesting in these last few pages is that good communication calls for language that accurately represents reality —and poor communication can often be characterized as language that distorts, deforms, or in some way fails to correspond to the thing or feeling being experienced by the sender.

LANGUAGE TO INDUCE DESIRED RESPONSES

The language of speechmaking, in addition to being characterized by the six features just discussed, has the auxiliary purpose of making the idea seem real and meaningful. It is not enough to have the idea expressed in everyday language; to have a lasting impression the message must be clear and vivid. The way the speaker selects and uses words—the proper word in the proper place—is often the first method of distinguishing the most able speakers from all the rest.

A person's style in using words is a highly personal matter and something which is developed over a long period of time. This does not mean that a person's language habits cannot be improved with practice. On the contrary, the basic elements of effective style and word choice can be amended and enriched by sincere and careful practice. What follows is a listing and discussion of those language elements which can help the speaker accomplish the overall objective, which, in most instances, is to secure a desired response.

YOUR LANGUAGE SHOULD BE CLEAR

As a speaker you must first of all know exactly what idea you wish to convey to your listeners. Then you must find those symbols that will enable you to be understood—to be clear. Clear language is language which is *immediately meaningful* to those who hear it. The speaker who can arouse definite and specific meanings has an excellent chance of being understood. Conversely, the speaker whose language suffers from ambiguity and confusion is not easily comprehended. Clarity can be fostered if the speaker's choice of language is **accurate** and **simple.**

ACCURATE LANGUAGE

Being accurate when one speaks involves selecting words which "say what you mean." How often we hear someone say, "I read this book one day," never indicating what book and what day; or someone refers to "that thing over there," without ever letting the listener know what "thing" is being talked about. In both cases the language lacks accuracy. Words have been selected which fail to correspond directly with the concept or thing being discussed.

Inaccuracy in word choice is normally brought about by carelessness. The speaker will often use technical language or uncommon words without stopping to realize that the symbols he or she has selected have very little meaning for the audience. Laziness may also show itself in our failure to seek words which are definite and exact. We may use ambiguous words, which, by their very nature, are not accurate and clear. We may also be guilty of omitting essential details.

Accuracy is enhanced if the speaker selects specific and concrete words. The listener will receive a much clearer picture of what is being talked about if the speaker will use names, dates, places, facts, and other details. For example, "On Tuesday John and I went to the Main Street exhibit" is certainly more accurate and meaningful than the phrase "I went away with a friend." Or we hear statements such as, "New York spends a lot on welfare for each family under its plan." The communicator who is concerned with clarity and comprehension would say, "In 1974 the maximum monthly welfare payment for a family on welfare in the state of New York would be three-hundred and fifty dollars." Here we can see the value of being accurate—the listener knows what we mean.

SIMPLE LANGUAGE

Short, simple words enhance clarity and understandability. Notice the difference in clarity between "moderate" and "abstemious," "money" and "legal tender," "top" and "ne plus ultra." Once again it is worth noting that the purpose of communication is to share ideas, information, and feelings. If your language distorts the concept you wish to convey, your communication act will fail. By being an exhibitionist with your vocabulary you run the risk of not being understood and, hence, of not accomplishing your purpose.

In closing, it should be remembered that being simple does not mean one is infantile and dull. It indicates that the speaker realizes that words which are vague and complicated can cause serious communication breakdowns.

YOUR LANGUAGE SHOULD BE
VIVID

Language which is clear will be understood, but if you wish also to hold attention, maintain interest, and create a favorable impression you must make your language vivid as well. This does not mean that vividness and clarity are necessarily separate. On the contrary, in order to achieve vividness you must first of all be clear.

When we talk of being vivid, we are normally talking about selecting those words and phrases which are sensory. Vivid language seeks to appeal to the senses of the listeners by having them see, hear, feel, taste, and smell the images the speaker tries to create.

IMAGERY

When we are employing imagery, we may be asking our listeners to reencounter a past situation, or to experience a new situation that we paint for them. In either case the main objective is to have the audience experience, vicariously, the particular sensation being described.

1. *Detail* is essential in painting word pictures for the audience. Notice the difference in effectiveness between "A water-skier hit the dock," and "The water-skier, gliding gracefully over the glass-top lake, failed to see the half-sunken dock protruding out into the still water and went crashing into the exposed wooden beams."

Consider these images:

   a. As we drove through the sandy and dusty area, we felt the earth beneath us tremble as the wild boars stampeded in front of us.
   b. I felt as cold as a piece of ice as I approached the half-open door of the broken down cabin.
   c. The dazzling brilliance of the setting sun made it difficult for me to see the large figure moving across the stream.
   d. His face, touched by time, was rough, scarred, and firm.
   e. As we entered the room an odor of sweet peppermint lead us to the copper pan sitting on top of the coal-fed stove.
   f. As I left the hospital I could still hear the piercing, penetrating cry of the wounded American.

2. Using *descriptive adjectives and adverbs* gives the listener a much more complete picture of what is being talked about. "A bitterly cold day," "a studious man," "a damaging admission," and "a sarcastic professor," all offer the listener a more vivid concept of what is being referred to.

3. Images should be selected in light of the listener's *background* and *experiences*. It is hard for someone to appreciate the "blue and rolling waves that break on the Solomon islands" if they have never seen the Solomons. Compare the idea to something from the listener's past and the image will be made more effective.

FIGURES OF SPEECH

Vividness is also achieved by using figures of speech. The figure of speech normally shows itself as a **metaphor.** This device compares objects which are basically alike. When Abraham Lincoln was talking about the danger of two Americas he used a metaphor: "A house divided against itself cannot stand." A speaker talking about John F. Kennedy's strength used a metaphor when stating, "Kennedy's heart is as gold, but his convictions are like pillars of marble."

The speaker may also find that his or her style can be made more vivid by using **antithesis.** In this figure of speech, contrast is emphasized by the position of words. For example, "The state exists for man, not man for the state." Former President Kennedy used this technique in his now famous phrase, "Ask not what your country can do for you—ask what you can do for your country."

The **simile** is yet another linguistic device that is available to the speaker. It normally uses *like* or *as* to compare and link similar ideas. For instance, vividness is enhanced when we say, "At times finding gasoline for our car is like hunting for a place to camp on the Hollywood freeway." As you can see, one of the advantages of the simile is that it clarifies as it adds variety and color to our language.

LANGUAGE SHOULD BE APPROPRIATE

When we explored the issue of audience analysis we stressed the importance of finding out as much as possible about the listener. That information will enable you to adapt your speech to specific audiences. Your language, as one aspect of that adaptation, may well be the most crucial. You know from experience that you often change words and phrases as you move from person to person and place to place. If a professor calls on you in class, you respond with one type of language, yet if a friend asks you a question, your remarks will be characterized by language that is far less formal. What you are doing when you move from phrases like "uptight" to "very nervous" is making your language appropriate to the receiver. We run the very real risk of not accomplishing our purpose when we use language that is not suited to our listeners. Imagine how you would feel if you had gone to hear a lecture entitled "An Introduction to Perception" and heard a speaker say, "Once we know that we can see electromagnetic radiation with wavelengths of 380 to 760 millimicrons, we should find out what the subjective experience is at each point between the upper and lower thresholds." If the entire audience was composed of people with very little background in perception, this would be a blatant example of inappropriate language.

As we indicated at the onset of this discussion, many of the problems presented by improper word choice could be avoided by a thorough and complete audience analysis. We have all seen sex education films that are aimed at different age levels. The notion of reproduction is explained in all the films, whether intended for fifth-grade pupils or college students. Yet the language in each of the films conforms to the educational level of the audience. The principles and the anatomy remain the same, only the words are changed.

When attempting to select appropriate language, we must also take the occasion into account. As we reflect on our own behavior we know that our vocabulary makes both obvious and subtle changes as we shift from context to context. A small informal meeting of friends would call for casual language, while a college commencement address might demand a more serious tone. For example, the commencement speaker could say, "The world has turned over many times since you entered these hallowed halls," but in a small group that same phrase would appear as pomposity, sarcasm, or stupidity.

One final note of caution. There might well be situations where patent attempts at adaptation will hurt rather than aid your cause. Two vivid examples are in the area of culture and age. Many blacks use language to produce a type of group solidarity. A white person using black argot would not be demonstrating ability to "speak the language," but rather a lack of tact. The same is true of the middle-aged person who expresses enthusiasm to a teenage audience by saying "out-of-sight." Trying to have our language be something other than what is natural to ourselves produces artificiality. This kind of sham is usually transparent and often results in embarrassment.

LANGUAGE SHOULD BE FREE FROM DISTRACTIONS

We all know from experience that we normally focus our attention on those things in our environment that either interest or distract us. For example, if someone is talking to you on the topic of saving money, you are likely to attend to every word. However, if during the explanation the speaker's fingers start to drum on the table, you are apt to move your focal point from the speaker's ideas to the noise being produced by the nervous mannerism. In many communication situations, words as well as actions serve as the distracting stimulus. What we are suggesting is that all of us tend to have some poor language habits that can interfere with our overall communication effectiveness. We inadvertently choose words or phrases that divert attention away from our main ideas. Because each of us personally selects the words we utter, it might be useful to examine some of the types of words that often cause communication problems.

Slang

Slang words and phrases are sometimes acceptable, but more often they tend to lower the status of the user. The person who must resort to slang is following the line of least resistance; it takes effort to find the right word. Phrases such as "guys," "cool," "sharp," "real great," and "behind the eight ball" do little to clarify an idea, make an image vivid, or raise the speaker's credibility.

Triteness

Closely related to slang is the problem of trite and hackneyed phrases. Speakers who are reduced to employing overworked expressions such as "pretty as a picture," "last but not least," "our hour of trial," and "it gives me great pleasure" clearly reveal their lack of imagination and education.

Jargon

When addressing a general audience, a speaker must avoid shoptalk, jargon, and highly technical language. Each profession has its own language, and the speaker must remember that what is clear to an engineer may be very confusing to the doctor. If the symbols selected are not easily defined, ambiguity will result. "Cognitive dissonance-consonance" may be quite meaningful to the

social psychologist, but it is only noise to the layman. Knowing your listener's
background and defining unfamiliar words will help you overcome many of
the problems of jargon.

"Big" words

There are many speakers who would rather exhibit their vocabulary than be
understood. These individuals will avoid the short, hard-hitting, accurate word
for the long and supposedly impressive one. They will say "edifice" instead
of "building," "surreptitiously" instead of "secret," and "imbibe" instead of
"drink." Admittedly, there will be occasions when the "big" word is appropriate, but good style calls for the best word at the best place.

Loaded words

There are those who would suggest that loaded and emotional words should
be used whenever possible. They would argue that such words assist the
speaker in the goal of "manipulating others." Although loaded words are
often colorful, they are in most instances ambiguous and vague. By playing
upon emotionalism these words, both implicitly and explicitly, ask the listener
to respond on a purely emotional basis. Notice the images which are called
forth by phrases such as "the savage and brutal senator," "the chiseling
miser," "the bureaucratic welfare state," and "a fanatical rightwinger." Grant-
ing that emotion is important in communication, the speaker should supply
adequate evidence and sound reasoning to justify any loaded word. The
speaker should remember that the words he or she uses must be consistent
with the real facts. If a colorful word can be selected that doesn't distort
reality, it should be used; but if the appeal is solely an irrational one, the
speaker is then violating ethical responsibility.

Empty words

In this day of the mass appeal we are constantly being exposed to superlatives
and exaggerations. This overexposure may well condition the unsuspecting
communicator to lean heavily on the overworked and meaningless term. Notice
the empty quality of the following words and phrases: *super, colossal, deluxe,
terrific, very good, fantastic, extra special,* and a *whole lot.* We are members
of an age where many people have been so bombarded with empty words that
they are tempted to discount them and pay little attention to the person who
uses them.

IMPROVING OUR
LANGUAGE HABITS

We have already observed that each of us has the freedom to select those
words we wish to employ at any particular moment. It is a matter of individual
choice as we decide to say "yes" instead of "yeah" or "sailboat" instead of
"yacht." Because word selection and style depend, to a large degree, on subjective factors, improvement is not an impossible task. The problem is that too

many people are guilty of believing the myth that orators are born, that the ability to use language effectively is a genetically endowed characteristic. This notion is simply not true! Even though language habits and vocabulary develop early in life, they are constantly open to change. And this change can be in the direction of improvement. However, this implies more than memorizing a few rules or formulas. It demands practice and hard work. If you are willing to put forth the energy, many of your efforts can be channeled into some of the activities discussed below.

1. *Learn to use a dictionary and book of synonyms.* These two sources are helpful in that they provide the student with clues to new words which are often more accurate and vivid than the ones he or she has been using. For example, turning to a book of synonyms and antonyms, such as *Roget's Thesaurus,* will increase your vocabulary while at the same time increasing your options when you have to find the right words to share an experience. Instead of having to say, "It was good," you could be more specific by utilizing one of the choices afforded by a *Thesaurus* such as "beneficial, valuable, edifying, salutary, capital," and *"rara avis."*

2. *Be alert to new words.* This means that you are aware of new words as you listen and read. Listening is an excellent method of improvement, for it allows you to perceive the overall impact of a word. Hearing someone say "glistening" instead of "bright" may persuade you that one strikes the ear more pleasingly than the other.

Reading novels, plays, speeches, poetry, and essays will illustrate how talented people use language. Probably most writers would avoid "the road was dangerous," preferring, instead, something like "the precarious nature of the highway made each new curve more menacing than the last."

Finally, improving your language habits implies that you remember the new words or phrases to which you are exposed. Remembering is often aided by the simple act of writing down those expressions that interest you. Many famous speakers carried a pencil and a pad of paper everywhere they went in order to jot down fresh and novel words they encountered.

3. *Develop a habit of careful writing.* Careful writing and revision tend to develop better expression. The diligent writer will not settle for the first word that comes to mind, but will search for the word or phrase that will promote clarity and convey the desired impression.

4. *Speaking often* is one of the obvious ways of learning to use language well. By actually "doing the thing," the speaker learns which words and phrases help in accomplishing a purpose and which words will retard his or her efforts.

5. *Be aware of words and make a study of language itself.* The field of general semantics, for example, seeks to examine the relationship between language and things. The sincere student will find this sort of study both rewarding and interesting. There is a whole new world to explore when one investigates how people use symbols to influence one another and the world they live in.

It is obvious by now that a large segment of the study of communication is necessarily a study of language. Therefore, it is well to remember that advice about language is not confined to this chapter alone. For example, our observation in this chapter that "language should be interesting to listen to and easy to comprehend" is treated under "informing" in chapter 8 and under "common language fallacies" in chapter 7. This is additional evidence that communication is a highly interrelated and overlapping process and not subject to clear-cut, isolated skills and techniques.

SUMMARY

Try to keep these general language principles in mind as you engage in both public and private communication: (1) Words are only symbols that are used to represent objects, ideas, concepts, experiences or feelings. (2) One word can have many meanings and many uses. (3) In using word-symbols as our communication code, we often omit essential details. (4) Word meanings reside within people; they have meaning only in terms of the associations established between the symbols and the object or concept to which they refer. (5) Words have denotative and connotative meanings. (6) Language tends to be static while reality is dynamic and ever changing.

Clarity, vividness, and appropriateness characterize effective language usage. Clarity derives from the use of words that are accurate, simple, and precise. Vividness derives from imagery, which is accomplished by use of details and descriptive words, and from figures of speech. Appropriateness derives from using language that is suited to the audience, occasion, and speaker, and avoiding slang, triteness, jargon, "big" words, loaded words, and empty words. One's language can be improved by sincere and conscientious study and practice.

Suggested Readings

Alexander, Hubert G. *Meaning in Language*. Glenview, Ill.: Scott, Foresman and Co., 1969.

Aly, Bower, and Aly, Lucile Folse. *A Rhetoric of Public Speaking*. New York: McGraw-Hill Book Co., 1973. Chapter 4.

Johnson, Wendell. *People in Quandaries*. New York: Harper and Row, Publishers, 1946.

Lee, Irving J. *How to Talk with People*. New York: Harper and Row, Publishers, 1962.

McCabe, Bernard P., and Bender, Coleman C. *Speaking Is a Practical Matter*. 2d ed. Boston: Holbrook Press, 1973. Part II, Step 3.

Monroe, Alan H., and Ehninger, Douglas. *Principles and Types of Speech Communication*. 7th ed. Glenview, Ill.: Scott, Foresman and Co., 1974. Chapter 16.

Reid, Loren. *Speaking Well*. 2d ed. New York: McGraw-Hill Book Co., 1972. Chapter 13.

Tubbs, Stewart L., and Moss, Sylvia. *Human Communication: An Interpersonal Perspective*. New York: Random House, 1974. Chapter 6.

Having An Influence

Part 3

Informative Speaking
Being Understood

8

Earlier in the text we noted that one of the primary functions of speech is to provide us with a means of transferring knowledge from person to person and from generation to generation. It shall be our concern now to discuss this vital function of speech—**the presentation of information in a fashion that makes it highly comprehensible.**

Situations requiring this type of discourse are numerous. Almost all teaching can be labeled informative speaking. Likewise, the instructions and training given to work forces and office and sales help can be placed in this particular category. Even the directions given by the person telling a friend how to get to Main Street must be labeled informative speaking. At all levels of communication, both formal and informal, informative speaking occurs.

Informative speaking seeks to impart materials that will increase the listener's knowledge of a given subject. If you know a great deal about astronomy and give a speech on the topic, you expect your listeners to know more about the subject when you complete your talk. Therefore, the **primary objective of informative speaking is to present information so that it will be easily understood and remembered by your audience.**

It may indeed seem unnecessary to document the importance of being able to convey complex ideas, for we are living in a time that has been characterized by the phrase "The Information Era." We are truly part of that history that has experienced an information explosion. Our world is constantly being flooded with new data, ideas, and concepts. A high premium is placed on the person who is able to understand and *share* information. It is the purpose of this chapter to offer you some theories and principles that will aid you in conveying information to other persons.

Like so many of the ideas discussed in this book, the issue of "informing" must not be viewed in isolation. Informing is but part of the entire and complex process we call communication. Therefore, principles discussed throughout the text apply to delivering the speech to inform. In addition, it must be remembered that any rigid distinction between speeches to inform and other types of speeches is impossible. It is perhaps more realistic to view discourse on a continuum with *many* gradations running from informing to persuasion. This orientation comes closer to reality than a philosophy that sees persuasion and informing in tight little boxes. The successful communicator realizes the subtleties of communication and the folly of believing that there are not countless occasions when informing and persuading overlap. For in the final analysis it is the response of the receiver that will determine whether the message is informative or persuasive, and in most instances it will likely be a bit of both.

TYPES OF
INFORMATIVE SPEECHES

While all informative speeches are alike in that they seek to give information and increase understanding, they may be separated into the following basic types: (1) *Descriptions*. You may wish to describe an indivdual, a
location, an event, a reaction, or a mood. In each of these instances you are
primarily concerned with having the audience see and experience what you
are describing. For example, if you wanted your listeners to have greater insight into the personality of Malcolm X, you might describe his youth, his
exposure to the Black movement, and his adult years. (2) *Reports*. Book reports, reports on articles, committee reports, and so forth, are commonly employed by the college student. You might report, for instance, on what your
research group decided to do about creating bicycle lanes on campus. Primarily, you have the responsibility to transmit what you have read, discovered,
or deliberated upon. (3) *Explanations*. This is a general term for information pertaining to the functioning of a process or the workings of some agent. You are
explaining how something works. A speech explaining the principles involved
in the operation of the electric car would fall into this category. (4) *Instructions*.
You may wish to tell others how to perform a specific act, such as how to ad-
minister first aid. Employers use instructions to show new employees how
certain tasks are performed.

STEPS IN PREPARATION

In chapters 1 and 2 we discussed some steps of preparation necessary for successful speech making. It was pointed out that before any behavior can be
changed, or any response secured, there must be both analysis and preparation.
Much of what we now say about the speech to increase understanding has already been examined under other headings. There are, however, some specific
principles of preparing the informative speech that bear closer examination.

DETERMINING THE PURPOSE
AND SELECTING A TOPIC

If you are to make ideas clear to an audience, you must first determine what
you want the audience to know about these ideas at the conclusion of your
talk. The specific purpose of any given informative speech is a statement of
exactly what the speaker wants the audience to understand. For example:

1. To have the audience understand how the North Atlantic Treaty Organization is financed.
2. To have the audience understand how to analyze dreams.
3. To have the audience understand the workings of a political party convention.
4. To have the audience understand the marijuana laws in California.

All of these specific purposes tell precisely what it is the speaker wishes the audience to understand and know.

In choosing and narrowing a topic for the informative speech, you should look to many of the criteria presented earlier in the book. Let us briefly review some of these. You should know more about the topic than do the members of the audience. During the course of the speech, and in a manner that does not border on boasting, you should tell them how you came to know as much as you do about this particular subject. For example, you might say, "Having worked as a page in the United States Senate, I was able to learn a great deal about the evolution of a new law, and today I would like to share some of those experiences with you."

The topic selected ought to be relevant. Intelligent people would not like to hear you talk about the night you raided the cookie jar. A comprehensive audience analysis (coupled with common sense) is perhaps your best guide to determining relevance. As always, we suggest you try to view the topic from the position of your receivers. This listener-centered approach should help you avoid trite and uninteresting subjects.

The topic should be stimulating as well as timely. Remember, you are seeking to increase the listeners' fund of knowledge. They have not selected this topic, you have! Therefore, it must be a topic that arouses curiosity at the same time it holds attention. It is often an exciting challenge to take what appears to be a dull subject and give it life and vitality.

Being able to locate sufficient material is yet another consideration in selecting and narrowing a topic. Think of how frustrating it would be if you wanted to discuss the types of rattlesnakes found in your region but could not find any information. You can be assured that your frustrations would be shared by your audience, for they would feel baffled as they listened but failed to hear anything new.

Select a subject appropriate to the occasion. A topic dealing with the uses of automation for carrying freight on trains would be out of place at a Teamsters convention.

Most important, you should select a subject that interests you. Could there be a more thankless task than having to explain the methods used in mounting butterflies if you are not interested in butterflies? Our pleasure is increased, and our burden lessened, when we deal with issues we enjoy.

GATHER AND SELECT MATERIALS

If you are to secure understanding, your speech must contain the materials that will contribute to clarity and comprehension. As noted earlier, in gathering the data for a talk you should be adaptable, selective, accurate, objective, and thorough.

In order to accomplish these objectives you should begin by making an inventory of what you already know and the material you have available to you. You will then be in a position to determine what additional materials you need. After the inventory, you are ready to locate and gather the necessary information. By realizing your aims, personal resources, and limitations, you can select the illustrations, examples, comparisons, definitions, statistical data, interest factors, forms of restatement, and the visual aids that will accomplish your specific purpose.

It should be underscored once again that an effective speaker gathers more material than he or she will be able to use. A thorough preparation and analysis will make you more knowledgeable about the topic and enable you to be more selective as to what you include and what you omit.

Objectivity is important in all phases of preparing the speech to inform. The speaker is not trying to convince others of the worth or value of one system over another, but, rather, is trying to expand the knowledge level of the listeners. Subjectivity, as we all know, is a characteristic of the human personality; so objectivity must be given special consideration when we try to inform. Unsupported inferences, value judgments, and the like, must be avoided or at least controlled. In short, the speaker should try to prepare and present a talk with an attitude of open-mindedness.

THE MATERIALS OF INFORMATIVE SPEAKING

Although increased understanding is the primary end of informative discourse, we know from our own experiences that information alone will not capture or hold attention. We seem to need a reason for listening—we have to be motivated. Therefore, the materials of informative speaking must serve two purposes—they must increase comprehension at the same time they hold attention.

There is a great deal of overlapping with regard to which features of a speech hold attention and which contribute to learning. What we might label an attention factor might also help to explain a key point in the speech. Nevertheless, we shall arbitrarily divide informative materials into those techniques and principles that seem to foster effective exposition and those items that tend to arouse interest and hold attention.

INCREASED UNDERSTANDING
What follows is a discussion of those materials that can often make an idea or a concept clear and understandable.

Definition
Mistakes are often made because people are confused about meanings. Because the speaker is usually very familiar with the subject matter, he or she may forget to define some of the basic and important terms, phrases, or concepts. In addition, because words are simply symbols, and usually interpreted differently by different people, listeners can become confused by the meanings of various words.

When trying to decide which words need defining, you should begin by examining those which are *abstract* or *unfamiliar.* If you were talking about democracy, it would behoove you to define what you mean when you use that particuar term. Words such as *democracy, freedom, socialism,* and *liberty* are so abstract that at times they may evoke any number of meanings. By defining such words we place them in a context that tells the listener what we mean when we use the word.

Confusion also results when we employ unfamiliar words or phrases. For example, if we say that "the congruity theory of persuasion is an effective tool for the advertiser," we might be hampering learning. However, if we were to define "congruity," we could make the unfamiliar become clear.

In defining words or phrases, the speaker should try to observe the following rules: (1) Define the unknown in terms of the known. Using language that is simpler than the original expression is an application of this principle. Going from the known to the unknown establishes a common frame of reference and allows the audience to see what you mean. For example, a veteran Navy radarman defined radar by comparing it to the action of a tennis ball being bounced off a garage door. (2) Define the word by placing it in the context in which it will be used; for example, you might say, "In discussing the problem of school dropouts we shall concern ourselves with the student who leaves school, for whatever reason, before graduation or before the age of eighteen." In this way the audience knows who you are talking about when you use the term "dropout." (3) Try to anticipate the knowledge level of your audience on the particular topic so that you will be in a position to decide which words need defining. If you were talking to a group of electronics experts and used the simple radar analogy cited above, you might find that you had insulted them, yet the same radar analogy might be very effective for a group of liberal arts majors.

Examples

The value of the example as a means of clarification cannot be overemphasized. Examples are not only the simplest and most common of all the devices, but they are the easiest to employ. In a very real sense they allow you to say, "This is what I mean."

The technique of using examples was explained in detail in chapter 5. And although we are now investigating informative speaking, what we said in earlier chapters applies directly to our current discussion. In short, examples can be helpful if we follow a few guidelines: (1) The example should be brief and pointed. (2) It should be relevant to whatever the speaker is explaining. (3) It should be adapted to the educational and interest level of the audience. (4) It should be consistent with the tone of the speech and not appear to be something the speaker has just added for no apparent reason.

An example may be either a specific instance or a detailed illustration and can appear as real or fictitious, in verbal form or in graphic form. In a speech on water pollution you might employ a graphic example by showing a large picture of some of the foreign matter found in many of our rivers and streams.

The important criterion is that it proves or clarifies the generalization being made. For instance, if you were speaking on the various funeral customs in Africa, you might offer the listener two or three factual examples of the rituals performed by some of the tribes. This would explain your point in a vivid and concrete form while holding the attention of your listeners.

Comparisons and Contrasts

Clarity may be enhanced through the use of comparison and contrast. Comparison shows how two things are alike, while contrast points out the way in which they differ. These devices are useful in that they lead the listener from the known to the unknown. In explaining the functions of the United States Senate, you might use comparison by explaining the relationship between the Senate and your college's Student Council. By pointing out the duties and functions of the Council (known) you would show the likeness in the Senate (unknown). Analogy is often a good form of comparison in that it also attempts to compare the known with the unknown.

The use of contrast may be of more help in some cases than the use of comparison. If the point from which the contrast originates is known by the audience, then the contrast will be particularly meaningful. For example, a student in a speech class recently used contrast to show the high increase in the cost of living in the United States. He contrasted the cost in 1975 to the cost in 1973 and 1974.

Statistics

It is frequently useful to explain an idea in terms of size or quantity. For example, if you were talking about income tax in the United States, it would be helpful to offer some statistics on the various programs and the numerous methods of calculating percentages.

In informative speaking, statistics are usually used for purposes of *counting* or *measuring*. If you were trying to explain that professional boxing could be considered big business in the United States, you could use statistics to point out that the Joe Frazier-Muhammad Ali fight grossed over 20 million dollars. Counting the number of motorcycles registered in California would be an example of how statistics could be used to clarify the extent of vehicle registration in that state.

Measuring is often used as a way of conveying size. We could highlight the vastness of Central Park by noting that it is situated on 840 acres.

In using statistics, a few rules and guides should be kept in mind. By themselves statistics are abstract and meaningless. To be useful they must be compared or contrasted with something else to show how many, how few, how large, or how small the idea or thing really is. If you were going to offer statistics dealing with the number of light-years to the nearest star, you might make such figures meaningful by explaining a light-year in terms of how many trips that would involve between the campus and the downtown area. Second, a large list of numbers is hard to comprehend. Therefore, whenever possible try to use round numbers. Third, it is important that you be very selective in citing statistics, for a listener will tire of a lengthy discussion of facts and figures.

Fourth, see that your statistics meet the tests advanced in chapter 6. Whether your aim be informative or persuasive, your material should be authentic, complete, and clear.

Description

There will be occasions when description will be the best method of explaining and clarifying the thought you are trying to develop. In description the speaker pictures or portrays an object, event, or person by stimulating the listener's sense of sight, sound, smell, taste, or feeling. The listener's mind is focused on the object by means of vivid word pictures. A speech on Canadian national forests might well employ descriptions of the wildlife, water sources, and vegetation that constitute the elements of the forest. For instance, clarity regarding water resources could be enhanced if a speaker said, "The waterfalls are everywhere; from any mountain and valley you can see and hear the crystal-clear water cascading and tumbling over the rocks."

We have already cautioned that the successful communicator is not abstract, vague, or general, but offers information and material that is clear, specific, accurate, and appropriate. In informative speaking, when the response sought is understanding, it behooves the speaker to use concrete data. An audience would have a difficult time remembering very much about a speech that tried to explain the entire subject of "Mental Health" in ten minutes. There simply wouldn't be time to supply the needed data to make the subject meaningful.

Reinforcements and Emphasis

We all know from our own experiences that as listeners we can never retain all that we hear. Therefore, by means of reinforcement and emphasis, the successful speaker underscores those materials that are deemed most important and compelling. Four of the most common reinforcement techniques are discussed below.

Restatement uses new words to convey and echo an idea already discussed in a speech. After giving a speech on "The Dangers of Cigarette Smoking" you might want to restate your main thesis to "cigarette smoking can cause you great physical harm." In this way the listeners hear the idea again, but expressed this time in a new manner. **Repetition** is the use of identical wording to repeat the idea. Through repetition the main point is better remembered. Both restatement and repetition have their roots in learning theory and should be used frequently in communication.

Calling attention directly to the idea you wish to stress is yet another device available to the speaker. Simply saying "this is important" or "now get this" can focus attention on the point you wish to emphasize. These two obvious phrases tell the audience that they are about to receive some significant information. Imagine how your attention would be arrested if, while you were daydreaming, someone looked directly at you and said, "It is important that you understand this issue."

The way we use our **voice** and **body** can also help us reinforce and emphasize those aspects of our speech that we would like our listeners to retain.

For example, we can reinforce an important idea by changing the loudness of our voice or by pausing. We can often add emphasis by moving toward our listeners. This activity seems to accent the verbal elements of our talk. It is analogous to someone firmly placing a hand on your shoulder while reprimanding you. The firm hand stresses the verbal portion of the message.

Partition, Enumeration, and Summary

Memory is short, and as the speaker moves through the speech, we frequently lose track of the main thesis. It is therefore of prime importance that a speaker aid the listener in remembering the main ideas as they are developed throughout the talk. **Partition, enumeration,** and **summary** are three such techniques that contribute to this increased understanding and retention.

A **partition** (often referred to as an initial summary or "preview") is a list offered early in the speech of the points that will be covered. In short, you simply tell your audience what main ideas you plan to treat in the body of your speech. For example, "In talking about how to insulate a room I shall first of all take up the procedures for insulating the floor, then those for insulating the walls, and finally the procedures for insulating the ceiling." Having highlighted what you plan to cover, you are now ready to move to the body of your talk.

Enumeration, which occurs during the body of your speech, is the numbering of each point as it is introduced. "First . . . , Second . . . , and Third. . . ." This technique is helpful in increasing clarity in that it alerts the audience to movements from one idea to another.

Summary is the reiteration of the main items at the close of the entire speech. For example, "In insulating a room we looked at the techniques used for insulating the floor, the wall, and the ceiling."

MAINTAINING INTEREST

The importance of listening attentively to any form of communication needs no demonstration at this point. We can all accept the premise that where attention is focused, concentration is most acute. In fact, the late James Winans of Cornell University built a theory of persuasion around "inducing others to give fair, favorable, or undivided attention to propositions."

We might, for our analysis, think of attention and interest as interchangeable. Admittedly, the dictionary may offer separate definitions of the two terms, but when we talk about human behavior, attention and interest have meanings that are interlocking and overlapping. Your own behavior proves that what interests you commands your attention and likewise, what you attend to interests you. In this approach to attention and interest, we are talking about the manner in which our awareness of a given stimulus is greatly heightened. All competing stimuli are secondary as the main message goes directly to what Psychologist William James called the "focus of consciousness."

We do not pretend to know any magic formula that will transform a dull message into a scintillating experience for the listener. Each speaking situation makes its own unique demands; hence, there could hardly be a universal formula for success. But we can profit from the findings of psychologists who have probed into the nature of attention and interest. These findings have enabled us to devise guidelines for minimizing the effort our listeners will have to exert in order to stay attentive to our ideas.

Noting That Which Is Impending

Not only are we interested in that which has just happened, but also in that which is soon to happen. A person who wants to discuss recent improvements in the safety features of automobiles might say, "I heard on the radio this morning that the first of the new model cars are due to hit the dealers' showrooms within the next ten days. It will be interesting to see how they measure up to the safety standards I'd like to discuss with you today."

You have probably noticed how much more interested people become in taxation on the eve of a school bond election, or how prognostications about the outcome of conference football standings take on greater interest the closer we get to the start of the football season. So look for ways of linking your subject to an event in the immediate future.

Alluding to That Which Is Physically
Near to Your Audience

Just as ideas involving temporal nearness tend to catch our interest more readily than those that are in the distant past or distant future, so ideas involving physical proximity tend to be more compelling than those that are remote. A news item that involves your immediate neighborhood probably will capture your attention faster than one concerned with the other side of town.

The immediate physical surroundings in which the communication act takes place may offer possibilities for applying this interest factor. For example, if you were trying to give the audience some conception of the size of the passenger compartment of a new supersonic jet airliner, you might compare its dimensions with the dimensions of the room (or building) in which the audience is situated. If you were discussing the principle of the microwave relay of telephone messages, you might say, "Look out the window at the bank building over there. See that large dish-shaped antenna on the roof? That is part of the coastal network of relay stations that enables you to talk with others in cities 800 miles to the north." Or a speaker who wishes to use a hypothetical illustration to explain some principle of boating safety might say, "Tim and Joan are going out to Mission Bay this weekend and rent one of those small sailboats for a cruise around the Bay." By giving the audience someone close at home to identify with, the audience will likely be more interested in following the illustration. Every teacher soon learns the attention value of a student's name to perk up that person's interest.

Referring to the Familiar

A parachutist once remarked, "Jumping out of a plane gives you somewhat the same sensation you experience when you unexpectedly reach the top step of a dark stairway. You raise your foot for another step, then discover it isn't there." By relating the unfamiliar (jumping out of a plane) to the familiar (reaching for a step that isn't there) the speaker enabled listeners to experience vicariously a small part of his or her favorite pastime.

This technique of relating the unfamiliar to the familiar is basic to effective speaking whether it be persuasive or informative in character. The listener's frame of reference must always be considered when we attempt to explain a new idea or concept. The use of reference to the familiar, however, does not mean that we simply tell the audience what it already knows. Rather, we tell the audience what it doesn't know in terms of what it does know.

Invoking the Listener's Personal Needs

Who is the most important person in the world to the listener? It's probably the listener. And what directly affects him or her will be of interest. Does your message have any bearing upon the listener's self-interests? Does it concern, directly or indirectly, the listener's health, safety, family pocketbook, status, personal comforts, or any of a long list of needs, wants, and desires? Every listener may subconsciously be asking the speaker, "What's in it for me?"

A speech concerning a nuclear power plant might be prefaced by remarks concerning possible cuts in the listener's light bill or new conveniences to enjoy as a result of cheaper electricity. Allusions to new food additives that will cut cooking time dramatically might enhance listener interest in an explanation of chemical compounds. A discussion of the proposed state budget takes on added impact when the speaker suggests that the children of the listeners may not enjoy "free" public education if certain amendments are adopted. Never overlook the possibility of relating your message to the personal concerns of the audience. In his book, *Persuasive Speaking,* Thomas Scheidel observes this of the listener:

> He will hear best those statements which are relevant to his needs,
> his expectations, and his experiences. They will be emphasized by him.
> The skillful speaker, aware of this fact, will take these sources of
> emphasis into account in adapting his message to his audience.

Imparting Activity

In our chapter on delivery, we pointed out how the speaker who uses meaningful bodily action and vocal variety tends to hold attention more readily than the speaker who fails to employ them. The content of the speech can also be infused with activity. If the speaker arranges ideas in a logical, easy-to-follow sequence, those ideas seem to *move* for the listener. A jumbled, helter-skelter lack of arrangement is one of the surest techniques for losing audience interest.

Words which suggest action should be fully employed by the speaker. "He staggered home" is more compelling than "He went home drunk." "The old pickup truck was doing seventy-five when it drifted over the divider strip into the oncoming lane" is more meaningful and interesting than "She was going too fast in that old truck."

The authors recall a classroom speech on memory improvement in which the speaker demonstrated a technique for memorizing a list of items. Among other things, the speaker asked the audience to visualize each item in motion—

the more absurd and exaggerated the motion the better. He explained that we tend to remember moving objects more readily than stationary ones.

Varying your developmental materials also imparts a feeling of activity to your message. Rather than dwelling at length on sets of statistics, add variety by inserting appropriate examples, analogies, and quotations from authorities. If you happen to be discussing a serious topic, avoid falling into a pattern of unrelieved sobriety. Insert a light note here and there (consistent with your purpose, of course) to lend refreshing variety.

Utilizing Reality

A student speaker was relating anecdotes about famous film comedians of the thirties. As he turned to W. C. Fields he unrolled a yellowing playbill he had found in the basement of a local movie theater where he was working. It advertised as "an outstanding coming attraction" one of Fields' early films. On a more somber note, the sister of an American student being held prisoner in Turkey for alleged possession of dangerous drugs was recounting the anguish of her brother's confinement. "This envelope I'm holding brought the first letter he was allowed to write from prison." Still another speaker, an apprentice bank teller, was explaining to an evening speech class how to recognize counterfeit currency. She asked each listener to take a dollar bill out of his wallet and examine it closely as she explained the telltale clues.

The film buff didn't need to display the W. C. Fields playbill in order to recount some of that comedian's hilarious escapades. The sister of the jailed student didn't need to hold up the envelope from her brother to make clear his ordeal. And the bank teller could have drawn a representation of the dollar bill on the board and made her instructions for counterfeit detection just as clear. But in all three cases a striking heightening of interest resulted from the use of an *actual* object. The real item is almost always more compelling than the best verbal description, pictorial representation, or mock-up that can be devised. By the same token, reference to an actual example tends to be more compelling than reference to a hypothetical example.

It isn't always possible or practical to produce "the real thing," whether it be an object or an example. In such cases we have to substitute that which is *realistic* for that which is *real*. For example, if we are trying to get our audience to visualize some circumstance in the future, we obviously can't produce the actual circumstance. But we can provide *lifelike* details that will cause the listener to respond, "Yes, that could very well happen." Putting real people in hypothetical circumstances or hypothetical people into an actual setting lends credibility *and interest* to such examples. You will recall our example of a few pages back where the speaker said, "Tim and Joan are going out to Mission Bay this weekend to rent one of those small sailboats for a cruise around the Bay." While the event depicted was hypothetical, the people and places were real. Thus the event bore a resemblance to reality.

Pointing Out Conflict

The speaker should be aware of the value of conflict as a means of holding audience interest on a subject. Perhaps conflict is implicit in the subject itself. A speech opposing a proposed course of action has built-in conflict. A problem-solving speech has built-in conflict. Subjects in which conflict is not implicit, on the other hand, require that the speaker superimpose it. A speech explaining what happens to a letter from the time it is mailed to the time it reaches its destination does not seem to have a built-in element of conflict. But by skillful use of a hypothetical illustration a postal worker did introduce conflict into that subject. He asked the audience to imagine that one of the men in the front row was carrying in his suit pocket an insurance premium he had forgotten to mail. To keep his insurance in effect the premium would have to reach the home office 1200 miles away within 36 hours. Would mailing the premium at this moment enable it to reach the company in time? For the remainder of the speech he followed the progress of that particular piece of mail until, happily, it reached its destination in the nick of time. The twin ingredients of conflict and suspense kept the audience interested throughout the entire speech.

Using Humor

Judicious use of humor can be perhaps the most effective means of holding audience interest. However, its effective employment requires real skill. Because of its unpredictable nature, we would caution you to use it sparingly and with propriety. Sometimes it succeeds too well, so that the audience's attention becomes focused upon the humor as an end in itself rather than as a means of making the message interesting.

A much more thorough treatment of humor will be found in a later chapter when we discuss special speech types. For the present we simply admonish you to label humor "Handle With Care."

ORGANIZING THE SPEECH TO INFORM

Systematic arrangement of material is crucial in informative speaking if the listener is to retain the information presented. Listen carefully the next time you hear an informative talk and you will discover that there are occasions when the educated as well as the uneducated forget the importance of organization and clarity. Speeches that seem to leap from point to point without offering any internal or external clue will seldom leave the listener with anything meaningful.

THE INTRODUCTION

The dual purposes of any introduction are to alert the audience to the subject of the speech and to arouse in the listener a desire for the detailed information contained in the body of the speech.

Specific methods of starting a speech were discussed in detail in chapter 6. The selection of a method will be determined by factors relating to the topic, audience interest, audience knowledge level, speaking time available, and the speaking occasion. When listeners are not vitally concerned with the topic, it is quite often profitable to begin with a rhetorical question, startling statement, or unusual illustration. These devices often arouse the apathetic and disinterested listener. For example, to stimulate audience interest in a speech dealing with "Hang Gliding" a speaker used the following introduction:

> The other day, while I was driving home from school, I noticed
> an extremely large bird gliding gracefully through the sky. As I
> looked again I realized that this was truly the largest bird I had
> ever seen. I pulled my car over to the side of the road so that I could
> get a closer look. As I gazed into the sky this third time I thought
> that I must be dreaming—for what was flying over my head was
> not a bird, but rather a person. A person with wings.

In all communication situations it is to your advantage if you can stimulate a desire on the part of the audience to want to listen to your presentation. In the introduction to the informative speech make it clear to your audience that your topic holds significance for them and that they will benefit by listening. For instance, recently a speaker used an introduction to demonstrate that paying attention to the speech could save the listener a great deal of money. The topic was "gasoline conservation," and the speaker said, "By following the few simple suggestions I will discuss today, you should be able to save enough money each week to treat yourself to a T-bone steak."

You can better hold attention during the body of your speech if you have already created an atmosphere of curiosity and interest. By motivating the audience early in the speech you also increase the probability that they will learn something by the conclusion of your talk.

In your introduction you should also provide a brief initial summary (preview) of the main points to be taken up in the body of your speech. By telling your audience that your speech on the subject of "How to Swing a Golf Club" will deal with the grip, the stance and the swing, you are allowing them a glimpse of your organizational pattern as a means of making their job of listening easier. You are preparing them for what is coming, and they will find it much simpler to locate your main ideas.

THE BODY

Since the introduction has (1) captured the listener's attention, (2) aroused his interest in the information to come, and (3) previewed your main points, you are ready to present the information itself. To promote the listener's comprehension of your ideas, and to maintain attention at a high level, you should organize the body of your speech into meaningful groupings. The division of the whole into its parts is an essential step in explaining any complex machine, process, or concept. No one, for example, can understand all aspects of public welfare, but most people could assimilate certain features if they were presented and explained separately. In most instances the classification and division of the speech is inevitable in light of the subject matter. These groupings will be more easily remembered if they can be worded into a logical pattern. Let us reexamine some of the patterns of arrangement discussed in chapter 6 in light of their application to informative speaking.

Chronological Pattern

The chronological, or time pattern, has its greatest value in explanations of processes, in presentation of historic events, and in relating personal experiences. In discussing "The History of Air Travel" you might develop your material under three headings:

I.   Early attempts at flying.
II. Air travel today.
III. The future of air travel.

When giving a speech on "The Legislative Process" the order might well be:

I.   Drafting a bill.
II. Committee hearings.
III. Debate on the floor of Congress.

Spatial Pattern

Use of spatial order is especially effective in speeches describing a scene, a location, or a geographical distribution. For instance, the body of your speech could be arranged from North to South, from top to bottom, or from center to outside. In talking on the topic of "Weather in the United States," your order might be:

I.   Weather on the East Coast.
II. Weather in the Middle West.
III. Weather on the West Coast.

For a speech on "The Life Under the Sea" you might select the following order:

I.   Surface sea life.
II. Sea life twenty feet below the ocean.
III. Sea life on the ocean floor.

Causal Order

In using the causal order you may tell of the causes of certain effects, or tell of the effects resulting from various causes. In giving a talk on "The Sun and the Individual," your pattern might appear:

I.   The effects of the sun on the skin.
II. The effects of the sun on the eyes.
III. The effects of the sun on the hair.

When treating the topic "Why World War II?" you might select the following arrangement:

I.   United States and German relations before 1941.

II.   United States and Italian relations before 1941.
III. United States and Japanese relations before 1941.

By examining the relationship of the United States to each of these countries, one is able to point out possible causes for World War II.

Topical Pattern

The topical pattern is probably the most frequently used of all patterns. This arrangement sets out several facets of a topic that are obviously related and consistent. If you are talking about "The Financial Structure of the University," your pattern might include:

I.   The university's assets.
II. The university's liabilities.
III. The university's endowments.

The key to the topical pattern is that the arrangement is rather apparent and the one that an audience most likely expects.

The speaker may wish to order the material so that it moves from the simplest to the most complex, the most familiar to the least familiar, the least important to the most important, or the most acceptable to the least acceptable.

THE CONCLUSION

Methods of concluding a speech were explained in some detail in chapter 6 and can profitably be reviewed as part of your training for informative speaking. There are, however, certain techniques of concluding that are especially valuable for the speech to inform. For example, it may be helpful to restate your main message and summarize its main points. You may desire to heighten audience interest once again and suggest areas where they will be able to add to or clarify some concepts you mentioned.

The most popular concluding technique is the final summary (or reiteration). People tend to pay close attention when they feel the end of the speech is near. The final summary takes advantage of this captured attention by reviewing the main ideas in the *same* order they were presented in the initial summary and in the body of the speech. In speaking on the topic of "College Registration," one might conclude by saying, "So we have seen that you can register for classes in three ways. First, you can register by mail; second, you can make special arrangements with the specific instructors; and finally, you can sign up in the Registration office on the first day of classes."

A SAMPLE OUTLINE

It might be helpful if we paused briefly at this point and looked at one form that organizational scheme often takes—the outline.

(Title)   Who Pays?
(General Purpose)   To Inform

(Specific Purpose)   To have the audience understand the major arguments for and against state aid to parochial schools.

Introduction

(Rhetorical question)

  I. How many of you realize that one of the crucial battles that raged during the founding of this country remains an unresolved issue even today?
     A. The early colonists were very insistent in their determination to separate church and state.
     B. Yet compulsory school attendance laws meant that some parents, who desired private schools, were forced into financing two separate institutions.

(Motivation towards topic)

  II. This highly emotional issue affects us today as much as it did hundreds of years ago.
     A. If the state would begin to pay the tuition fees for private schools, it would mean that millions of additional dollars would have to be found.
        1. Money from our taxes.
        2. Money now being used to pay for our public education.
     B. If the state supported parochial schools, some say it would bring church and state closer together.
     C. Yet what about the person who believes that under the Fourteenth Amendment we can educate a child in any way we deem appropriate?
        1. Is it not a denial of our freedom to be forced to pay dual taxation?
        2. What if you believe that our public schools are "Godless?"

(Preview)

  III. To better understand this important issue of state aid to parochial schools, I should like to look at the arguments which are frequently made in favor of tax support for these schools and then examine the arguments advanced by those who oppose such aid.

Core Statement: Opinion is strongly divided on the issue of state aid to parochial schools.

Body

  IV. The arguments that support tax aid for parochial schools are twofold.
     A. Denominational schools offer an important religious, spiritual, and ethical element that is not found in public schools.
        1. Only religious schools can teach Christian values.
        2. Public schools are Godless.

B. The right of parents to determine the education and religious instruction of their children is a fundamental one.
   1. Failure to provide public funds for denominational schools is a partial denial of that right.
   2. This denial may well make some families second-class citizens who are not benefitting from their taxes.

V. The arguments advanced by those who oppose tax support for parochial schools are threefold.
   A. It is urged that the appropriation of public funds for denominational schools would be a long step towards breaking down the unique American policy of separation of church and state.
      1. Part of an early colonial policy.
      2. An idea contained in the First Amendment to the Constitution.
   B. It is contended that the organization of American public schools along denominational lines would make education a divisive rather than a unifying factor in our life.
      1. Schools now teach a variety of opinions and views.
      2. Denominational schools would tend to teach dogma and one-dimensional attitudes.
   C. It is argued that the present arrangements promote healthy growth among various religions.

(Use visual aids)

   1. A recent religious census reveals that 53 percent of the population hold church membership—the highest mark in U.S. history.
   2. Approximately 78 million persons now belong to some religious group.

Conclusion

(Summary)

VI. Today, by looking at both sides of an important issue, we have gained some insight into the pros and cons of tax support for parochial schools.
   A. Those in favor of tax support suggest the following:
      1. Denominational schools can do a better job of teaching values and ethics.
      2. It is unfair to deny a basic right to people who select parochial schools.
   B. Those opposed counter by saying:
      1. Granting funds for these schools would bring church and state closer together.
      2. Denominational education is divisive.
      3. The status quo is beneficial to both church and state.

VII. In the final analysis you must seek out additional information before deciding how you personally feel about this important historical and religious problem.

VISUAL AIDS

The value of visual aids as a means of support was suggested in chapter 5 when we discussed the forms of support. Visual aids are useful in informative discourse in that they make ideas more vivid, more lasting, and more understandable. Visual aids are helpful in clarifying new terms or ideas which are not readily understood or meaningful to many in the audience. The word "larynx" might be unfamiliar to the listeners, but a model or diagram would quickly offer the audience a definition of the term, and "steam generating plan" would be more meaningful when accompanied by a diagram. A common principle of learning maintains that it is worthwhile to employ as many senses as possible, that the more associations one has with an idea the better are their chances of remembering it. Being able to see the idea, as well as hear it, contributes to both of these objectives. We have stressed throughout this chapter the importance of interest and attention as part of the informative process. A pretty picture, a shiny object, or a drawing provides the listener with an object upon which attention can be focused, and the listener is usually anxious to hear what the speaker has to say about it.

TYPES OF VISUAL AIDS

Objects, Specimens, and Models

If at all possible, use the *actual object*. Reality is usually more compelling than a mere representation of that reality. If the actual object can be seen, it can help explain an idea or a principle while it captures and maintains attention. An audience could better understand how to develop film from a camera if all of the essential objects (pans, acid, and so forth) were in front of them. Or a speech on "football protection gear" would be aided by displaying a football player's shoulder pads, hip pads, and helmet. In short, effective communicators are not content to merely talk about an idea, they want the listeners to see the actual concept in question.

There will be times when you cannot bring the actual object to the speaking situation. On those occasions you will have to settle for a *specimen*, a sample of the real object. The speaker who could not bring the audience an entire rock collection had to be satisfied with showing a few specimens. Even so, these specimens were useful in that they shortened the time needed to explain what certain rocks looked like.

Because they are often replicas of the real thing, *models* can serve three useful purposes. First, they can help *explain* a complex idea. For example, a model of the human heart can greatly simplify this intricate organ without distorting any of the heart's main functions. Second, models can be made into any size or shape; therefore, they can be *moved* from place to place. We could not bring the *U.S.S. Nautilus* to class, yet seeing a disassembled model of that nuclear submarine would be helpful to any audience. Third, because models have to be constructed, the model-makers can *emphasize* whatever aspect of the process they wish to stress. Notice in the communication model below how

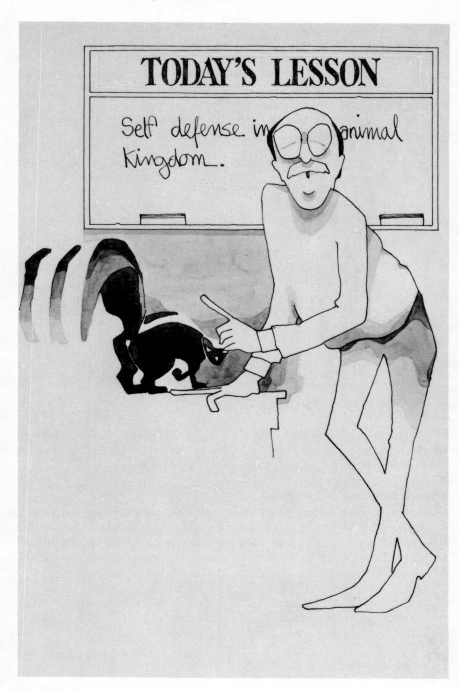

Visual aids help explain, clarify, and
hold attention.

messages and feedback are emphasized while such concepts as encoding, decoding, and channels are not even shown.

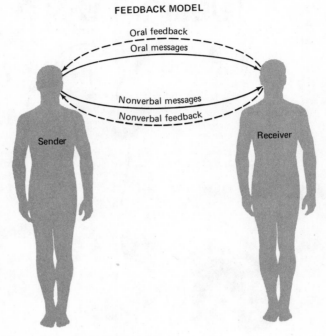

Figure 8–2   Feedback Model

With this particular visual aid the speaker was concerned with defining feedback. As you can see, the model helped demonstrate that feedback is the response the receiver makes to the sender's messages.

Posters, Diagrams, and Pictures

Speakers who want to make their own visual aids normally find that *posters* are very useful. They can clarify and/or reinforce any idea selected by the speaker. For example, if you are using statistics in your speech you might well say, "In 1971 the price for a gallon of regular gasoline in our city was 29.9¢,

PRICES OF REGULAR GASOLINE IN OUR CITY	
YEAR	PRICE
1971	29.9
1972	32.9
1973	41.7
1974	52.9
1975	58.9

Figure 8–3   Poster

in 1972 it was 32.9¢, in 1973 it was 41.7¢, and in 1974 it was up to 52.9¢." The same point could be given added emphasis by a poster.

Some speakers use posters to help their listeners remember the key elements in the speech. Figure 8–3 demonstrates how a speaker, talking on the subject of fire prevention, used a poster to stress the important ideas he wanted the audience to retain.

> **HOME FIRE PREVENTION PLAN**
>
> 1. Eliminate rubbish in halls and closets.
> 2. Use container when storing inflammable materials.
> 3. Check all electrical wiring.

Figure 8–4   Poster

In some ways *diagrams* are like models—both attempt to explain and clarify that which is complex. However, models are often three-dimensional while diagrams are composed of line and geometrical forms. The blueprints for an underground watering system would be an example of a diagram using such forms.

Pictures and photographs are extremely helpful and are readily available to all speakers. Imagine how clarity would be enhanced by pictures if you were speaking on either the history of the American automobile or modern architecture for the 1980s.

Charts and Graphs

Abstract or complicated ideas can often be made more understandable through use of *charts* and *graphs.* The increase in personal income taxes over the last twenty years can be well illustrated on a graph that shows, on the vertical axis, the years involved and, on the horizontal axis, the average amount of taxes paid by each individual. The four most common graphs and charts are: (a) the **organizational** chart, which shows, by means of blocks and interconnecting lines, the hierarchy of control and responsibility; (b) the **comparison** chart, which compares or contrasts two or more quantities, usually of a statistical nature, in terms of each other or in terms of other predetermined quantities; (c) the **"pie graph,"** which is a circle divided into several pie-shaped segments, each segment representing a classified item and its relationship to the other items; (d) the **bar graph** and the **line graph,** which are usually employed to represent trends, as in a sales graph.

Blackboards

The main advantage of blackboards as visual aids should be obvious to anyone who has attended school: they are *convenient;* items can easily be added or removed at any time. They are usually found in conference rooms and auditoriums as well as in classrooms. We would caution the conscientious speaker to check the speaking environment before the speech to be sure that a chalkboard will be available. The authors remember one speaker who very casually

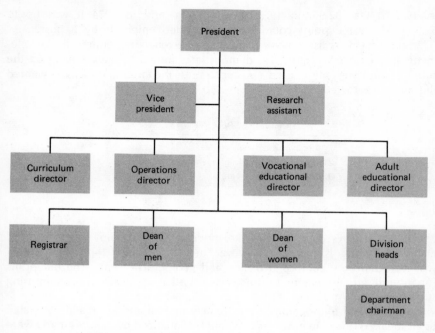

Figure 8–5   Organizational Chart

WELFARE EXPENDITURES 1970-75	
1970	$1,200,000.
1971	$2,700,000.
1972	$2,900,000.
1973	$3,400,000.
1974	$4,100,000.
1975	$5,800,000.

Figure 8–6   Comparison Chart

said, "Now let me diagram how this system will work," only to turn around and find there was not a blackboard in the room. Both the speaker and the audience were greatly embarrassed.

There will be occasions when the blackboard will offer an opportunity to present a step-by-step development of the process you are explaining. By adding material as you go along, you could visually demonstrate how a ship is built from the inside to the outside. Moreover, because chalk is easy to erase, you could eliminate certain items as a means of clarifying your point.

Blackboards are handy and helpful, but some words of advice are in order concerning their use and abuse. Remember that it takes time to write, and you may well lose the audience's attention while you are lettering and

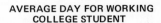

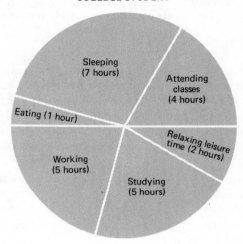

Figure 8–7   Pie Graph

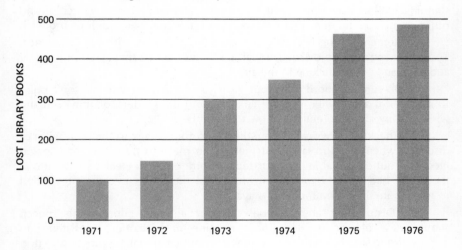

Figure 8–8   Bar Graph

diagramming. Therefore, you should try to continue talking and maintaining eye contact while you are at the board. If you put your material on the board before you speak, you may find that your audience spends more time looking at it than at you.

The content and mechanics of a particular chalk drawing should be planned well in advance of your presentation. You may want your efforts to appear to be spontaneous, but in actuality you should be as rehearsed with your drawings as you are with your speaking.

USING VISUAL AIDS

By following some simple guidelines in the use of visual aids, you will discover that your material will be clearer, more meaningful, and more interesting.

1.   In preparing and selecting your visual aid make certain that the aid is pertinent to the subject and serves a real purpose.

2.   The material on the visual aid should be completely accurate in both representation and authenticity. This does not mean that some forms of exaggeration cannot be used to show emphasis.

3.   The visual aid should not contain any distracting elements. For example, nonessential details or details that are so poorly depicted that they can't be accurately interpreted may well obscure rather than clarify your ideas.

4.   In most instances it is best to display only one visual aid at a time. To have more than one aid in front of the audience at one time encourages the listeners to divide their attention between the aids and perhaps miss certain important points about the one you happen to be discussing.

5.   See that the lettering, artwork, or other main features are large enough, clear enough, and of sufficient contrast for all viewers to see.

6.   Make the aid attractive enough so that it adds to clarity and understanding while helping you secure and hold attention. Try to use color and other creative techniques that can keep your aid from being dull or ordinary.

7.   Remember the necessity of maintaining contact with your audience. Too many speakers enjoy their visual aid to the degree that they forget their audience and end up talking to the aid.

8.   Be sure to coordinate your visual aid with your words. Don't point to a wheel of a car when you are talking about the fenders, or show one aid while talking about something shown by another.

9.   Check the physical surroundings and furnishings so that you will not discover, when it is too late, that there is no place to put your chart, or no electrical outlet available for your tape recorder. Many speakers have found they have had to hold their aids throughout their talks because they failed to investigate the accommodations available.

10.   Distributing any material to your audience during the speech should, as a rule, be avoided. The circulating material offers the listener an easy excuse to stop listening. If you must distribute material, be sure to give it to every person in your audience. Trying to read over someone's shoulder can cause confusion in the audience.

SUMMARY

The principles of communication discussed throughout this book are directly applicable to informative speaking. There are, however, certain steps that must be applied when sending someone a message intended to increase his knowledge of a particular subject. In outline form, these steps are:

I. Introduction
    A.   Arouse attention.
    B.   Stimulate interest.
    C.   Summarize the main points to be covered in the speech.
II. Body
    A.   Adapt material to the audience—audience analysis.
    B.   Employ clear organization.
    C.   Strive for audience comprehension.
        1.   Use definitions.
        2.   Employ concrete examples.
        3.   Use comparisons and contrasts.
        4.   Dramatize essential points with statistics.
        5.   Utilize vivid and complete descriptions.
        6.   Reinforce and emphasize main points.
        7.   Use partitions, enumerations, and summaries.
    D.   Arouse and maintain interest and attention.
        1.   Note that which is impending.
        2.   Allude to that which is physically near to the audience.
        3.   Refer to the familiar.
        4.   Invoke the personal needs of the audience.
        5.   Impart activity in body, voice, and content.
        6.   Utilize reality.
        7.   Point out conflict.
        8.   Use humor.
    E.   Employ effective visual aids.
III. Conclusion
    A.   Present summary of the main points.
    B.   Arouse interest in further investigation.

Suggested Readings

Baird, A. Craig; Knower, Franklin H.; and Becker, Samuel L. *General Speech Communication.* 4th ed. New York: McGraw-Hill Book Co., 1970. Chapter 20.

McCabe, Bernard P., and Bender, Coleman C. *Speaking Is a Practical Matter.* 2d ed. Boston: Holbrook Press, 1973. Part IV.

Olbricht, Thomas S. *Informative Speaking.* Glenview, Ill.: Scott, Foresman and Co., 1968.

Oliver, Robert T., and Cortright, Rupert L. *Effective Speech.* 5th ed. New York: Holt, Rinehart and Winston, 1970. Chapters 14 and 18.

Reid, Loren. *Speaking Well.* 2d ed. New York: McGraw-Hill Book Co., 1972. Chapters 14–17.

Rogge, Edward, and Ching, James C. *Advanced Public Speaking.* New York: Holt, Rinehart and Winston, 1966. Chapters 12–14.

Wittich, Walter A., and Schuller, Charles F. *Audio-Visual Materials: Their Nature and Use.* 4th ed. New York: Harper and Row, Publishers, 1967.

9

Persuasive Speaking
Changing Beliefs, Attitudes, and Behavior

It is virtually impossible to draw a clear-cut distinction between informing and persuading. Examination of the form and substance of a speech message does not yield a reliable clue to its identity as persuasion or exposition because a given message may produce a variety of effects depending upon who receives the message. For example, if the doctor says to the patient, "Jerry, you weigh 225 pounds," Jerry's reaction to that simple statement might be, "I guess you want me to start dieting." Or perhaps he might say, "Great! I've lost another ten pounds!" Or conceivably, "I'll never get a pro football contract unless I gain at least twenty more pounds." Unless we know Jerry's reaction we are hard put to classify the doctor's statement as persuasive or informative. A speech which is intended to be informative may be persuasive in impact. Or one segment of a message may have an informative effect while another segment of the same message may have a persuasive effect. So the distinction between informing and persuading is not to be found in *what the speech is* but in *what the speech does*.

If the discourse produces clarification of ideas or concepts, or an increase in understanding, then we may say that it has informed. If it produces changes in belief, attitude, or behavior, then it has persuaded. It can be argued, of course, that increased understanding may precipitate attitudinal or behavioral change; thus a speech that has the immediate effect of informing may have the long-range effect of persuading.

Thomas Olbricht, author of *Informative Speaking,* offers a distinction between persuading and informing in terms of the predisposition of the audience. He suggests that if the audience is "predisposed to accept without argument what the speaker has to say," then the discourse is perceived by the listener as informative. If it is predisposed to view the speaker's ideas as controversial, then the speaker has a persuasive task. For example, consider how a speech explaining the advantages of offshore drilling would be perceived by an audience of environmentalists versus an audience of oil producers. The former would probably see the message as controversial and manipulative while the latter would probably view it as purely informational.

Perhaps an examination of representative definitions of "persuade," "persuasion," and "persuasive speaking" may help us differentiate the functions of persuading and informing. *Webster's Seventh New Collegiate Dictionary* says that to persuade is "to move by argument, entreaty, or expostulation to a belief, position, or course of action." Brembeck and Howell, in *Persuasion,* state that "Persuasion is the conscious attempt to modify the thought and action by manipulating the motives of men toward predetermined ends." Bryant and Wallace, in *Fundamentals of Public Speaking,* define persuasive speaking as "verbal communication whose prime purpose or goal is the influencing of attitude, belief, or behavior." Thomas Scheidel, author of *Persuasive Speaking,* defines it as "that activity in which speaker and listener are conjoined and in which the speaker consciously attempts to influence the behavior of the listener by transmitting audible and visible symbolic cues." J. Jeffery Auer, in *The Rhetoric of Our Times,* defines persuasion in public speaking as "the process of securing acceptance of an idea, or an action, by connecting it favorably with the listener's attitudes, beliefs, and desires." And Gary Cronkhite, author of *Persuasion: Speech and Behavioral Change,* defines persuasion as "the act of manipulating symbols so as to produce changes in the evaluation of approach-avoidance behavior of those who interpret the symbols."

Let us examine some of the patterns that seem to emerge from these definitions. In every case the end sought by persuasion is stated or implied:

"move . . . to a belief, position, or course of action"

"modify the thought and action"

"influencing of attitude, belief, or behavior"

"influence the behavior"

"securing acceptance of idea, or an action"

"produce changes in the evaluation or approach-avoidance behavior"

Change seems to be the essence of the reaction sought. The elements one seeks to change are beliefs, attitudes, and actions or behavior. The definitions also suggest the instrumentality for effecting the change:

"by argument, entreaty, expostulation"

"by manipulating the motives"

"by connecting it favorably with listener attitudes, beliefs, desires"

"by transmitting audible and visible symbolic cues"

"manipulating symbols"

There are certain other features of these definitions that should be noted as well. Brembeck and Howell call persuasion the *conscious attempt* to modify thought and action. This qualification suggests that changes wrought by accident rather than by speaker design fall outside the realm of the *art* of persuading. Speaker intent to persuade therefore must be present if the discourse is to be labeled with accuracy as an example of persuasion. Scheidel's definition of persuasive speaking contains the qualification that the parties be *conjoined,* that speaker and listener be joined together for a common purpose whether by radio, television, or by face-to-face confrontation. The use of expressions such as "connecting it favorably" and "manipulating the motives" suggest that persuasion is concerned with inducing a *willing* change of belief, attitude, or behavior rather than a grudging acquiescence resulting from force, threat, or coercion. At the same time, there is an implicit notion in the definitions that the listener's field of choices is restricted in persuasive communication. Unlike informative communication, where the listener has greater freedom to draw whatever inference he chooses from the information presented, persuasive communication attempts to restrict the listener to inferences (and attendant behavior) that are predetermined by the speaker. Finally, the definitions imply that if any attempt at persuasion is to succeed, there must be interaction of all elements of the communication situation. There can be a situation calling for persuasion, a time and a place for communication to be attempted, an audience ripe for persuasion, a speaker with an intent to persuade, and a message designed to persuade, but until the message is presented, perceived, interpreted, and a reaction produced which is consistent with the speaker's intent, then persuasion cannot occur.

In this chapter, then, we shall focus upon that communication activity which is consciously aimed at inducing willing changes of belief, attitude, or behavior in the listener. For the remainder of this chapter we shall be discussing the elements the speaker wishes to change, various ways of inducing the desired changes, and the prospects of achieving change.

THE TARGETS AND TOPICS OF PERSUASION

When we say that the targets of our persuasive efforts are beliefs, attitudes, and behavior of others, what do we mean by these terms? Belief is defined in Webster's New Collegiate Dictionary as "a conviction of the truth of some statement or reality of a fact, especially when well grounded." Fishbein (see suggested readings) maintains that we display beliefs in and beliefs about objects. Thus, if you were to say, "Poverty exists in the United States," you would be expressing a belief in the probability of its existence. If you were to say, "Poverty in the United States is intolerable," you would be expressing a belief about its existence.

Attitudes, according to Fishbein, "are learned predispositions to respond to an object or class of objects in a favorable or unfavorable way." How do you react when you find out that the friendly stranger seated next to you at the lunch counter is an off-duty police officer? An undertaker? A minister? An ex-convict? A debt collector? Your instinctive reaction is probably reflective of a learned predisposition toward the person's particular occupation or status.

Behavior, as we shall use the term, refers to the listener's observable state of activity. The observable state will range somewhere between total inactivity and hyperactivity. Changes in behavior may be from action to inaction or vice versa, or they may involve an increase or decrease in the intensity, duration, or magnitude of an action. For example, if you were to urge a friend to stop smoking, you might observe one of these changes in behavior: your friend might give up smoking entirely, might cut down on consumption, might ignore your advice, or might increase consumption out of defiance or some other motive. Furthermore, your friend's behavioral change might take place immediately, or it might be delayed. The change might be short-lived or permanent.

If beliefs, attitudes, and behavior are the targets of change, with respect to what fundamental issues do we wish to effect change? Generally speaking, people hold differing views on (1) the reality of facts, (2) the validity of value judgments, and (3) the advisability of adopting proposed courses of action. If speaker and listener differ over the reality of a fact, the speaker espouses a *proposition of fact;* he attempts to prove or disprove the existence of something. For example, you might support or attack the following allegations:

The CIA is spying on American citizens.

Multinational corporations control the world's economy.

Capital punishment is a deterrent to crime.

Environmentalists oppose all land development.

The Internal Revenue Service is being used to harass political enemies of the administration.

President Kennedy was struck by bullets fired from two separate locations.

California will suffer a major earthquake within two years.

It is important to bear in mind that propositions of fact deal with *alleged* facts —matters whose reality people dispute. Moreover, propositions of fact may deal with past, present, and future circumstances. "The movie *Jaws* caused a decline in the number of swimmers at the nation's beaches in the summer of 1975" alleges the existence of a circumstance in the past. "TV violence is causing an increase in juvenile crime" asserts a present condition. "The Communists will control all of Southeast Asia in two years" alleges a future condition.

If speaker and listener differ over the validity of a value judgment, the speaker espouses a *proposition of value,* that is, the speaker maintains that something is good or bad, is better or worse than something else, is right or wrong, is justified or unjustified, and so forth. The following are examples of propositions of value:

Solar energy is better than geothermal energy.

The U.S. decision to withdraw from Southeast Asia was wise.

Flying is safer than driving.

The defense budget is too big.

Penalties for possession of marijuana are too severe.

To lower taxes when the cost of government services is increasing would be irresponsible.

Aristotle's *Rhetoric* was the best speech book ever written.

The governor was justified in vetoing salary increases.

Like the proposition of fact, the proposition of value may concern itself with judgments about something in the past, the present, and the future, as can be seen in the examples cited above.

If speaker and listener differ over the advisability of adopting a proposed course of action, the speaker espouses a *proposition of policy;* that is, the speaker argues that something should or should not be done. Thus, one might recommend or oppose the following proposals:

The sale of garments made from the skin of animals on the endangered species list should be prohibited by federal law.

The construction of buildings in excess of 20 feet in height should be prohibited in any area within 1500 feet of the seashore.

The manufacture of passenger-car engines rated at more than 280 HP should be prohibited by federal law.

The United States should withdraw from NATO.

The 55 *mph* speed limit should be abolished.

The college bookstore should be prohibited from selling textbooks at a price in excess of that charged by off-campus bookstores.

The petroleum industry should be nationalized.

Issues of fact, value, and policy, then, constitute the common topics of persuasion. Within the compass of a single speech, the speaker may be called upon to defend all three kinds of propositions. For example, a speaker trying to win support for a proposed policy will have to prove several propositions of fact and value in the process:

A need exists for the policy. (proposition of fact)

The proposed policy will fulfill the need. (proposition of fact)

The proposed policy is better than any other proposals advanced. (proposition of value)

While the foregoing example by no means exhausts the list of propositions of fact and value that have to be established before a proposition of policy can be proved, it does illustrate the point that several propositions may occur within one speech.

TYPES OF PERSUASIVE SPEECHES

Persuasive speeches may be classified according to the kinds of audience response sought. If your aim is to secure audience agreement with your position on a proposition of fact, value, or policy, then we say that you are making a *speech to convince*. Thus you might want your audience to agree that industrial spying is taking place, or that industrial spying is bad, or that industrial spying should be declared illegal. In each case you would be trying to convince your audience. If your aim is to get audience action on some matter, then we say that you are making a *speech to actuate*. If you want your listener to sign a petition, donate to a charity, write to a legislator, buy an insurance policy, take a course, or see a play, then you are attempting to actuate that listener. If your aim is to reinforce or rejuvenate existing attitudes or beliefs held by the listener, then we say you are making a *speech to stimulate*. Inspirational messages, ranging from sermons to pep talks to commencement addresses, are usually concerned with stimulating audience attitudes, beliefs, and emotions.

There may be occasions when it will be necessary to convince, stimulate, and actuate all within the same speech, but only one of these will constitute your *ultimate* aim. A sales presentation is an example of a speech whose ultimate aim is to actuate—to get the customer to buy the product or service. In the course of the presentation the salesperson will probably have to convince the customer of a number of points—that the product is needed, that its purchase is feasible, that it is better than competing products—and will probably have to stimulate existing attitudes and beliefs in order to intensify the customer's desire for the product. But the acts of convincing and stimulating are merely instrumental to the ultimate aim which is to actuate.

PREPARING THE
PERSUASIVE SPEECH

The process of preparing a persuasive speech is in many respects similar to that used in preparing an informative speech. A topic is chosen, the audience is analyzed, the specific purpose is determined, the materials for achieving the specific purpose are discovered, the speech is organized and rehearsed, but the application of each of the steps of the process to persuasion involves certain unique procedures.

CHOOSING THE TOPIC AND
POSITION

Ideally, the choice of a topic for a persuasive speech should arise from the speaker's recognition of some condition that requires change and the further recognition that change cannot be effected without the help of others. Perhaps you feel that student activity fees at your school are too high, but you despair of ever seeing any reduction take place until students get together to bring pressure on those responsible for setting the fees. Such a situation calls for a persuasive speech. Or perhaps you live near a factory and suffer from the noise of its operation. You want the noise level reduced but know that such a reduction will not take place until people unite to bring pressure on the management. Again, the need for a persuasive speech arises. In each case you become aware of a disturbing element. Then you take a *position* or *stance* with regard to the correction of that disturbing element.

Doubtless you have already taken a position with respect to a number of analogous disturbances. Why not draw upon one of them as the topic for a persuasive speech? As we observed in chapter 1, one of the basic principles of subject selection is to choose a subject that is interesting to you—that *involves* you.

There may be times when the topic and position is chosen for you. Perhaps a friend will ask you to assist in campaigning for some person or some cause. Perhaps you will become a salesperson and will be told what to sell! But regardless of whether you originate the subject or someone else does, you should not undertake a persuasive task unless you are interested in the subject and motivated to persuade.

ANALYZING THE AUDIENCE

We have repeatedly called attention to the importance of audience analysis in this text. If the aim of persuasion is to induce a change in the listener, then it behooves us to place particular emphasis upon knowing the listener. It is probable that the majority of failures in persuasive attempts can be traced to insufficient or inaccurate analysis of those the speaker wishes to influence. Perhaps the speaker has taken pains to find out about his listeners as individuals but has failed to take into account what they are like when they become members of a group. The group imposes codes of behavior upon the individual that are not necessarily operative when he is removed from the group. The salesperson who is accustomed to dealing with one person at a time sometimes finds it a difficult experience to deal with a crowd, so different are people in their public and private behavior. On the other hand, there are those who find it easier to deal with the crowd than with the individual because of the tendency of most people to become less critical in their thinking when they become members of a crowd. At any rate, the speaker should become familiar with what *motivates* the listener as an individual and as a member of a group.

In analyzing your audience for a persuasive speech it is advisable to seek answers to these questions: (1) What is the audience's general attitude toward my topic and position? (2) What is the audience's attitude toward me as a spokesperson? (3) What beliefs does the audience hold about my topic? (4) What has influenced the audience to take its current position on the topic?

1. *Audience attitude toward topic and position.* The following are some of the possible individual and group attitudes that will confront the speaker at the outset of a persuasive speech. (1) Individual listeners or the audience as a whole may be apathetic toward your proposition. If that be the case, you may have to place particular stress upon the link between your proposition and the listeners' self-interests in order to overcome the apathy. (2) Individual listeners or the audience as a whole may be hostile toward the point of view you are espousing. This may involve your starting with those items with which you and the audience are in agreement and then moving on to the areas of disagreement. (3) Individual listeners or the audience as a whole may be interested but undecided, in which case you may decide to place particular emphasis upon the use of factual evidence which supports your position. (4) Individual listeners or the audience as a whole may be favorably inclined toward your position. Your job, in that case, is to reaffirm for the listeners their basis for agreeing with you.

2. *Audience attitude toward the speaker.* Individual listeners or the audience as a whole may be primarily concerned with your personal credibility. If you have a good reputation preceding you to the platform, then your task is to confirm that reputation. If you have a negative reputation before the speech, your job is to supplant it with a positive reputation. If you have no reputation

preceding you to the platform, then your job is to create a good one through the speech itself.

   3. *Audience beliefs.*   The precise issues with which you should deal in a given communication will depend upon the audience. Through careful analysis of the audience you should determine *where they are in their thinking about the subject.* What beliefs do they presently hold? If you are planning to urge the adoption of a policy, you should ask:

> Does the audience know that a problem exists? Do they *doubt* that a problem exists? Do they *deny* the existence of a problem?
>
> Are they aware of the seriousness of the problem? Do they *doubt* the seriousness of the problem? Do they *deny* its seriousness?
>
> Are they aware of the causes of the problem? Are they likely to *doubt* my interpretation of the causes?
>
> Are they aware of the possibility of solving the problem? Do they *doubt* that a solution can be found? Do they *deny* that a solution can be found?
>
> Are they aware of the various solutions that have been advanced? Are they aware of the advantages and disadvantages of some or all of the proposed solutions?
>
> Do they doubt the efficacy of my proposed solution?
>
> Do they doubt the superiority of my proposed solution over other proposed solutions?

It should be evident that persuasion should not be attempted until one has tried to secure an answer to the foregoing questions. It would be folly to try to convince an audience that you have the best solution when they don't believe that a problem even exists! Your answers to these questions may tell you that more than one speech will be required before the audience is ready to accept your proposal. Finding out where the audience is in its thinking will tell you the point at which you should launch your argument and will enable you to make a more reliable prediction of just how far you can move the audience from its present position.

   If you are planning to limit your purpose to winning audience agreement on a proposition of fact or value, then you should try to find answers to these questions:

> By what criteria does the audience measure the "truth" of the fact in question (or the value judgment in question)?
>
> Is each criterion valid?
>
> Are there criteria that the audience has overlooked?
>
> Are there better criteria available?

For example, if you wanted to convince an audience that the Datsun is superior to the Toyota, you would be well advised to discover how your audience measures a car's superiority. By its economy? Stability? Comfort? Safety? Beauty? Speed? Its aura of prestige? Unless you discover the criteria (and the *priority* of criteria) that the audience uses, you may be wasting your time. This does not mean that you will necessarily *use* the audience's criteria. You may try to convince them that there are criteria that are even more important. For example, you might convince the audience that the efficiency of a car's smog control equipment is a more significant criterion of superiority than the car's beauty, speed, comfort, or economy.

The criminal court case furnishes an example of criteria used to measure the truth of an alleged fact. The prosecution contends that the defendant is guilty. Then it offers as criteria of guilt such elements as motive, means, and opportunity: "Henry is guilty of murdering Margaret because he needed the $50,000 that her life insurance would yield, he possessed a weapon capable of dealing the deathblow, and he was known to be in her house at the time of the murder." The defense counsel concedes that motive, means, and opportunity are indeed criteria for measuring guilt but adds that they are not the *only* criteria or necessarily the *important* criteria: "Even though Henry had a motive, a means, and an opportunity, he didn't possess the *physical capacity* to deal the deathblow."

So discover whether your audience has criteria for measuring the truth of the fact you are alleging or the value judgment you are urging. Then you will be in a much better position to offer your audience convincing reasons for agreeing with you.

4. *Forces influencing audience position.* While it is of great importance to try to discover what your audience feels and believes, it is of equal importance to try to ascertain the principal sources of influence operating upon the listener. *Why* does the listener believe and feel a certain way? While there are any number of forces that may be influencing the listener's position, we would like to single out two categories for discussion. The first deals with pressures brought upon the listener from without, and the second deals with pressures brought upon the listener from within.

Group membership and audience position. Much interest has been shown of late in the social pressures which influence the adoption, retention, modification, and abandonment of our attitudes. The reference groups with which we identify, the small groups with which we interact directly, and leaders to whom we look for guidance exert pressures upon us to believe, feel, and act in certain ways.

Each one of us probably identifies with numerous reference groups. We identify with a particular race, political party, religion, age group, economic class, philosophical orientation, occupational group, regional group, to cite some of the more common reference groups. Some have no determinate structure or goal, such as age group, economic class, regional group. Others display varying degrees of organization and orientation. Our "membership" in a particular group may be by reason of our parentage—religious and political affiliations are often inherited; our membership in others may be the result of voluntary actions which place us within the group. Whatever the circumstances of our "joining," a feeling of kinship with the *group* (but not necessarily with the *individuals* within the group) tends to develop, in some instances resulting in a kind of blind loyalty. Donald K. Smith (see Suggested Readings) points out that the "individual's perception of his membership in certain groups is likely to be accompanied by a contrasting recognition of groups with which he feels little or no identification." In fact, he points out, it "may sometimes be accompanied by hostility toward other groups."

We also belong to small groups which involve us in direct interaction with other members of that group. Our families, our circle of friends, our associates at work, our fellow club members, our church congregation are representative of those groups which exert the most direct pressure upon our behavior.

Our leaders in all those areas where we join with others in a group exert varying degrees of influence upon our attitudes, beliefs, and behavior. The greater the confidence we place in the leader, the greater our propensity to emulate that person's behavior and accept his or her attitudes and beliefs on certain matters as our own.

What are the implications for persuasion in the social pressures exerted by reference groups, small groups, and leaders? Depending upon the particular circumstances involved, the speaker may find that the listener's consciousness of group pressure is an asset that can be used or is a detriment that must be offset. In some situations an individual may consent to believe, feel, or act in a particular way if informed that others of the group are doing likewise or have given approval to such behavior. The "bandwagon technique" of the propagandist is built upon this very principle. It attempts to intensify the listener's awareness of membership in the group. In those situations where the speaker's proposal runs afoul of the social pressures operating upon the listener, then the speaker must seek for means of minimizing those pressures. The speaker will attempt to get the listener to disassociate from the force bringing pressure.

It is important, then, for the speaker to try to discover the identity of the reference groups, small groups, and leaders that may be exerting an influence upon the listener's position.

Ego-involvement and audience position. Muzafer Sherif and his associates have conducted extensive investigations into the relationship between our ego-involvement with an issue and our willingness to modify our position on that issue. Sherif maintains that the greater the degree of ego-involvement we experience, the narrower are our "latitudes of acceptance," and hence the less likely we are to change our existing opinions on the issue.

The listener's proprietary interest in the issue, then, poses a considerable problem for the persuader who aspires to change the listener's position on the issue. Feature the difficulty of trying to convince a schoolteacher that teachers should accept less pay for more work. "More pay for less work," will be the likely response.

Our degree of familiarity with an issue and our willingness to change position was also studied by Sherif. His findings suggest that the less familiar we are with an issue, the more amenable we are to changes in our position on that issue (if, indeed, we hold a position at all).

Extreme devotion to a position, he maintains, virtually blinds one to any suggestion of change. Even a moderate point of view is perceived with some hostility by the fierce believer, because "it falls squarely within his latitude of rejection."

Try to discover, then, what "vested interest" your listeners may have in the issue under consideration. This information will enable you to set a more realistic persuasive goal.

DETERMINING THE SPECIFIC PURPOSE

Having analyzed the audience carefully, you are now in a position to devise a strategy of persuasion. You know what beliefs and attitudes have to be modified or overturned, you know what influences have to be enlisted or counteracted, you know how the audience perceives your personal credibility —in short, you know the magnitude of the task that lies ahead. You may decide that more than one speech will be necessary for you to attain your ultimate persuasive goal. In any case, your audience analysis has equipped you to determine how much you can accomplish in a given communication encounter. Therefore, your next move is to formulate a statement of the specific purpose of the upcoming speech.

You will recall that a statement of specific purpose indicates the exact audience response sought. In a persuasive speech, the statement of specific purpose indicates exactly *what you want your audience to believe, feel, or do.* For example:

> To have my audience believe that steel traps are inhumane.
>
> To have my audience feel that the telephone company is acting in the best interests of the public.
>
> To have my audience purchase tickets for the Charity Fair.
>
> To have my audience believe that the municipal airport should be relocated at least ten miles further from town.
>
> To have my audience sign a petition urging the governor to veto the bill legalizing the sale of fireworks.

Once you have formulated your specific purpose you can undertake the selection of those materials which will enable you to accomplish that purpose.

CHOOSING THE MEANS OF PERSUASION

Twenty-four centuries ago Aristotle in his *Rhetoric* observed that there are three instruments of persuasion: (1) ". . . persuasion is effected by the **arguments,** when we demonstrate the truth, real or apparent, by such means as inhere in particular cases." (2) ". . . persuasion is effected through the audience, when they are brought by the speech into a state of **emotion;** for we give very different decisions under the sway of pain or joy, and liking or hatred." (3) "The **character** of the speaker is a cause of persuasion when the speech is so uttered as to make him worthy of belief; for as a rule we trust men of probity more, and more quickly, about things in general, while on points outside the realm of exact knowledge, where opinion is divided, we trust them absolutely." The durability of Aristotle's classification may be seen by a cursory examination of rhetorical treatises from his day to the present. Perhaps different labels are affixed to the modes of persuasion, and perhaps some of the modes have been subdivided, but all are essentially Aristotelean in their origin. In this section we shall be concerned with finding convincing arguments, impelling psychological appeals, and ways of manifesting personal credibility.

It should be emphasized that the separation of persuasion into three modes is purely arbitrary. In most communication situations the speaker's persuasive attempts will be a composite of all of the modes. So we suggest that you view these three as being fused together in practice, even though we are analyzing them separately.

I. CONVINCING ARGUMENTS

To be convincing an argument must meet the audience's test of reasonableness. We all like to think that any action we take or any belief or attitude we hold rests upon a rational foundation. In fact, we search for reasons to justify our behavior, whether past, present, or future behavior. The speaker, then, is obliged to meet the listener's rational requirements.

Let us examine now the materials of argument— evidence and reasoning— and some of the possible requirements for a rational argument.

Evidence

A thorough analysis of evidence (forms of support) was undertaken in chapter 5. It would be well for you to review that material as part of your introduction to this view of persuasive communication. What follows, therefore, is a description of how various forms of evidence apply specifically to persuasive speaking. We shall group the forms of evidence into the following two general categories: (1) evidence of **fact,** and (2) evidence of **opinion.**

Factual evidence may be drawn from the speaker's own personal observation or from external sources. Each of us has witnessed some event and then reported to others what we have witnessed. Perhaps we were on the scene of an automobile accident and we tell the investigating officer the details of what happened. Or we argue with a friend over which supermarket has the lowest prices and we cite the actual prices we have paid for a particular grocery item. The validity of factual evidence drawn from our own personal observation is dependent upon two factors. First, how well equipped are we to be good witnesses of the "facts" we report? Do we have the necessary physical capacities, such as keen eyesight, or acute hearing? Is our perception colored by the emotional state we happen to be in? Do we see only what we want to see? In short, are we objective observers? Second, how well equipped are we to report what we have seen? Do we alter the story from telling to telling to make it more interesting? Do we relish the lurid details out of proportion to their importance? Do we possess the kind of vocabulary needed for relatively objective reporting?

Factual evidence drawn from external sources must meet these and other tests of validity. Is the fact being reported directly by the original observer? If so, that observer should be judged in light of the same questions we ask ourselves when we are the primary observers. Is the fact being reported by a secondary source? If so, what is the secondary source's reputation for reliability? When was the fact observed and when was it reported? What is fact today may not be fact tomorrow (witness population figures!). Is the fact represented out of context? Do other sources report the same fact?

Opinion evidence also has two sources—the speaker's own personal opinions based upon direct experience and the opinions of others, presumably experts. The acceptability of the "educated guess" is, of course, dependent upon whether the audience views the speaker as a person qualified to voice an informed opinion. If by reason of your occupation or your major field of study, you do possess the necessary qualifications for expertness—and if your audience recognizes these qualifications as adequate—then you may with impunity use yourself as a source of opinion. By and large, however, the student speaker will utilize the testimony of a recognized authority. Whether the opinion cited is his own or an expert's it should meet the criteria for valid testimony discussed in chapter 5.

Reasoning

The mere possession of valid evidence of fact and opinion is, of course, valueless unless we do something with it. The process of "doing something with" evidence—that is, drawing conclusions from it—is called **reasoning.** As you have doubtless seen, the same set of facts and opinions can lead to more than one conclusion. The persuasive speaker attempts to show that his or her conclusions are nearer to "truth" than the opponent's.

We generally recognize four forms of reasoning: (1) deduction, (2) induction, (3) reasoning from analogy, and (4) reasoning from causation.

1. *Deductive reasoning.* This is also called reasoning from axiom and reasoning from the general to the particular. The familiar syllogism,

> All men are mortals.
> Socrates is a man.
> Therefore, Socrates is a mortal.

is often cited as an example of deductive reasoning. The first line, "All men are mortals," is the axiom, or general statement. The second line is the particular case in point, "Socrates is a man." The third line states the conclusion, which shows the relationship of the particular to the general. Much of our reasoning follows this pattern. We have countless axioms which we employ in making everyday decisions. We have axioms to guide us in selecting a movie to see—"Movies starring Faye Dunaway are interesting movies. I see one is playing at the Lyric. Let's go!" Others guide us in where to eat out—"The tacos at Nina's are fabulous. I'm hungry for a taco. Let's go to Nina's."

Others guide in picking professors—"The Faculty Register is a reliable guide. I'm going to follow its advice and crash Professor Tower's class." Needless to say, our reasoning is not 100 percent foolproof!

Several tests should be applied as a means of detecting potential weak spots in our use of the deductive method. First of all, is the axiom or general rule usually true? Are Faye Dunaway's movies usually interesting? Why do you say so? How many of her movies have you seen? Is your axiom based on personal experience or on the judgment of a friend or perhaps a professional movie critic? Unless the axiom is usually true, then the conclusion will not be usually true. (You will note that we use the word *usually*. The persuasive speaker deals in the main with what is probable rather than what is certain.) Secondly, does the particular case in point fall within the scope of the axiom? Does the movie playing at the Lyric really *star* Faye Dunaway, or does she simply play a cameo role? Is it a feature she made sometime before she was regarded as a star? Unless the case in point falls within the scope of the axiom, we cannot validly conclude that the movie at the Lyric will probably be interesting.

Persuasive speaking is replete with use of deductive reasoning. When we urge others to defeat welfare legislation "because it's socialistic," we are saying in essence:

> Socialism is bad.
> Welfare legislation is socialistic.
> Therefore, it is bad. (And we don't support bad things.)

It behooves us as speakers and as listeners to examine critically any use of deductive reasoning. Unless the deduction can meet the tests mentioned above, it is spurious.

2. *Induction.* Also called reasoning from examples, reasoning from the specific to the general, or simply generalization, induction is the reverse of deduction. The pollster interviews 500 voters and concludes that "The American voter is more conservative today than compared to ten years ago." We read that four locals of the International Speech Fabricators are rife with corruption and conclude that all the other locals are probably corrupt, or possibly that all labor unions are corrupt. We meet a beautiful exchange student from Sweden and then tell our friends that Sweden has the most beautiful women in the world. All of these examples are imperfect inductions in that the generalization is based upon a limited number of examples. However, it is usually impossible for us to investigate every single part of the whole; so we must rely upon what we feel is a representative sampling. The professional pollster has perfected the means of obtaining a representative sampling to the extent that the services command high respect (and high prices).

All of us engage in inductive reasoning. In fact, many of the axioms we employ in deductive reasoning have been arrived at through a prior process of induction. The axiom, "Movies starring Faye Dunaway are interesting movies," was probably arrived at after the viewer had witnessed three or four of her movies.

Since we all use induction we should be familiar with the tests of its validity. The following questions are pertinent. (1) How many examples are used in arriving at the generalization? To sample two watermelons from an entire truckload and then generalize about the whole truckload is to trust to luck rather than to logical reasoning. There must be *enough* examples to warrant the conclusion drawn. (2) How representative of the whole class are the examples which are used in generalizing about the class? While the *quantity* of examples is important, even more important is the *quality* of the examples. Permitted by the indulgent storekeeper to sample three apples from a bushel basket, could you choose a representative sampling of the entire basket? Perhaps not because of the limited quantity. But at least you could make an intelligent attempt. Would you choose your three apples from the top? From the middle layer? From the bottom layer? Very likely you would choose one from each layer. Or if the storekeeper has a reputation for packing fruit of uniform quality, then conceivably one apple from the basket might warrant a generalization about the whole. (3) Is the generalization confined to the class from which the examples were drawn? Alluding to our apple-sampling example, any generalization we draw should be concerned only with the basket from which the sampling was made, not with all the baskets in the store. Yet this is a common error in induction. One renegade labor union gives a black eye to all organized labor. The misbehavior of a few teenagers in Denver is used as the basis for a generalization about all teenagers, when at best it should be used as a basis for generalizing about certain Denver youngsters. As a listener you should apply these tests of inductive logic to the remarks of the speaker. As a speaker you should make certain that your inductive reasoning meets these tests before employing it.

3. *Reasoning from analogy.* "It will never work here. It didn't work in England." "Try my headache remedy. It'll make you feel better in a hurry." "I don't see why I can't have a new car. George's dad bought him one." In each of the examples cited, the speaker is drawing upon comparisons to reach a conclusion. In the first example there is an implied comparison between England and "here." In the second, there is a comparison between "you and me" or my headache and yours. And in the final example, George and "I" or George's dad and my dad are things compared. Reasoning from analogy, then, suggests that because two things are alike in certain known respects, they will also be alike with respect to the issue in question. Of all the forms of reasoning, this is perhaps the one most subject to error—and for a very simple reason. The validity of any argument based upon comparison is contingent upon a high degree of similarity existing between the circumstances compared. A perfect analogy would demand identical circumstances with no variables involved. Such circumstances are seldom ever found to exist. Thus the person using analogical reasoning must be extremely careful to avoid overlooking pertinent points of *dissimilarity* between two otherwise comparable things.

What are the *relevant* points of similarity that should exist in the items compared? The physician is trained to recognize relevant points of similarity between the patient at hand and a patient already treated. Thus Dr. Evans can reason that "Joe has the same symptoms as Harry. Penicillin treatment worked for Harry; so I'll prescribe it for Joe." But speakers all too often do not take the time to analyze the constituents of relevancy. Noting that a great *number* of similarities exist between two situations, they don't take the time to ask if the similarities are pertinent. Don't be fooled by quantity; look for quality.

If you expect to employ reasoning from analogy in a speech, it would be advisable to utilize one or more of the other forms of reasoning as well because of their higher probative value. If you rely solely upon the analogy, your audience may note points of dissimilarity that you have overlooked.

4. *Reasoning from causal relationships.* Causation may appear in at least three forms. We may reason from a known set of circumstances to a probable set of consequences, that is, from cause-to-effect. Conversely, we may reason from a known set of consequences back to their probable cause, effect-to-cause. Or we may reason from one set of consequences to another set of consequences, that is, from effect-to-effect.

Cause-to-effect reasoning can be readily illustrated. We read in the newspaper that the auto workers have been granted a wage hike; so we predict that the prices on new-model cars will be higher. Or in election years we hear Democrats saying, "Don't elect the Republicans unles you want another depression." The Republicans, in turn, say, "Don't elect the Democrats unless you want to get us in another war."

Effect-to-cause reasoning is just as common. The accident scene reeks of alcohol; so we reason that the accident was the result of drunken driving. The next-door neighbor sports a beet-red complexion; so we reason that he stayed too long at the beach. The stock market moves sharply upward; so we conclude it is the result of the president's latest observation on the state of the nation's economy.

Effect-to-effect reasoning is actually a special form of reasoning from analogy. It says that because two sets of circumstances are similar (similar "causes"), their consequences will be similar. The doctor who prescribed penicillin for Joe because it worked for Harry, who exhibited the same symptoms, was using both analogical and causal reasoning.

Reasoning from causation should be subjected to the following tests. (1) Does the alleged cause always produce the same effect? (2) Can the effect result from more than one cause? (3) Are there any conditions that can interfere with a causal connection?

Thus we have examined some of the ways people reason and the kinds of evidence from which they reason. As you frame arguments to support your persuasive proposition, bear in mind the tests of reasonableness that your audience may require you to meet.

There is only one answer to the question, "How much proof will an audience require before it believes something?" That answer is, "Enough." If you have studied your audience well, if you have tried to put yourself in the role of the listener, then you have a pretty fair idea of what constitutes "enough."

II. IMPELLING PSYCHOLOGICAL APPEALS

A speaker may, with faultless reasoning and unimpeachable evidence, convince you that a problem exists and that there is an ideal solution to the problem. Yet you may fail to take the steps necessary to implement that solution. You have been convinced, but you haven't been actuated. Why? The answer may lie in the fact that the speaker talked in terms of "a problem," rather than *your* problem, and has offered a solution to "a problem" rather than a solution to *your* problem. In short, the speaker has overlooked the psychologically impelling reasons that spur people to action. Unless the listener can feel some identification with the problem, action isn't likely to be taken to solve the problem however logical a given solution might be.

How does the speaker get the listener to **identify** with the problem and the solution? There are two general means. First, if the problem and its solution have a direct bearing upon the life and welfare of the listener, the speaker simply has to point this out. Second, if the problem and its solution affects the listener only indirectly, then the speaker can point out how someone close to the listener is affected (or possibly how someone *who can be made to seem close* to the listener is affected). Perhaps an illustration will clarify these avenues of identification. If you are making a plea for contributions to the cancer fund, and your listeners are themselves cancer victims, then your approach will probably be to point out that augmentation of the cancer fund may mean direct assistance to the listeners. If the audience is made up of those who have relatives or friends who are sufferers, then you will probably stress the warmth of helping out a loved one. If the audience is made up of those who have no connection with anyone who is afflicted, then you may, through a vivid narrative, introduce them to a "typical" cancer victim through whom they can identify with the problem and its solution. **The listener should be made to feel the problem directly or vicariously if action is to be forthcoming.**

An examination of some of the basic needs, wants, and desires that lie behind human actions may suggest ways in which you can get the audience to identify with your persuasive messages.

1. *Self-preservation.* The person who uses automobile seat belts is typical of those who are motivated to act out of a desire for self-preservation. Safety devices, physical fitness courses, life-prolonging medications are examples of goods and services that provide a partial answer to our need to stay alive and enjoy physical well-being. Pleas to control population growth may be rooted in one's desire to preserve the sources of survival. It is the familiar tactic of those soliciting support for an increase in military expenditures to use self-preservation as the appeal: "With the enemy stockpiling nuclear warheads twice as fast as we are, we stand to move into a hot war unless we build up an equivalent deterrent."

2. *Sex attraction.* A cursory glance at any magazine, newspaper, billboard, or television advertisement will confirm the power of sex attraction as

a motive impelling us to buy an astonishingly wide range of goods and services. Purchase of that new car suggests a bevy of glamorous companions. The new electric typewriter conjures up fantasies of a happy, and hence glamorous, secretary. The public speaker, however, is well-advised to employ this motive more discreetly than the advertiser. People in a group would probably be made to feel uncomfortable by an overt appeal to the sex motive while the same appeal appearing in print would not cause a raised eyebrow. The difference probably lies in our reluctance to acknowledge publicly our susceptibility to this appeal. Therefore, it is preferable to plant a suggestion rather than to openly link your argument with sex attraction.

3. *Acquisition of property.* The appeal to the pocketbook is as popular as the appeal to sex attraction in advertising. Bargain sales, "giant, economy sizes," higher interest rates on savings accounts, real estate speculation are all manifestations of the universal desire among people to acquire property. The spokesperson for the school bond drive points out that a better educated citizenry will be a more prosperous citizenry, suggesting that money spent now will be returned many times over as a result of a healthier economy. Even the Rolls Royce ads have occasionally appealed to our desire to save money—in the long run.

4. *Self-esteem.* Sometimes we will sacrifice personal safety, eschew sex attraction, and spurn the acquisition of property if it means that our self-esteem can be increased. The desire to be "looked-up-to," to be well-regarded by one's peers, or one's superiors, is a powerful motivating force. It may be manifested in such diverse actions as enrolling in night school, swimming the English channel, donating a large sum to charity, or indulging in conspicuous consumption. Self-esteem, extended to groups, takes the form of civic pride, the desire to be "first in the nation," to be the alfalfa-baling center of the country, to have the world's finest zoo.

5. *Personal enjoyment.* Our love of good food and drink, of comfortable accommodations, of labor-saving devices, of all the so-called good things in life becomes a dominant motive once our basic needs for food, clothing, and shelter have been satisfied. We don't buy sugar for its life-sustaining qualities but for its power to bring pleasure to our taste buds. We don't buy a ninety thousand dollar home just to keep out the elements but to satisfy our love of the "nicer things." Trailers, campers, power boats, works of art, and videotape recorders are acquired primarily to satisfy our need for personal enjoyment.

6. *Constructiveness.* The weekend mason erecting a concrete-block retaining wall, the housewife making dresses for her daughters, the retired captain fashioning a brigantine from toothpicks, cloth, and pasteboard are manifesting human desire to be constructive, creative, inventive. The speaker enlists support for a community cleanup campaign by appealing to the civic club's collective desire for constructive effort.

7. *Destructiveness.* We are also motivated by an urge to destroy that which is felt to be detrimental to self, to family, to society. So we are urged

to "stamp out crime," conquer disease, rid the nation of poverty, break down the barriers of race, creed, and color, and fight pollution. In short, we are asked to put our destructive instincts to constructive effort.

8. *Curiosity.* Many things we undertake not simply to gain some tangible benefit therefrom, but rather to satisfy our sense of curiosity. We flock to the balloon-launching, patronize the freak show, buy the paperback book with the enticing cover, or try a "new taste sensation" because we find the unusual and the novel so enticing.

9. *Imitation.* The desire to "be just like" some person we admire may prompt us to buy the breakfast food recommended by the leading ground gainer in the National Football League, to acquire the same kind of color television set as our neighbors, to vote for the political candidate recommended by our favorite movie actor. The speaker must be cautious, however, in appealing to our imitative instincts. Pains should be taken to discover whether or not the model we are to imitate is really admired by us. If the model is envied by us, we may go to great lengths to avoid imitation.

10. *Altruism.* We like to think that some of our actions are not selfishly motivated. We make anonymous donations to charity, we send CARE packages abroad, we volunteer to read to the blind.

The speaker should consider using as many appropriate appeals as possible, for not all members of an audience are motivated by the same appeal. The hierarchy of needs, wants, and desires differs from one individual to another. Furthermore, most of us are occasionally impelled by motives we'd rather not admit; so we appreciate the speaker who gives us a "legitimate" motive for doing what we already want to do. Our propensity to rationalize has long been recognized by persuaders on and off the platform.

Even though we have discussed the preceding ten motive appeals as though they were separate entities, they are, in reality, seldom as simple or fixed as we have, for explanatory purposes, suggested. For, in essence, human beings are complicated creatures and not subject to simple stimulus-response relationships.

Most human behavior is motivated not by a single act, but rather by a large complex of behavior patterns. For example, most of our actions are related to our past experiences, our emotional tendencies of fighting, fleeing, and pairing, our biological needs, our psychological needs (such as security, recognition, affection, and new experiences), our personal goals and beliefs, and, most of all, our self-concept. It should be obvious, therefore, to the trained speaker that the receiver should not be viewed as a simple responding organism but rather as a highly intricate individual.

Before leaving the area of psychological influences that may be made operative in persuasion, we should examine two other phenomena: (1) our need for consistency, and (2) our susceptibility to suggestion.

1. *Our need for consistency.* The theories of attitude change advanced by such men as Fritz Heider with his "balance" theory, Leon Festinger with his theory of "cognitive dissonance," and Charles Osgood and Percy Tannenbaum with their "congruity" theory are all concerned essentially with our apparent

need to maintain consistency with our beliefs, attitudes, and knowledge—
"cognitions." If something acts to introduce an element of inconsistency (im-
balance, incongruity, or dissonance), then, according to these theories, we
make adjustments necessary to restore a state of consistency.

For example, if I harbor the notion that salespeople are not to be trusted
and then I am told that one of my trusted friends has become a salesperson,
an element of inconsistency has been introduced into my cognitions. Perhaps
I will resolve this inconsistency by changing my belief about salespeople or
my attitude toward salespeople. Thus my unfavorable predisposition toward
salespeople may be transformed into a neutral or (less likely) favorable disposition. My belief that all salespeople are untrustworthy may be transformed
into the belief that most, or some, or a few salespeople are untrustworthy. I
might resolve the inconsistency by rationalizing that my friend does not really
fit into my concept of "salespeople," and thus my old beliefs and attitudes are
allowed to remain intact. Or I might resolve it by refusing to believe the news
that my friend has become a salesperson. I might say to my informant, "You're
mistaken," or "My friend was just kidding when you were told that," or "You're
lying!" Or, conceivably, I might start disliking my friend if my beliefs and
attitudes with respect to salespeople as a class are deeply entrenched.

The application of the consistency principle to persuasion can readily
be seen in selling. The basis of much selling is rooted in the introduction of a
dissonant note to the prospective buyer. Let's say that Charlie is very happy
with the set of tires on his car because he believes them to be very safe. Into this
picture of contentment intrudes the salesperson who raises serious questions
about the durability of the tires. Charlie's cognitions are thus thrown out of
balance. The salesperson has the answer which will restore the balance (or, at
least hopes to!).

Sometimes the job as the persuader is to help the listener live with an
existing inconsistency by offering a means of reducing it in intensity or rationalizing its existence. Wartime propaganda furnishes an example. The people of
a peace-loving nation are besieged with a sense of guilt at becoming involved
in a war. They are offered the palliatives, "This is the war to end all wars," or
"We must not desert the cause for which so many of our people have died,"
or "We must fight so that our children can live in peace," or "If we don't stop
them here, we'll have to stop them somewhere else." In these instances the
persuaders have attempted to offset the severity of the listener's cognitive dissonance—"I don't believe in war, but here I am supporting a war"—by re-
minding the listeners of other beliefs or attitudes they hold which are consistent
with supporting the war—"I believe in safeguarding our children," or "I believe in honoring our dead," or "I believe that the achievement of peace is
worth any price," or "A stitch in times saves nine."

Our apparent need to maintain consistency, then, would seem to offer
a wellspring of opportunities for the person who would alter our beliefs, attitudes, and behavior.

2. *Our susceptibility to suggestion.* We are all familiar with the chain
reaction set off by the first person in a group to yawn. We recall the delight
of "conning" our elders into looking upward at a tall building. We have ex-

perienced the magnetic pull toward the carnival barker as we see a small crowd gathering. And the sight of a child carrying a box of popcorn stirs our desire for the same thing. The power of **suggestion** is operative in all of these cases.

Suggestion may be defined as the arousal of a response by indirect means. It may operate through channels that are external to the message, such as the decor of the surroundings, flags, paintings, posters, giant photographs, acts of ritual, music, and prominently displayed collection plates or cannisters. These factors may operate to condition the listener to respond positively to the speaker's message.

Suggestion operates as well through your appearance, your voice, and your manner on the platform. If you appear to be confident (but not cocky), you tend to stir confidence in what you have to say. If you *seem* to lack assurance (whether you actually do is beside the point), the listener tends to be wary of your message. If your posture is slouchy, your ideas, by association, may seem superficial or your thinking sloppy.

Suggestion operates through your message. If you stress positive ideas, if you avoid mentioning ideas contrary to your position, if you keep "personalities" out of controversy, you condition the audience to respond favorably to your point of view (or at least you condition them against a negative response).

Further ramifications of the influence of suggestion will be apparent in our discussion of the next means of persuasion.

III. MANIFESTING PERSONAL CREDIBILITY

"What you are stands over you the while, and thunders so that I cannot hear what you say to the contrary." Emerson's familiar statement epitomizes the impact of the speaker's **ethos** upon the listener's reception of the message. The way the audience perceives the speaker, as well as the way it perceives the message, determines the nature of its response.

Why do you take your automobile to a certain mechanic for repairs? If you know something of the intricacies of an automobile engine, then your selection of a mechanic may rest on logical grounds. If you are mechanically naive, you may have chosen the mechanic simply because *something about that person* inspired confidence.

Speakers on two separate occasions attempt to convince you that a right-to-work law in your state should be repealed. Both use essentially the same arguments and the same evidence. But you want to agree with one of the speakers, while the other speaker cannot manage to budge your convictions. What is the difference? *Something about* the one speaker inspired believability.

What are the constituents of personal credibility? What are the clues we as listeners subconsciously look for in speakers? The following list, while by no means exhaustive, does suggest some facets of speaker behavior to which audiences respond favorably.

1. *Intelligence.* The extent to which a speaker seems to have mastery of the subject matter is a determinant of our response. If the speaker marshalls

Our perception of the speaker's credibility
affects our response to the message.

an impressive amount of evidence, shows insight into all aspects of the question, uses reasoning that meets the tests of logical validity, and displays "common sense," then the speaker's believability is enhanced.

2. *Poise.* As we observed earlier in our comments about the power of suggestion deriving from the speaker's delivery, the speaker who seems to be in command of himself inspires confidence. President Kennedy inspired confidence in his answers to hostile questions because he never appeared to become unsettled by the hostility.

3. *Modesty.* This trait should not be confused with self-effacement or "false" modesty. In the sense in which we use it here, it suggests the absence of self-congratulation in any form. Genuinely great people don't have to tell others of their greatness. Speakers who take themselves too seriously can only inspire contempt.

4. *Moderation.* We tend to be wary of those who indulge in overstatement, in personal abuse, in unseemly emotional displays. Moderation is usually equated with reasonableness.

5. *Tact.* Closely associated with moderation is tact. It is defined as the ability to deal with others without giving offense. In application to persuasion, it means such things as disagreeing without being disagreeable, admonishing without scolding, enlightening without insulting the audience's intelligence.

6. *Friendliness.* Goodwill is contagious. The speaker who shows a good disposition toward the listeners, even though there may be matters on which they disagree, clears one of the obstacles to persuasion. It is well to remember, however, that a mere *pose* of friendliness can have extremely adverse effects, if the audience detects it as a pose.

7. *Sincerity.* The used-car salesperson tells the customer, "I'd like to sell you this car because, quite frankly, I stand to earn a good commission. Furthermore, you stand to get a good car in the process." The salesperson's candid disclosure of the real motives may well have a disarming effect upon the customer because we tend to place credence in the remarks of those we regard as sincere and open in their dealings with others. Of all the traits of character, sincerity may well be the most important to persuasion. We will often overlook a person's vices if we know that person is sincere.

8. *Genuine concern for the listener's welfare.* The speaker who shows himself motivated by something more than personal gain, who shows a genuine concern for the listeners as well, will more readily receive our confidence than the speaker we suspect of selfish motives. Here again, the concern should be *sincere.*

These, then, are some of the marks of personal credibility. One word of caution is in order. Speakers who wish to show themselves worthy of respect and emulation must not, in the process, place themselves beyond the possibility of emulation.

ORGANIZING THE PERSUASIVE SPEECH

As you doubtless realize by now, every persuasive situation has its own unique demands. Therefore, the organization of one persuasive speech may radically differ from that of another. One may be organized as if it were an informational speech while another may be as obviously manipulative as a television commercial. We simply cannot say to you, here is *the* way to organize a persuasive speech. What we shall attempt to do instead is to suggest some of the more popular organizational strategies. Your good judgment will tell you if a given strategy is applicable to the persuasive situation you are facing.

As we indicated in chapter 6, most speeches do have one structural characteristic in common—they are usually divided into three parts. Let us explore briefly the principal functions of the introduction, the body, and the conclusion of the persuasive speech.

The basic functions of the introduction to any speech are to get attention and prepare the audience for what is to follow. In the persuasive speech these two functions have to be accomplished in a way that is conducive to the creation of a climate of acceptance. It is usually a good policy for the speaker to refrain from assertiveness in the early stages of a persuasive speech because such behavior may generate suspicion and hostility. A spirit of inquiry is much less likely to erect barriers. If the speaker decides to announce the proposition in the introduction, consideration should be given to the possibility of putting it into the form of a question. Compare these two ways of orienting your audience to the nature of your talk:

1. Today I would like to discuss with you the question, "Are penal institutions justified in a modern society?"
2. Today I will attempt to demonstrate that penal institutions are not justified in a modern society.

The body of the persuasive speech contains the speaker's defense of the persuasive proposition. For example, if you are defending a proposition of policy, you will probably offer arguments that show the need for a policy and demonstrate the capacity of your policy to satisfy that need. If you are defending a proposition of fact or value, you will probably offer criteria for measuring the truth of the fact or value judgment in question and then apply those criteria. In the next segment of this chapter we shall discuss in much greater detail some of the possibilities for designing the body of the speech.

The conclusion to the persuasive speech should serve to place the audience in the state of mind most conducive to the accomplishment of the speaker's purpose. For example, if your purpose is to actuate, the audience should be ready to act. If your purpose is to convince, the audience should be ready to give you assent.

With these general considerations before us, let us turn now to some specific strategies of design that have been found useful.

1. *Organizational strategies for propositions of policy.* In chapter 6 we discussed two organizational patterns that can be utilized when one is urging

the adoption of a policy, the Problem-Solution Order and The Motivated Sequence.

   a. *The Problem-Solution Order*   This pattern is based upon a tripartite division of the body of the speech. After an introduction designed to gain attention and orient the listener, the speaker moves into the body of the speech where (1) the problem area is presented, (2) the solution to the problem is explained, and (3) the solution is defended. The speech concludes with a call for appropriate belief or action. An example of proposition of policy organized around this mode of arrangement follows:

Introduction

I.   The mid-channel collision of a Navy destroyer and the island ferry last week underlines the existence of a long-standing problem in our area.

Body

I.   The ferry is an unsatisfactory means of commuting between the mainland and the island.
   A. It is costly.
       (support)
   B. It is inconvenient.
       (support)
   C. It is dangerous.
       (support)

Core Statement: A bridge should be built from the mainland to the island.

II. A bridge would represent a solution to the commuting problem.
   ing problem.
   A. It would be less expensive.
       (support)
   B. It would be convenient.
       (support)
   C. It would be safe.
       (support)

III. It would be practical to build a bridge.
   A. It would be practical from an engineering standpoint.
       (support)
   B. It would be practical from a financial standpoint.
       (support)

IV. The disadvantages a bridge would bring are minor compared to the advantages.
   A. Residents who would be displaced by construction of bridge-approaches are few.
       (support)

B. Displaced ferry employees could find employment locally.
   (support)

V. A bridge would be the best solution.

A. It would be less costly to build than a tunnel.
   (support)

B. It would not present a navigational hazard as would a causeway.
   (support)

C. It would be more aesthetically pleasing than a tunnel or a causeway.
   (support)

Conclusion

I. Next week when petitions are circulated calling for the construction of this bridge, I hope you will be one of the signers.

    b. *The Motivated Sequence.* This organizational strategy is basically a variant of the Problem-Solution order. As its name suggests, The Motivated Sequence has a psychological orientation. It consists of five steps to be taken up in this order: Attention, Need, Satisfaction, Visualization, and Action. The Attention step must be the speaker's first concern. Unless the listeners are made to focus their attention on the speaker, all else is to no avail. The Need step involves the introduction of an element of dissonance. The listeners must be made aware of the existence of a problem which affects them in some way. The Satisfaction step is that segment of the speech where the solution to the problem is explained and defended. The Visualization step projects the listeners into the future where they are made to visualize the solution in operation, especially as the solution concerns the listeners personally. The Action step, as its label suggests, calls upon the listeners to implement the solution. An example of the Motivated Sequence might look like this in skeletal form:

Attention Step

1,500 of your fellow citizens are suffering from a form of pollution that can't be seen, smelled, tasted, or touched.

Need Step

Statement of problem: The noise level at the assembly plant is dangerous to the workers.

I. The 115 decibel noise level is 30 decibels higher than the maximum level set by the Industrial Safety Commission.

II. It can cause hearing loss, cardiovascular problems, partial loss of vision, and mental disturbance.

III. Many of your neighbors are in the affected work force.

Satisfaction Step

Statement of Solution: Acoustic shielding of the metal presses would reduce the noise to a safe level.

  I.   Acoustic shielding is feasible.
 II.   Acoustic shielding is advantageous.
III.   Acoustic shielding is the best solution to the problem.

Visualization Step

Many of your neighbors will suffer needlessly if this problem isn't corrected. If acoustic shielding is provided, those same neighbors will be healthier, more productive, and happier workers.

Action Step

Join me in writing to Don George, General Manager, Ajax Motors.

2. *Organizational strategies for propositions of fact and value.* In chapter 6 we discussed two patterns that are commonly employed in the development of propositions of fact and value, the Deductive Order and the Inductive Order.

a. *Deductive Order.* This mode of organization involves disclosure of the proposition prior to the presentation of materials supporting the proposition. For example, if a speaker wished the audience to agree with the proposition, "Magum X is better heating fuel for our clubhouse than Sagum Y," the speech might be organized in this order:

Introduction

  I.   By the end of this month we have to make a decision about heating fuel for our clubhouse.
 II.   There are two alternatives available to us, Magum X and Sagum Y.

Statement of Proposition: Magum X is superior to Sagum Y.

Body

  I.   Magum X is cleaner.
 II.   Magum X is cheaper.
III.   Magum X is safer.

Conclusion

I hope you'll give careful consideration to Magum X.

b. *Inductive order.* When using this pattern of organization, the speaker withholds disclosure of the proposition until *after* the presentation of materials supporting the proposition. Using the same proposition, "Magum X is superior to Sagum Y," the Inductive Order of presentation might appear this way.

Introduction

  I.   By the end of this month we have to make a decision about heating fuel for our clubhouse.

Body

I.   The heating fuel we choose should have these qualities:
     A.   It should be clean.
     B.   It should be cheap.
     C.   It should be safe.
II. We have two fuels from which to choose, Magum X and Sagum Y.
III. Magum X is cleaner, cheaper, and safer.

Statement of Proposition: Magum X is superior to Sagum Y.

Conclusion

I hope you'll give careful consideration to Magum X.

In choosing between Deductive Order and Inductive Order the speaker should be guided by knowledge of the audience's predispositions. If the speaker feels that the direct approach exemplified by Deductive Order would make the audience defensive, then Inductive Order should be chosen. There are occasions when the direct approach is to be preferred. For example, if two speakers are debating a proposition of fact or value, the audience might view a late disclosure of position as ridiculous.

3. *Further consideration of idea placement.*   Behavioral scientists have attempted to find answers to some of the persistent questions of organizational strategy. Of particular interest to students of persuasion are their *tentative* answers to the following questions:

Does an argument exert a more lasting influence if it is heard first or heard last in a series of arguments? If the audience is familiar with the issue or if it is involved in the controversy, then it is influenced more by the argument heard first. If the audience is disinterested or if it is relatively uninformed about the issue prior to hearing the arguments, then it will be influenced more by the argument heard last.

When both sides of a controversy are presented in succession, will the side presented first or the side presented last be in the more advantageous position? Some studies have concluded that the side presented first has the "natural" advantage. Other studies, however, were inconclusive.

Are attempts to persuade helped or hindered when "the other side" is presented as well as the speaker's own side? If listeners are initially opposed to the speaker's position, the strategem exerts a persuasive effect. The same is true if listeners are well educated. Less educated listeners, however, are moved more rapidly by a one-sided presentation.

Is it more effective to imply the conclusion one wishes the audience to accept or to state it explicitly? Results indicate that an explicit statement exerts a more persuasive effect upon the majority of listeners.

Please be reminded that the foregoing "answers" are only tentative. A multitude of variables operate in any given communication situation; so it is virtually impossible to design an experiment which will take them all into account.

One final note concerning the overall structure of the persuasive message is in order. Jesse Delia, writing in the *Quarterly Journal of Speech* visualizes a persuasive structure "beginning with arguments highly congruent with the existing predispositions [of the audience] and gradually moving through a series of accepted linkages to the persuader's recommended opinion or course of action."

EXPECTATIONS

If a speaker commands all of the pertinent information needed about the listeners, subject, and occasion, what are the chances of persuading? They will probably be good if the speaker remembers that beliefs and attitudes are not apt to change suddenly and dramatically, that many attempts may have to be made before signs of change become evident; if realistic goals are set for each encounter with the listeners; if intelligence, patience, and persistence are exercised; and if the speaker has a little luck as well.

SUMMARY

Persuasion is the process of inducing willing changes of belief, attitude, and behavior in the listener. Successful persuasion rests upon a thorough knowledge of the audience and its attitude toward the speech topic, the speech purpose, and toward the speaker as well. The objects of change are the listener's learned predispositions, convictions, and manifest behavior, particularly with respect to issues of policy, fact, and value. The speaker's choice of position should rest upon a knowledge of where the audience is in its thinking about the subject. The means of persuasion, according to rhetorical tradition, lies in logical appeals, psychological appeals, and the listener's perception of the speaker's personal credibility. The constituents of logical persuasion are evidence and reasoning. Evidence should be derived from an authoritative source, it should be fairly presented, it should be recent, it should be capable of corroboration. Reasoning takes four forms, according to the traditional view. Deductive reasoning moves from the general rule or axiom to the specific case at hand. Inductive reasoning proceeds from particular cases to a generalization about all cases. Reasoning from analogy is based on the supposition that because two things are alike in certain known respects, they will also be alike in the point at issue. Causal reasoning may appear in at least three forms—from cause-to-effect, from effect-to-cause, or from effect-to-effect.

Persuasion through psychological appeals traditionally is thought to involve the use of motivation and suggestion. The needs, wants, and desires to which the speaker may link the message include self-preservation, sex attraction, acquisition of property, self-esteem, personal enjoyment, constructiveness, curiosity, imitation, and altruism. Suggestion is the arousal of a response by indirect means. It may operate through channels external to the speaker, through the speaker's delivery, and through the verbal message.

Persuasion through personal credibility is possible when the speaker manifests poise, modesty, moderation, tact, friendliness, sincerity, and genuine concern for the listener's welfare provided the listener perceives these factors.

While the persuasive speech may be organized in a variety of ways, certain methods seem to enjoy high popularity. The Problem-Solution Order and the Motivated Sequence are particularly appropriate for developing propositions of policy. Deductive Order and Inductive Order are among those patterns well suited to the development of propositions of fact and value.

Suggested Readings

Andersen, Martin P.; Nichols, E. Ray, Jr.; and Booth, Herbert W. *The Speaker and His Audience.* 2d ed. New York: Harper and Row, Publishers, 1974. Chapters 6 and 12.

Auer, J. Jeffery. "The Persuasive Speaker and His Audience." *The Rhetoric of Our Times.* Edited by J. Jeffery Auer, pp. 255–75. New York: Appleton-Century-Crofts, 1969.

Baird, A. Craig; Knower, Franklin H.; and Becker, Samuel L. *General Speech Communication.* 4th ed. New York: McGraw-Hill Book Co., 1971. Chapters 21 and 22.

Bryant, Donald C., and Wallace, Karl R. *Fundamentals of Public Speaking.* 4th ed. New York: Appleton-Century-Crofts, 1969. Chapters 16–21.

Cronkhite, Gary. *Persuasion: Speech and Behavioral Change.* Indianapolis: Bobbs-Merrill Co., 1969.

Delia, Jesse G. "The Logic Fallacy, Cognitive Theory, and the Enthymeme: A Search for the Foundations of Reasoned Discourse." *Quarterly Journal of Speech* 61 (April 1970): pp. 140–48.

Fishbein, Martin. "A Consideration of Beliefs, Attitudes, and Their Relationships." *Current Studies in Social Psychology.* Edited by Ivan D. Steiner and Martin Fishbein. New York: Holt, Rinehart and Winston, 1965.

Fisher, Walter R. "A Motive View of Communication." *Quarterly Journal of Speech* 56 (April 1970): 140–48.

Gruner, Charles R.; Logue, Cal M.; Freshley, Dwight, L.; and Huseman, Richard C. *Speech Communication in Society.* Boston: Allyn and Bacon, 1972. Chapter 11.

Hovland, Carl I.; Janis, Irving L.; and Kelley, Harold H. *Communication and Persuasion.* New Haven: Yale University Press, 1953. Chapter 3.

Martin, Howard H., and Colburn, C. William. *Communication and Consensus: An Introduction to Rhetorical Discourse.* New York: Harcourt Brace Jovanovich, 1972. Chapters 4, 7, and 8.

Mudd, Charles S., and Sillars, Malcolm O. *Speech: Content and Communication.* 3d ed. New York: Thomas Y. Crowell Co., 1975. Chapters 3, 8, 9, 10, and 17.

Nadeau, Ray E. *A Basic Rhetoric of Speech-Communication*. Menlo Park,
    California: Addison-Wesley Publishing Co., 1969. Chapter 10.
Scheidel, Thomas M. *Persuasive Speaking*. Glenview, Ill.: Scott, Foresman
    and Co., 1967.
Sherif, Muzafer; Sherif, Carolyn W.; and Nebergall, Roger E. *Attitude
    and Attitude Change*. Philadelphia: W. B. Saunders, 1965.
Smith, Donald K. *Man Speaking: A Rhetoric of Public Speech*. New York:
    Dodd, Mead & Co., 1969. Chapter 7.

Changing
Environments

Part

4

Special Occasions
The Unique Communication Situation

10

Most occasions for public or private discourse call for speeches whose primary purposes are to inform or persuade. The principles and techniques of informing and persuading are basically the same regardless of the occasion which dictates the speech. That is to say, all speaking situations call for messages that utilize supporting details or evidence, factors of interest and attention, organization, language, and delivery. There are occasions, however, when the situation demands an extension or combination of the basic elements found in informing and persuading. Knowing that all forms of communication have a great deal in common, the trained and conscientious speaker can quickly adapt skills to the unique and different situation.

No list or treatment of special occasions could ever be complete, for in one sense each communication situation and occasion is novel and original. Yet there are some very specific occasions that the speaker might be in when moving from environment to environment. It is on these occasions that the speaker must remember all of the past speech training while at the same time utilizing the items that relate directly to the special occasion. In this chapter we will examine some of these common types and forms of discourse and deliberation.

We have selected the entertaining speech, the after-dinner speech, the impromptu speech, the manuscript speech, and the question-and-answer session to treat in some detail, for it is these forms of discourse and deliberation that you are most likely to encounter.

THE ENTERTAINING SPEECH

All speeches, to some extent, may entertain the listener. Yet there are specific occasions when the objective is not to increase someone's knowledge or even change the destiny of civilization, but rather to have the audience relax in a lighthearted mood and in an enjoyable atmosphere. Perhaps you will belong to an organization or club that has occasional meetings of a purely social nature where speeches provide part of the entertainment. Maybe you will be asked to recount some interesting experience you've had, or tell about an unusual person you've met, or perhaps help "roast" a fellow club member. Then again, you may be asked to talk on a subject of your own choosing. Whatever the case, a careful audience analysis is one of the most important steps in the preparation of the speech to entertain.

CHARACTERISTICS OF
ENTERTAINING

The speech to entertain may well show itself as a humorous talk, but all speeches to entertain need not be funny. The one basic requirement for all speeches of **entertainment** is that **they must hold attention and interest in themselves.** The speaker can best accomplish this objective by incorporating into the speech many of the factors of attention and interest we have discussed in the chapter on informational speaking.

The dominant characteristics of the speech to entertain are as follows:

1.   In presenting the speech to entertain *the delivery should be lively, enthusiastic, and animated.* If the speech is delivered extemporaneously, a spontaneous and natural effect will be produced.

2.   *Stories, illustrations, and humorous anecdotes are liberally used* in this type of speech. The fully-developed example is often so vivid and real it serves to capture and maintain attention. Remember these illustrations should be fresh and original and free from any appearance of triteness. Furthermore, "canned" illustrations and anecdotes should be avoided.

3.   The speech to entertain, like all speeches, is *well organized and easy to follow, and is normally constructed around a central theme or idea.* The theme for the speech to entertain should be appropriate to the audience and occasion. In many instances it may deal with a common topic in a unique and different manner, such as the problems of eating three meals a day while orbiting the earth in a space capsule.

4.   *The response sought by the speaker who is entertaining is immediate and momentary.* The audience may remember some of the information long after the speech, but the speaker's primary concern is the covert or overt behavior *at the time* of the talk.

THE USE OF HUMOR

Humor is indeed the most common ingredient found in the speech to entertain. It holds our attention and, if used correctly, creates an enjoyable and friendly atmosphere. The problem of what constitutes humor has been discussed for centuries. People have long asked, what makes us laugh? Several of the more common aspects of pleasure and enjoyment will be examined at this time as a means of trying to supply the speaker with some guidelines in the selection and use of humor.

Exaggeration

Take a possible occurrence, make it larger, and overstate it, and you have a potentially humorous situation. As long as the exaggeration has a touch of reality, we can enjoy its obvious distortion. To describe the successful assembly of a child's toy as though it were a major scientific achievement would be perceived as obvious exaggeration (and hopefully, as humorous). One of the tactics used by "roasters" is to seize upon some very minor fault of the "roastee" and make a major crime of it.

Incongruity

In a very real sense incongruity consists of any situation in which the parts do not fit together. The unusual, the sudden and unexpected twist, and the inconsistency are all potential sources of humor. You've probably heard sportscasts where the final score of a game involving two little-known schools was used to conclude a "roundup of the major games of the day." To hear the Hueyville-Lukenburg score immediately after the USC-Ohio State score is probably going to startle the listener (unless they happen to live in Hueyville or Lukenburg). A meal of caviar and Fritos topped off by rare-vintage champagne and Twinkies sounds incongruous because of the casual mixing of exotic and ordinary items.

Attacking Authority

We all know how much we enjoy seeing the boss, the sergeant, the police officer, or some other figure of authority as the target of a joke. Even the mother-in-law jokes are instances of having fun at the expense of someone or something that is normally regarded reverently. In poking fun at others it is always important to use good taste and not offend anyone's morals or standards.

There are many other devices that lend themselve to humor. For example, *the pun, irony, sarcasm,* and *burlesque* can all be effectively used. Yet the greatest source of humor comes from the creative and imaginative work all of us do when we sit and reflect. In short, *thinking* about what is humorous usually produces some excellent and rewarding examples and situations.

DEVELOPING THE SPEECH

A primary consideration in the development of the speech to entertain is your knowing the exact makeup of the audience. In addition, your audience analysis should include some information on the occasion. It is important to know if the audience came only to listen to you, to laugh, or if they expect some concrete information to take home. Once these questions have been answered you are ready to determine your central theme, decide upon an introduction, an organizational pattern for the body, and your conclusion.

Introduction

Your opening remarks in the speech to entertain have the task of arousing attention, setting the mood, and establishing the main point. In the speech to entertain you must make it quite clear that you do not plan to develop any profound concepts, for if the audience expects you to "get somewhere," they will be confused as you continue to provide only entertainment. If you return to chapter 6, you will find a discussion of some of the methods that can be used in starting the speech to entertain. The illustration is a very popular opening device in entertaining.

Body

In choosing your speech plan, or approach, you must keep in mind the nature of the audience, the occasion, and your speaking talent and limitations. There are endless varieties in the organization of the speech to entertain. The topical order or the chronological order are especially appropriate in serving the objectives of entertaining. (A review of chapter 6 might be helpful in adapting these two patterns.)

The single, long narrative is a popular device in entertaining. As we noted in chapter 5, the narrative, when presented as an illustration, holds attention, makes a point, and is interesting. A good narrative tells a story; for the entertaining speech, the story should be humorous.

You can also use a series of short narratives developed around a central theme. A series illustrating registration problems in college is an example of this type of approach. In any case, the speech to entertain should not lead off in many different directions, but rather should be built around a central theme. Remember too that interest may be derived from associating your ideas with things that are recent, impending, physically near, familiar, vital, active, unusual, suspenseful, concrete, real, humorous, or conflicting.

Conclusion

The conclusion is usually very brief and continues to carry forth the general mood. The devices for concluding were discussed in chapter 6 and should be reviewed as a means of determining which technique best applies to the specific communication situation the speaker faces.

PRESENTING THE SPEECH TO ENTERTAIN

Although the subject of delivery was discussed in some detail in chapter 3, there are some special features of the entertaining speech that influence the way it is presented.

The speaker's mental set is of vital importance. The speaker must *want* to give the talk and enjoy the experience as well, or the audience will not be able to relate to the humor and will miss the spirit of the talk. We have pointed out many times before that moods are contagious, and if the speaker is not relaxed and at ease, it will detract from the mood of enjoyment.

In the speech to entertain the speaker should also try to be animated. A lively feeling must be communicated to the audience, and animation seems to contribute to that atmosphere.

THE AFTER-DINNER SPEECH

The after-dinner speech, which is, in many instances, considered a speech to entertain, is perhaps the most widely used occasional speech. It should be stressed, however, that many speeches that take place after a meal may be very serious and vital. Yet there seems to be a tradition that seeks to establish a relaxed and friendly atmosphere after a meal. In these cases **the after-dinner**

speech is characterized by a short, genial, and humorous talk. Because of its
relationship to the speech to entertain, the after-dinner speaker should heed
the advice offered those who seek to deliver the entertaining speech.

There are a few special considerations to keep in mind as one prepares and
delivers an after-dinner talk.

1.   After having enjoyed a meal and conversation with friends, an audience is normally in a good mood by the time the after-dinner speaker begins
to talk. In most instances, because this friendly atmosphere prevails, the
speaker should try to be optimistic and good-humored. Pessimism, bitterness,
gloom, and denunciation make a poor combination with a full stomach. Therefore, the selection of an appropriate topic is essential in after-dinner speaking.
This, in turn, puts an added emphasis on audience analysis. A story or a joke
that is funny to one group of individuals may fail to arouse even a smile from
another group.

2.   The relationship between speaker and audience in the after-dinner
situation should be more informal than formal in its organization, language,
and delivery.

3.   The after-dinner talk is normally quite brief. Attention spans grow
short after a pleasant meal.

4.   The material should be interesting and easy to understand. Humor,
interesting stories, examples, and unique experiences are at the root of
after-dinner speaking.

5.   Most after-dinner speeches are well prepared. The speaker does not
have to hesitate or grope for ideas or words. The speaker must be careful not
to let this thoroughness of preparation be carried to the extent that he loses
spontaneity and thus destroys the friendly and casual mood essential to effective after-dinner speaking.

THE IMPROMPTU SPEECH

There will be occasions when you are called upon to deliver an offhand response to a demand or a request for a "few remarks" on a specific subject. The
impromptu (or spur-of-the-moment) speech is delivered in just such a situation.
It is a speech that simply cannot be thoroughly prepared. We see this type of
speaking every day. In discussions in meetings, at conferences, in classes and
in conversation, we are asked to give our ideas and opinions on countless
subjects. Because of the lack of specific preparation, many view impromptu
speaking as the most difficult of all speech forms. If you can learn to remain
calm when called upon to give a talk, you will discover that the impromptu
situation is not nearly as menacing as first anticipated.

The trained speaker soon strikes upon the idea that there are three different times when you can prepare for the impromptu speech. First, if you are
fortunate enough to possess a large storehouse of information, you can usually

find something worthwhile to say. A broad background of reading and experience are invaluable in meeting the challenge of impromptu speaking. Second, if you suspect that you might be called upon, you can pay close attention to what is going on at the meeting and what is being said at the platform. By observing what is going on you may be able to think about what you would say if called upon. Third, you can learn to utilize the brief period between the time you are called upon and the time you have to utter your first words. Although this period of time may range from a few seconds to a few minutes, it can still be put to good use.

The following suggestions, if practiced, will help you overcome your fears and get on to the task of accomplishing your purpose.

1.   Try to adopt a positive mental attitude toward the impromptu situation. Remember, those who ask you to speak impromptu don't expect you to produce a polished oration on the spot; so listener expectations of you are not as demanding as they would be under different circumstances. They are more concerned with hearing your off-the-cuff observations about the subject than they are about watching a display of speaking skill.

Consider, too, the likelihood that when someone asks you to speak on the spur of the moment it is because that person knows you are knowledgeable about the topic. Otherwise, why should your comments be solicited?

2.   Listen carefully to the remarks of others. There is a good possibility that you can build upon their remarks when you are called upon to speak. Avoid daydreaming to spare yourself the agony that comes when you are jolted into the present by someone's announcing, "Let's hear what your opinion is." Listening is a part of the preparation for any speech and especially so for the impromptu speech.

3.   When called upon to speak, you should first try to formulate a central statement or position on the subject. Perhaps you can agree with a previous speaker's position and add more examples, statistics, or testimony. Or you might disagree with another and build your speech around the reasons for your disagreement. What if you happen to be the first or only speaker? Then perhaps you can design a speech that answers one of these stock questions about the general topic on which you are asked to speak: What is it? Who is connected with it? Where can it be found? When did it come into being? Why should you be concerned with it? How can you cope with it? Of course, there are many other questions that could be applied to a given topic, the answers to which could provide the main theme for an impromptu speech. The important thing is to try to confine yourself to one main theme so that your speech will have unity.

4.   Select an organizational plan that will let you develop your main point. Here are a few of the commonly-used patterns:

a.   Refer to what has been said by a previous speaker. State your position on the issue. Develop your position by illustration, analogy, or any appropriate form of support.

b.   Tell the audience what you plan to do. Tell them why it is important. Carry out your plan.

Many view impromptu speaking as the
most difficult of all speech forms.

c. Start with an illustration. Explain how it clarifies or proves your point.

d. Develop the theme chronologically, such as past history, present state, future prospects.

e. Develop the theme according to spatial or geographical considerations, such as impact on Europe, Asia, or Africa.

f. Divide the topic into component parts, such as economic, social, and political aspects or mental, moral, and physical aspects.

5. Try not to hurry into the main part of your presentation. This will give you valuable time in which to think of what to say and will help you relax and gain your composure.

6. Don't prolong the conclusion. Too many impromptu speeches are characterized by the conclusion that is apologetic and embrassed. Why not simply summarize what you've said, restate your position and sit down?

7. The ability to cope with an impromptu speaking situation can be greatly improved if one is willing to practice. One good method is to read the editorial page of your local newspaper and frame a reaction to each of the editorials or letters to the editor that deal with some subjects about which you feel strongly. Valuable, too, are speeches developed around a word or phrase such as sexism, integrity in public office, consumerism, or business ethics.

MAKING INTRODUCTIONS

A **speech of introduction** is another common type of occasional speaking, yet it is one that is often poorly done. People often forget that the introduction serves to link the guest speaker with the audience. It should not be used to demonstrate the introducer's cleverness or "superior knowledge."

The introduction has two main purposes. First, it should acquaint the audience with the guest speaker and, second, it should arouse interest in the talk. In order to see to it that the speaker and the speech secure a favorable reception, the introducer can follow a few simple rules.

1. *Be brief.* As noted earlier, the introducer subordinates his or her own speech for the sake of the main talk. In most instances, thirty seconds to two minutes is normally the time allotted to the person making the introduction.

2. In planning your introduction, see to it that your information concerning the speaker and his or her background and topic *is accurate.* Errors in pronunciation, particularly of the speaker's name or personal data, can cause a great deal of embarrassment to you, the speaker, and the audience. It is worthwhile to secure the essential and personal information from the speaker well in advance of your formal introduction.

3. It is often quite effective if you can begin the introduction with a brief reference to the nature of the occasion. This may well serve as a bond between

the speaker and the listeners. There may also be occasions where it will be of value to emphasize the importance of the subject.

4.   Once you have established rapport with the audience by humor, reference to occasion, or by some other form of motivation, you are ready to give the biographical data necessary to identify the speaker and to make that person sound interesting and authoritative to the audience. In most cases the biography should include: (a) the speaker's place of residence, (b) achievements (publications, honors and awards, etc.), (c) background on the topic (professional and educational), (d) relationship to the audience, (e) and the reason this person was selected to deliver the talk.

5.   If the occasion allows for it, you should try to hold off the speaker's full name and/or subject until the end. In this way the speaker's name and topic can be presented as a climax.

6.   Avoid hackneyed words and phrases. Introductions such as "Our speaker needs no introduction . . ." and "without further ado . . ." are much too common.

7.   Pay close attention to the speech so that at the close of the address you can make reference to the ideas and their value to the audience as you thank the speaker.

THE MANUSCRIPT SPEECH

The reading of a speech that one has written is more popular today than ever before. There are a number of reasons for this recent rise in popularity. People are discovering that they are called upon to give speeches at rather formal and professional occasions. Professional conventions, business meetings, and appearances before government agencies are all occasions when one could benefit from a "polished" speech, a speech where every word is carefully selected for its accuracy. Such a speech is part of the manuscript occasion.

PREPARING THE SPEECH
In preparing the manuscript speech remember that you are preparing a *speech*, not an essay. The characteristics of good speechmaking and good writing are quite different. Therefore, the principles of successful speaking, discussed throughout this book, apply directly to manuscript preparation.

Because there is something very special about the occasion that calls for the manuscript speech, most people are willing to put forth a great deal of energy in preparing their manuscript. The following sequence, although it is time consuming, may be helpful in preparing the manuscript.

Develop the Outline
You should begin by going through many of the same steps we discussed in the section called "The Organization of Your Ideas" (chapter 1). After ques-

tions of purpose, audience analysis, and analysis of occasion are asked, you should begin to develop the outline. The outline for the manuscript, like the outline for the extemporized speech, should be concerned with matters such as an introduction, body, and conclusion.

Writing the First Draft
Once the outline is researched and completed, you are ready to write your first draft of the manuscript. Given the luxury of time in preparation, the speech should be characterized by an excellent vocabulary and vivid images.

Revising the First Draft
After reading the first draft aloud you will want to make changes. Many sections that would be acceptable in an essay fail to have the effect you want when read aloud. Having a friend listen to an early draft of the speech can also be of value.

Developing the Final Draft
After making the necessary corrections and additions you should now have a well-written and highly polished speech. The manuscript from which you read can be made even more useful if you follow a few simple guidelines: (1) Use stiff paper, (2) write on only one side of the paper, (3) number your pages, (4) type your manuscript and use triple spacing, and (5) try to use short paragraphs—they are easier to locate when you return to the manuscript after establishing and maintaining eye contact.

You should practice using the final draft a number of times. This will enable you to become familiar with the material and will aid you in developing the skill needed to handle the paper. You might also find it helpful to mark the manuscript in those places where you want to pause or provide special vocal emphasis and variety.

DELIVERING THE MANUSCRIPT SPEECH
In addition to recalling the principles of good delivery discussed in chapter 3, you should also be aware of practices that are somewhat unique to manuscript delivery.

1.   Don't try to conceal the manuscript. In reading from a manuscript many speakers have tried to feign total spontaneity only to discover that such deception only works against them. In addition to having trouble locating their places in the speech, they incurred audience dislike at being deceived.

2.   Establish and maintain eye contact. The fact that you have a manuscript should in no way detract from your initiating and maintaining rapport with the audience. Eye contact can be fostered by your becoming very familiar with your speech.

3.   Concentrate on ideas rather than words. You must keep in mind that

it is a speech you are delivering. If you start to read every word and forget the influence of ideas, you will no longer have the unique effect of speech communication.

ANSWERING QUESTIONS

Jan Morris is explaining the process of setting a time lock on a bank vault to a group of bank equipment specialists. She is interrupted by a member of the group: "Before you go any further, Jan, could you tell me what the function of that third switch is?"

Ralph Snyder is urging a group of spectators to boycott a local grocery until it stops selling nonunion lettuce. As he concludes, one of the spectators asks, "What makes you think this boycott will work any better than the one you led against that store in Anaheim?"

John Garcia has just finished a classroom speech on the subject of transcendental meditation. A number of students call out questions simultaneously: "Why can't you tell us your mantra?" "Where can I sign up for a course?" "What kind of religion is it?"

Fielding questions from the audience is often a routine part of communication encounters. The speaker who seeks to instruct will often invite the audience to pose questions whenever appropriate; the speaker who attempts to persuade will very likely be questioned or challenged by some listeners; the speaker who rouses the curiosity of the audience with unusual subject matter may be bombarded by questions after the address. In fact, except for speeches delivered under circumstances which preclude immediate feedback, such as televised and broadcast messages, almost all speech situations lend themselves to a question-and-answer session. Because the audience's impression of a speaker is based not only upon what happens during the speech but also upon the speaker's prespeech and postspeech behavior, it is important for us to examine ways in which the question-and-answer session can promote a favorable final impression of the speaker.

CHARACTERISTICS OF THE
EFFECTIVE REPLY

Politeness, straightforwardness, and brevity mark the ideal reply to a question. Politeness cannot be overstressed as a desirable ingredient in replying to the questions of another. Every person who asks a question feels that it is important. So regardless of how naive, irrelevant, or poorly worded the question might be, always treat the questioner with dignity. If other members of the audience laugh in derision at a poor question, it is wise for the speaker to refrain from joining in that laughter. Show that you respect the questioner's feelings, and you will deserve the goodwill that follows from such a gesture. Even hostile questions should be answered without rancor. You can disagree politely with your questioner. Issues, not personalities, should be the substance of your replies. Moreover, meeting hostility with politeness may serve to disarm the hostile questioner while minimizing that person's influence upon other listeners.

Straightforwardness is another desirable feature in answering questions. Audiences are usually quick to sense evasiveness; sometimes the favorable impression left by a speech can be negated by a shifty answer to a question asked afterward. If you don't know the answer to a question, it is better to say so than to try to divert the issue elsewhere. Likewise, if you don't wish to answer a question, then say so, adding an explanation for declining. When a question is asked, then, come directly to grips with it and avoid diversionary tactics.

Brevity should characterize your answers, too—that is, brevity consistent with completeness. Some speakers are guilty of "overkill" in their answers. Not only do they reply to the question asked, they move into tangential areas and answer questions that haven't even been asked! If there appears to be a number of questions forthcoming from the audience, then brevity in answering is an absolute necessity.

DETERMINANTS OF A
STRATEGY OF REPLY

Choice of a suitable strategy to employ when answering a question will be governed in part by the nature and specificity of the question and by the apparent motive of the questioner.

1. *The nature of the question.*   Most questions can be classified under one of the following headings:

   a.   A request for clarification. Perhaps the listener did not understand your explanation of some concept or process and wants you to explain it in other terms.

   b.   A request for more information. Here the problem is not in what you have said but in what you haven't said. Such questions are usually a good sign that you have generated a high level of curiosity in your listener.

   c.   A challenge to the validity of your point of view. The listener may be dissatisfied with the kind or amount of evidence you have employed or with the inferences you have drawn.

The nature of the question, then, will be one factor which determines the kind of reply needed.

2. *The specificity of the question.*   How specific the question is will be a determinant of how much latitude you have in answering. Some questions or requests are very general in nature, such as "What's your reaction to the feminist movement?" or "Tell us about your stay in Vienna." Given such general questions, your problem is one of delimitation. The suggestions we offered for coping with the impromptu speaking situation are applicable in such instances. The important thing is to narrow the topic down to one manageable central idea and develop that idea.

In other cases, the questions may be very specific, affording you little difficulty in deciding upon a unifying theme for your answer. Examples of such questions are: "In your opinion, is acupuncture a defensible medical practice?" "What kind of batteries do you recommend for a portable electronic calculator?" "Where can a person obtain free legal aid?"

3. *The motive of the questioner.* A person's real reasons for posing a question are not always easy to discover. We look for signs of motivation in the wording of the questions and in the questioner's nonverbal behavior. Does the questioner appear to be displaying a neutral, friendly, or hostile attitude? Is the question constructive? Does the questioner seem to want your information or want to find out the extent of your information? Is the questioner apparently intent upon lowering your credibility in the eyes of the audience? Is the questioner apparently more interested in getting the spotlight than in getting an answer to a question? Our perception of the questioner's motive may not be accurate, but it is nonetheless influential in shaping the tenor of our reply. Perhaps it is safest to assume that the questioner is a cynical friend. Then let your answer be logical enough to satisfy a cynic and congenial enough to satisfy a friend.

ORGANIZING THE REPLY

The nature of the question will probably dictate the format most appropriate for your answer. In all instances, however, you should make a practice of repeating the question before beginning your reply. This will serve to give your audience a chance to hear the question again in case it was inaudible when first posed. It also lets the questioner know whether you heard the question correctly. Moreover, the few moments spent in repeating the question may give you valuable time in which to formulate an answer.

Here are some general suggestions for organizing answers to the three principal kinds of questions:

Request for Clarification

1. Refer to the section of your speech requiring clarification.
2. Utilize the appropriate clarifying devices, such as definition, restatement, examples, illustrations, analogies, diagrams, or demonstrations.
3. Ask the questioner if the point is sufficiently clarified.

For example: "I've just been asked to define the word 'decibel' which I used earlier in describing the noise level at the assembly plant. A decibel is a unit for measuring the relative loudness of sounds. The faintest audible sound detectable by the human ear is placed at 1 decibel. Then the range runs upward to about 130 decibels. So when I said that the noise next to the metal press was about 115 decibels, I meant it was really loud. Does that explain it clearly enough?"

Request for More Information

1. Refer to the point on which you have been requested to offer further information.

2. Relate the information utilizing an appropriate sequence such as chronological, spatial, topical, or logical order.
3. Ask the questioner if you have answered the request sufficiently.

For example: "Bill asked where the nuclear generating plant is located in relationship to Camp Pendelton. Bill, since Camp Pendelton runs for a number of miles along the coast, I'll use the main gate as a reference point. As you know, the main gate is located at the northeast edge of Oceanside. Well, the plant is approximately fifteen miles northwest of that gate, right on the oceanfront. Can you visualize that now?"

Challenge to Your Position

1. Refer to the point that has been challenged.
2. State the nature of the challenge.
3. Answer the challenge by offering additional evidence in support of your position and/or by showing the fallacious character of the questioner's objections.

For example: "The gentleman in the back row has challenged the source of my data on the number of missles deployed along the coastline of our state. If he questions the source I cited, let me refer him to a statement made by Senator Neeland which was quoted in the most recent issue of *U.S. News and World Report*. I think he'll find the identical figure cited by the senator, who is a member of the Senate Armed Services Committee."

SUMMARY

In this chapter we have sought to deal with special communication situations. Although all communication is in a sense special, and therefore utilizes similarities in form and style, there are certain situations that demand a different degree of proficiency if the speaker is to accomplish a given purpose. The most common of these occasions are entertaining speeches, after-dinner speeches, the impromptu speech, making introductions and manuscript speaking.

The major purpose of the speech to entertain is to have the listeners enjoy themselves. The speaker, by employing the concepts of attention and interest, has the audience relax in an enjoyable atmosphere. Humor is often a trademark of entertaining. This means that the successful speaker must learn to use the humorous illustration, exaggeration, incongruity, attacking of authority, and other such devices.

The after-dinner speech is similar to the speech to entertain. Here again the speaker strives for a lighthearted and congenial atmosphere. This speech is usually brief and "fun to listen to."

The impromptu speech is given on the "spur-of-the-moment" or when the speaker has little time to prepare. To keep from being completely overwhelmed, the speaker can call forth a few simple techniques such as remembering what was said just before being asked to speak, thinking about past reading and speaking experiences, or working out a suitable organizational pattern.

The main task of the speech of introduction is to create a rapport between speaker, subject, and audience. By stimulating interest in both the speaker and topic, you will create a climate which is friendly and one in which the audience is interested in hearing what the guest speaker has to say.

The manuscript speech is unique in that it offers the speaker an opportunity to write out the speech in detail before delivering it. In preparing this type of speech it is important to remember that it is basically a speech and not an essay. Once an outline is completed, you are in a position to start the manuscript. You will find it beneficial to rewrite and finalize your wording and phrasing. The final draft should be highly refined and polished. In presenting the speech, the essentials of good delivery must be kept in mind. Eye contact, vocal variety, gestures, and the like are as important to good manuscript speaking as they are to good extemporaneous speaking.

The question-and-answer session is a common part of communication encounters. Politeness, straightforwardness, and brevity are desirable qualities in replying to questions. The nature and specificity of the question as well as the perceived motive of the questioner will affect the speaker's strategy of reply.

Suggested Readings

Barrett, Harold. *Practical Methods in Speech*. 2d ed. New York: Holt, Rinehart and Winston, 1968. Chapter 13.

Hance, Kenneth G.; Ralph, David S.; and Wiksell, Milton J. *Principles of Speaking*. Belmont, California: Wadsworth Publishing Co., 1962. Chapters 15 and 16.

Harral, Stewart. *When It's Laughter You're After*. Oklahoma: University of Oklahoma Press, 1962.

Mudd, Charles S., and Sillars, Malcolm O. *Speech: Content and Communication*. 3d ed. New York: Thomas Y. Crowell Co., 1975. Chapter 18.

Oliver, Robert T., and Cortright, Rupert L. *Effective Speech*. New York: Holt, Rinehart and Winston, 1970, Chapters 22 and 23.

Reid, Loren. *Speaking Well*. 2d ed. New York: McGraw-Hill Book Co., 1972. Chapter 21.

White, Eugene E. *Practical Public Speaking*. New York: Macmillan Co., 1964. Chapter 15.

11

Discussion
Group Communication

You have probably already discovered that there are many communication situations that call for a *sharing* of ideas and a willingness to "talk things over." Whether it be in business, at school, at church, or at social functions, we are constantly having to get together with other individuals in order to discuss items of business or solve mutual problems. When you engage in a situation that brings you face-to-face with others, you should be aware of the influence of communication upon the final outcome of the meeting. Being able to communicate effectively on these occasions can make the difference between an "aimless bull session" or a productive communication experience.

The concept of group thinking is fundamental to the democratic process for a number of reasons. In a democratic society it is only natural that decisions should be made after considerable deliberation and discussion. We pride ourselves on being fair—that various points of view are presented and considered before judgment is given or a decision rendered. We maintain, as part of our democratic philosophy, that each person counts and has the right and the responsibility to contribute to the resolution of both individual and public problems. Group discussion affords us an opportunity to conduct our own social, political, and vocational affairs in a democratic manner utilizing maximum participation of other trained and interested citizens. In short, we can say that **discussion is the systematic and objective sharing of ideas and information by two or more persons who work together in an effort to solve a problem or to gain a better understanding of a problem.**

The uses of discussion are obvious when we reflect on the occasions and situations when we are in the position of sharing ideas and information with others. In education, for example, many classes function by means of the discussion process. In countless situations, by either chance or design, we meet with others to resolve problems, share feelings, or gather information. It is therefore the purpose of this chapter to investigate the theory, principles, and techniques that will make us more effective participants in small group communication.

TYPES OF GROUP DISCUSSION

Although the main emphasis of this chapter will be devoted primarily to problem-solving discussion, it might be useful to note some of the various forms of *public discussion*.

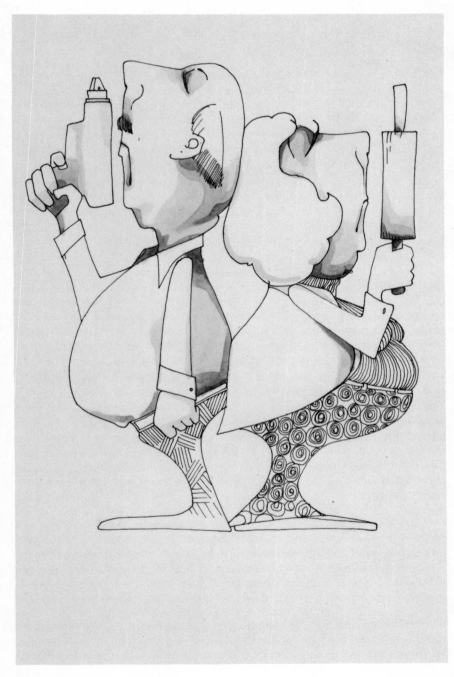

Discussion demands a willingness to
talk things over.

Traditionally people have tried to classify various types and forms of public discussion. These classifications are not hard and fast, for in many instances one form may overlap another.

1. *Lecture-forum.*   This is the simplest form of public group discussion. A speaker addresses the audience who is the speaker of the evening—the lecturer. After the speech the lecturer is expected to answer questions directed by members of the audience. The audience may contribute opinions of their own during this period. Hence, we have discussions—ideas are being exchanged. Normally there is a chairperson to introduce the speaker and to guide the discussion period.

2. *Symposium.*   In the symposium each of several speakers, generally two to five, delivers a talk. These speeches center around one topic, theme, or issue. Each speaker may explain the position and thoughts on the subject as a whole, or perhaps may be limited to a specific phase of the subject. Frequently the audience is allowed the privilege of asking questions at the conclusion of all of the talks.

3. *Panel.*   During the last few years the panel has become a very popular method of group discussion. In a very general sense, a panel is a discussion within a discussion. In this ararngement a limited number of persons, usually four to seven, sit before the audience and discuss a given topic. There are no planned and set speeches; all the remarks are short and spontaneous. When the panel finishes its discussion, there are normally questions from the floor which are answered by the panel members.

4. *Informal group discussion (round table).*   This is the most common of all the forms of discussion. It is frequently a nonaudience type of discussion and tends to be more informal than the other methods. It consists of a small group seated around a table. In this setting they exchange their views and their information in a spontaneous and free manner. The stimulus-response pattern is constantly changing as attention is directed from one person to another. This type of pattern is well suited for either decision-making or information-sharing and is the type of discussion situation in which we most often find ourselves.

The four types of discussion mentioned above represent what we call *public discussion.* They seem to be the types of discussion that are often held before audiences and are usually somewhat formal. We also engage in many discussions that take a more common and less formal procedure. We can call these *private discussions.* These often have overlapping purposes, but as a means of classification we might list two of the most common types.

1. *Therapy groups.*   This form of group discussion has many different names—encounter groups, sensitivity sessions, T-group training, and the like. These are basically groups made up of people who have come together to study themselves and group interaction. No group solution is sought, but rather the aim is to learn about such questions as, "How do I function in groups?" (group interaction), "How do I communicate?" and "What do others

think of my communication behavior?" It should be noted that there are times when many of these same questions should be asked in other types of groups.

2. *Problem-solving groups.*   Problem-solving groups can take many forms. The form may be a committee, a conference, or simply a group of individuals who share a common problem and join together as a means of solving their problem. This is by far the most common of all group discussions in which you will find yourself.

Because of the widespread nature of problem-solving groups, we shall make this type of group activity the central focus of this chapter.

CHARACTERISTICS OF SUCCESSFUL PROBLEM-SOLVING GROUPS

Although problem-solving groups share many of the same ingredients of other groups, they nevertheless are characterized by some rather unique features.

1. *Cooperation is stressed in group discussion.*   Cooperation and not competition are the attributes of good problem-solving discussions. The rationale for cooperation seems to be built into the very fiber of problem-solving discussion. The members have gathered together because they all share a common concern, and it is this concern that is manifested in a spirit of cooperation.

2. *Analysis and investigation are part of the discussion process.*   The various members of the group have joined together because they are all vexed by the same problem. To find the best answer to that problem the members must be willing to analyze and investigate the issues involved. The person who already has all of the answers does not belong in the group, for it is the analytical and systematic search for those answers that gives the problem-solving group its life.

3. *Group discussion is objective.*   Members of the group should be willing to examine all sides of issues and questions. They should be open-minded and not fearful of giving all points of view a fair and just hearing.

4. *Discussion is a method of reflective thinking.*   Rather than engaging in random and aimless behavior, the problem-solving group seeks to follow a thought process that is purposeful, systematic, and organized. The most common pattern of group reflective thinking is one that was developed from the phases of reflective thought described by the educator and philosopher John Dewey. These phases, which will be discussed in greater detail later in the chapter, consist of (1) defining and limiting the problem, (2) analyzing evidence for causes and effects of the problem, (3) proposing solutions for the problems, (4) evaluating and analyzing *all* solutions, and (5) deciding upon ways to put the chosen solution into operation.

5. *Discussion groups attempt to strike a balance between emotionality and rationality.*   This balancing of our feelings with our logical arguments is

essential if the group is working towards the resolution of "real-life" problems. Imagine how difficult it would be to talk about an emotional problem, such as abortion laws, without having our personal feelings fusing with our rational research. It is this blending together that serves as one of the essential components of successful problem solving.

6. *Sincere scepticism is encouraged.* Although the group strives for a high degree of solidarity, individuals should feel free to question and criticize those ideas that they believe are weak and void of substance. A group of individuals that spend all their time simply nodding heads in argreement usually end up with rather shallow conclusions. Therefore, phrases such as "I'm not sure that is a very good plan," or "Are you certain of that?" should be used by all members.

7. *Discussion groups are in touch with their immediate needs.* Successful groups can detect, and respond to, various shifts in moods, fatigue, and tension. Being able to take the necessary measures to control these rhythms demands that each member be aware of what is going on within the group.

8. *All members are aware of the wide range of roles that must be performed.* A group does not move toward its goal by centrifugal force; the members supply the energy that enables things to happen. This energy reflects itself through various group roles. These roles range from leadership duties to asking questions. What is important is that these roles be manifest to all members and the acting out of these roles diffused throughout the group. For example, everyone must know and be willing to perform the role of arbitrator if interpersonal conflicts are to be resolved.

9. *Intergroup communication channels are informal and open.* Communication is essential in problem-solving groups. The members must feel free to say what they want. If, for any reason, the participants become reluctant to take part, the entire group suffers. This freedom to communicate is stimulated and nurtured when the group climate is informal.

10. *Individual needs are integrated with the group goals.* Group productivity and member satisfaction will be hampered if the group fails to strike a balance between its members' personal needs and the overall goal of the group. We all know from personal experience that our enthusiasm is diminished when we are in groups that do not offer us some positive motivation. What we strive for in any group experience is an atmosphere that enables us to accomplish personal aims and desires at the same time we are working with others to solve a mutual problem. In short, we need group cohesiveness coupled with individuality.

PREPARING FOR
DISCUSSION

Discussion will be an aimless, purposeless activity if the participants engage in conversation without preparation and forethought. The steps in preparing for discussion involve three closely related activities—selecting a subject, wording a subject, and gathering material.

SELECTING THE SUBJECT

On most occasions the members of a private discussion group will be in a position to select their own subjects. In deciding what to talk about, and what problem to investigate, the participants will find it helpful to follow a few guidelines.

1. Select problems in which the participants have an interest. If the members of the group feel personally involved, they will be far more active in both research and participation. There is ample experimental evidence to point out that we tend to work harder for those causes we feel most strongly about. In addition, we seem to enjoy the experience with added enthusiasm if we are sincerely committed.

2. The topic should be important and worth discussing. Time is too precious and serious questions too numerous to waste time on trivial and frivolous matters.

3. Choose a topic on which ample resource material is available. Sitting around and offering information from the "top of our heads" will result in a "pooling of ignorance."

4. Problems should be selected that can be investigated prior to the discussion and that can be discussed in the time allotted to the group. A group that is rushed, both before and during the discussion, will usually produce a solution that reflects just such a hasty analysis and lack of deliberation.

5. The subject selected should present a problem. If the group is going to be motivated in the problem-solving discussion, they should feel a common need to find a solution. The topic should provide *at least* two sides of investigation. If the solution is obvious at the outset, there is no valid reason to engage in the time-consuming steps of the reflective process.

WORDING THE SUBJECT

The correct wording and statement of the problem area is as important as the problem itself. For if the group formulates the problem in a way that distorts the real issue, confusion and misunderstanding will result. In addition, the general subject area must be worded into a workable topic if all members of the group are to deal with the same problem. The student of discussion might well consider some of the following suggestions for wording the subject.

1. The subject-problem should be phrased as a question. The question highlights a specific problem while it motivates persons to seek answers to the problem. Phrasing such as "price fixing" and "war and peace" are so general and vague that they cannot be discussed in a specific manner. On the other hand, a question such as "What should be the economic role of the United States in Israel?" or "What can our college do to improve the parking

situation in the student lot?" call for an answer—hence discussion can take place.

2. The question should be clearly phrased. If the wording is ambiguous, the group may have to spend long periods of time trying to decide what to talk about. A question such as "What should be the current status of business?" is an example of ambiguity. The group must stop and decide what "business" and "current status" mean before they can even start working on the problem. Careful wording of the problem, even before the group begins discussing, also serves the dual role of limiting and restricting the scope of the problem. A topic worded "What are the graduate fellowships offered at San Diego State University?" indicates precisely what the group will talk about.

3. Whenever possible avoid wording the problem-question in a "yes-or-no" form. The "yes-or-no" response limits the available solutions and also leads to debate instead of cooperation. Questions such as "Should our school adopt a year-round session?" places restrictions on the group and limits the responses the participants can make.

4. The topic should be worded in an impartial way. We all know that one can state a topic in such a manner that it favors one side or the other. We can also word a topic so that the conclusion appears obvious at the start. Both of these evils should be avoided in wording the topic for discussion. We can all see the restrictive nature of a topic that is stated, "Since all students would like a Democrat to be elected president, how can we raise money for the campaign of our Democratic governor?" That example, and others like it, reflect partiality, state the conclusion at the start, and therefore greatly limit the group's latitude.

GATHERING MATERIAL

The amount and depth of preparation in discussion is as vital as in preparing for a speech. If the participants are ill-informed and poorly researched, very little productive deliberation can take place. Each member of a group depends on the other members for different and fresh ideas; if one member fails to gather specific and concrete data, the entire group suffers.

We have already written about the processes of gathering and preparing material. The same principles apply to discussion: (1) think carefully on the subject before you start your research; (2) decide what you already know on the subject and what you must research further; (3) gather the additional information you need; (4) accurately record your findings; and (5) organize your material around a purposeful and meaningful pattern.

You will notice that the fifth principle in the preceding paragraph suggests that the material should be built around a "purposeful and meaningful pattern." This means that the materials you gather should be organized in the same general order that the group deliberations will follow. Most problem-solving groups will utilize the reflective pattern as their organizational scheme. If you were going to be in a group whose basic aim was problem solving, it might be helpful to organize your research around the following phases:

I. Definitions and limitations of the problem.
    A. Provide definitions of important words and phrases that
        are found in the problem.
        1. You can use the dictionary.
        2. You will want to use authoritative sources and experts
            as a means of defining the topic.
    B. Find those materials that help limit the scope and range of the area.
II. Analysis of the problem.
    A. Material related to the history of the problem should be
        researched and placed next in your outline.
    B. Information, evidence, and the like must be provided to highlight
        specific incidents of the problem. (These are usually called effects or
        symptoms of the problem.)
    C. Evidence must be gathered that reveals and explains the
        causes of the problem.
III. All possible solutions should be listed.
IV. The solutions should be evaluated and analyzed.
    A. Exploring the advantages and disadvantages is often helpful.
    B. Evidence that examines the effects of all the solutions is normally
        treated in this portion of the outline.
V. Evidence and research that discusses the best method of putting
    the solution into practice should be treated next.

UTILIZING REFLECTIVE
THINKING

In most instances group discussion follows the steps of problem-solving developed by John Dewey, American philosopher and educator. Dewey developed a simple pattern that allows the discussants to adapt the steps of problem-
solving to group deliberation. These are, briefly, (1) recognition of the problem,
(2) description of the problem, (3) discovery of possible solutions, (4) evaluation of solutions and acceptance of the best solution, and (5) plan of action
for the preferred solution.

Most problem-solving groups can derive numerous benefits from utilizing the steps of reflective thinking. Two of the more common advantages are
worth mentioning. First, it is assumed that by treating each of the five phases
in a systematic order we will progress *logically* from a problem to a solution.
By analyzing the key issues step by step, reflective thinking seeks to eliminate
the random and haphazard decision-making processes so characteristic of
many deliberations. Think of all those occasions when you were in a group
that chose the first solution proposed only to find out later that the final
decision would have been much better, had judgment been suspended until
all alternatives had been examined.

The second advantage of Dewey's five steps is manifest in the group
itself. With all the members concerned with the same step of the reflective
thinking process at any given moment, we can be somewhat assured that all
the participants will be talking about equivalent issues at the same time. In this
way we hope to be spared the person who commences the discussion by say-

ing, "Now the best way to solve this problem is to . . ." Because each person knows what phase the group is in at every instance, it is a simple matter to tell this person that "We should define our terms at the start of the discussion."

RECOGNITION OF THE PROBLEM

Before we can solve a problem we must be aware of the fact that a problem exists. Therefore, the first step in trying to resolve or understand a problem is the defining and limiting of the specific problem area. By defining the problem early in the discussion, the group can set certain limits if the topic is too broad for the amount of time allotted. By analyzing certain crucial terms and key concepts, they are also in a better position to comprehend the scope and seriousness of the problem. For example, if a group was going to discuss the topic of high school dropouts, it should use the initial period of its discussion to decide such things as a definition of "high school dropouts." Is it anyone under sixteen years old, or is the age to be eighteen and below? Deciding issues such as these early in the discussion helps a group avoid the all too common problem of nearing the end of the discussion only to discover that there was not a common definition agreed upon.

DESCRIPTION OF THE PROBLEM

Now that the members of the group have stated, defined, and limited their problem they are ready to analyze the nature of the problem. This analysis and evaluation normally demands that the participants discuss and exchange ideas and information on three topics—history of the problem, effects of the problem, and causes of the problem.

1. *History.* What has led up to a situation may offer insight into how that situation can be remedied. If, for instance, a group is discussing student parking fees, it might be helpful to explore the history of these fees as a method of finding out when they were first initiated and the rationale behind their introduction. Whenever possible the history of the problem should extend as far forward as the *status quo*.

There may be occasions when the history phase will have to be omitted. Problems that call for immediate action may not offer a group the luxury of a historical review. In addition, problems that are very new may not have any relevant history.

2. *Effects.* Using the various forms of support mentioned in chapter 5, the group should discuss how serious the problem is and who is being affected. By reporting observed effects the members can see the outward manifestations of the problem and how widespread it is. For example, if the group was discussing "what can be done about the increased crime rate among teenagers?" someone might ask if the problem was serious; in response, another participant would attempt to substantiate the seriousness of the problem by stating that

"the governor indicated that the crime rate among teenagers in California has doubled in the last ten years." By knowing *what is happening* (effects of the problem), the group can later decide how to remedy the problem.

3. *Causes.*   The group, having examined and verified the effects of the problem, now concerns itself with the conditions which caused the effects. In deciding what caused the increased crime rate (effect), someone might offer support that establishes broken homes as a cause of teenage crime.

DISCOVERY OF POSSIBLE SOLUTIONS

After the group has determined the specific problem to be solved and has examined the effects and causes of the problem, it is ready to suggest possible solutions. *All* possible solutions should be identified. Solutions suggested can be singular in nature ("The courts should be stricter with teenage offenders.") Multiple solutions can also be listed ("Stricter courts, better probation procedures, and parent counseling programs are what is needed.").

EVALUATION OF SOLUTIONS

One of the most important characteristics of reflective thinking is the practice of withholding judgment until all possible solutions can be objectively and completely considered (a concept often referred to in the literature of group processes as "suspended conclusions"). The participants should talk about each solution in detail, testing their remarks with concrete evidence, and analyzing their conclusions in light of logical reasoning. In this deliberation the advantages and disadvantages of each solution should be discussed and evaluated. How will the solution offered solve the problem? What will the solution do to the causes and effects mentioned earlier in the discussion? What will the solution do to the **status quo?** Once these, and other questions, have been answered, the group is ready to decide which of the solutions will best eliminate, or at least minimize, the problem. The acceptance of the "best solution" is tentative and related only to the problem mentioned in the discussion. It does not necessarily represent a decision that is fixed and static.

PLAN OF ACTION

As a final step the group must decide whether or not its preferred solution can be put into effect. If the solution seems workable, desirable, and practicable, the group should determine the most effective means of implementing their findings and conclusions

Specific plans are influenced by such factors as the topic, time, and the power of the group. For example, a group discussing a local campus problem might well present its solution to the college administration or to the student council. By contrast, a group dealing with an international topic might have to be content with writing a letter to representatives in Washington.

COMMUNICATING IN
SMALL GROUPS

Although we have been talking about group structure and procedure, it should be stressed once again that *this book is about human communication*. It is about the ways we send and receive messages. Because of this focus it is only natural that the section on communicating in small groups should serve as the main thrust of this chapter. For whatever else group discussion may be, it is primarily concerned with the activity we have been calling human communication.

Group interaction, personal relations, and sensitivity are highly complex concepts and cannot accurately be taught in a single session or by reading a few pages of techniques. However, there are some essential tasks and responsibilities that can be learned by the participant who is motivated and willing to practice.

1. Each member of the group should be well informed on the topic. Research is *everyone's job*. Unsupported generalizations and unwarranted assertions harm the entire group. A successful participant brings not only ideas to the group, but also information that he has gathered from sources other than his personal experiences.

2. Make your presence known throughout the discussion. The amount of time the group has and the number of participants will obviously influence the frequency and length of your contributions, but basically you should feel free to participate as often as you have something to say.

3. See that your contributions relate to what is being said or to something that has already been said. Remarks that are simply "tossed out to the group" will often result in confusion or even force the group to depart from their established agenda. Think of how frustrating it is for the entire group when progress is interrupted by someone who begins to recount a personal experience that is completely off the subject. On those occasions all members have the responsibility to see to it that the transgression is noted and the group is returned to the topic.

4. In discussion, as in all communication, it is crucial that one use index numbers and dates as reminders that *no word has exactly the same meaning twice*. This means that one must try to make all remarks as specific as possible. For example, "a few weeks ago" is not the same as "January 7, 1975." To say "that man" is not the same as "Dr. John Jones." The other participants in a discussion must know exactly what the contribution means. In short, one must narrow and define the symbols that are used so that they will call up an image that is common to all who hear it.

5. Many controversies among participants in a group discussion are accompanied by assertions—assertions where one party maintains that something is truth, while the other person maintains it is not truth. The problem for participants in a group discussion becomes one of determining how controversies based on assertions can be solved. Two of the many methods of resolving

these conflicts are worth noting at this time. First, it is necessary to know what the controversy is. In other words, what the assertions assert. This involves a critical examination of basic premises inherent in the assertions. Second, the participants must see to it that they are not mistaking assertions about the speaker for assertions about things. It is confusing to our listeners if we say "Nancy, you are wrong," when in reality we should have said "Nancy, your *information* is wrong."

6. It must be kept in mind that communication is a two-way process; therefore, the listener also plays a key role in discussion. It is unfair to place the burden for understanding completely on the speaker. Participants in a discussion cannot sit back and contentedly assume they have nothing to do but wait their turns to talk. The listener must pay close attention to what is being said. Participants must ask questions and attempt to narrow and define all ambiguous and nebulous concepts. (A review of the chapter concerning listening would be helpful at this time.)

7. "Loaded language" or emotionally toned words and phrases should be avoided in group discussion. These words bring to mind a variety of meanings and images. When such words are used, they often confuse the real meaning in the mind of both sender and receiver. Once again the solution becomes one of using words that are specific. We are taken off the track and often lose our concentration when someone says "What would she know? She is not only vicious and stupid, but she was once a Communist."

8. The discussants should work toward establishing an atmosphere that stresses questioning. The various participants must realize that a lack of understanding as to what is said and what is meant hampers the reflective process. By asking questions of one another whenever there is a basic misunderstanding or need for information, the group can overcome many of its obstacles. Many groups, we fear, move ahead in the discussion only to discover later that they did not understand the earlier premises that lead to the current stage of the discussion. By raising questions, the group can also encourage silent members to take part. For example, someone might say to a reticent member, "Roger, what did you find when you looked at the effects of the problem?" Roger would have a difficult time remaining silent!

9. Whenever possible the participants should endeavor to keep their contributions and exchanges brief and precise. Long and detailed contributions, although sometimes needed, frequently bore the other participants.

10. Try to remain open minded. Your prejudices should be left outside the door. The closed mind has difficulty cooperating and objectively evaluating ideas and issues.

11. Adhere to the logical pattern selected by the group. If Dewey's reflective pattern is selected, see to it that the group "stays on the track." Jumping from effects to solutions and back to definition of terms will only waste time and frustrate the participants.

12. Work for a decision by majority. Remember, cooperation is one of the key elements of successful discussion. This does not mean that honest

differences have no place in group deliberation but rather that debate and disagreement should be over ideas and data, not over personalities.

13. Try to employ role-taking (empathy) towards all members of the group. To understand the thoughts and feelings of others is an essential ingredient of successful group participation. To know the reasons why people behave as they do will enable you to know what to say, when to say it, and how to say it.

14. An active participant offers verbal and nonverbal support for the other members. If by your attitude (facial expressions, posture, utterances, and so forth), you reveal a lack of interest and enthusiasm, the other members will be inhibited and defensive. No one likes to feel unimportant and without regard. If the receiver of messages lacks expression and animation, the speaker is apt to feel that what is said is futile and not worthy of the group's time. A lack of recognition and support of our ideas hampers a free and spontaneous flow of communication. In short, by our silence and our remarks we can aid or destroy communication.

15. Supply leadership for the group whenever needed. There is a tendency among many participants to rely solely on the judgment of the leader for decisions that are basically the responsibility of the participants. There are, in addition, many "functions" of a leader that can easily be performed by any alert member of the group. For example, any participant can offer summaries whenever that person feels they are appropriate and would aid the group. Don't make the mistake of assuming the leader, because of the title held, has all of the answers.

16. Try to create an atmosphere that is conducive to constructive and purposeful discussion. A relaxed and friendly atmosphere is far more productive than one that is characterized by tension. Simply ask yourself this question: "Is it not true that I am at ease and do my best work when I am in a situation that is free from hostility and anxiety?" If the answer is "yes," then do your part to make the communication environment a pleasant one. What we are saying is that discussion should not be conducted in an authoritarian atmosphere, but rather in a climate where each person is honest and speaks freely. It is a healthy attitude when each person says, "The discussion belongs to all of us—it is a chance to say what we think and feel." This openness and frankness among all participants is not only good for the group, but often helps the individual. You know from experience that if someone says or does something that bothers you and you feel constrained to keep silent about it, you are apt to brood silently while allowing the incident to be distorted completely out of proportion. What are we suggesting is that in those circumstances you immediately confront the idea or behavior in a spirit of candor.

17. All of us work very hard to protect, enhance, and maintain our self-concept. If someone sends us a message that we interpret as an attack on our ego, we will immediately call forth our entire arsenal of defensive strategies as a means of protecting ourselves. In a group we face a number of challenges with regard to ego-defense. First, we must try to avoid sending the types of messages that force others into defensive positions. For example, we

can be honest with others concerning their opinions without attacking their egos. Imagine how you would feel if someone said to you "That is sure a stupid idea." Once we utter phrases like that all further communication is doomed to failure. Second, we must be sensitive enough to recognize ego-defensive behavior when we see it. A person criticized for being late to the meeting is likely to respond in a defensive manner by saying "Nothing very important ever happens at these meetings anyway." When we observe these kinds of responses we should try to aid the person and the group during this uncomfortable period. Finally, we ought to be alert to defensive reactions on our own part. If we are the ones reprimanded for tardiness, we must be in touch with ourselves so that we can arrest those defensive reactions that are likely to impede the group's progress and make us subject to the development of an ulcer.

18. As long as communication involves people, we must be aware of individual and perceptual differences that will appear in the group. Each of us is unique; we come from different backgrounds and therefore bring different personal past histories to the group. These individual differences will be manifested in countless ways. What one person finds humorous another may consider offensive. What is "planned growth" to you may well appear to be "stifling free enterprise" to the person sitting next to you. From judgments of beauty to issues of "truth," our decisions are influenced by our past experiences, and thus having had different experiences, we often reach different conclusions. Effective participants are aware of this truism and are constantly telling themselves that perceptual differences are not only beneficial, they are natural.

19. The watchful participant is aware of the *total* communication situation and is cognizant of the fact that symbols other than words can send messages. Therefore, it is important to be alert to all aspects of nonverbal communication —facial expressions, body movements, eye contact, spatial relationships and seating arrangements. Someone in the group might well be "talking" with their body as they become upset with the group and slowly edge their chair from the inner circle.

20. Because discussion is basically a communication activity, the way we communicate is often as important as *what* we communicate. For example, many of our best ideas can be lost if our delivery is distracting or dull. We all know how hard it is to listen to someone who speaks in a monotone or who shifts aimlessly in the chair. These violations of basic communication skills, the improper use of the voice and body, can often obstruct communication.

21. All participants should employ clear and concise feedback. This simply means that we respond directly, either verbally and/or nonverbally, to the remarks of others. We all know how frustrating it is when we make a statement to someone and receive only silence. In a group the problem is compounded, for there are now eight or ten people who are not responding to what is being said. By nodding, smiling, or talking, we let our colleagues know our reactions to what was presented. It not only keeps the group moving, but it allows other people to know we are interested in them and their ideas.

STYLES OF LEADERSHIP

Perhaps we should begin our analysis of leadership by pointing out that learning how to lead a group is much more complex than simply memorizing a series of techniques. Each group, because of its unique personality and choice of topic, requires a type of leadership specifically suited to its special needs. While one group may work best with a strong leader, another group might be hampered by such control. Therefore, what has evolved are various styles of leadership. We believe that the best treatment of these styles was offered by William M. Sattler and N. Edd Miller in their book *Discussion and Conference*. They examined five of the most common styles found in discussion groups. Let us briefly examine these five approaches to leadership so that you will be able to decide which style would be most appropriate for your particular group. We shall begin with that type of leadership that seeks control of its members and moves gradually to a type that permits complete and total freedom.

At one end of the continuum we have a type of leadership pattern called *authoritarian*. As the phrase implies, in this orientation nearly absolute power rests with the leader who not only conducts the meeting and leads the group, but also makes most of the important decisions concerning content.

When time is short and group efficiency crucial, *strong supervisory* leadership is often employed. Although this type of leadership is not as radical as the authoritarian approach, it is nevertheless based on the philosophical premise that groups need a strong and aggressive leader. The leader will usually ask specific questions and generally direct the flow of the meeting in a direction that has personally been predetermined. In essence, the leader is concerned with procedure and solutions and spends little or no time treating issues of group maintenance, member satisfaction, and interpersonal relationships.

The *democratic* style of leadership is the type most often found in group discussion. The leader plays an active role, but this role is to see to it that a democratic atmosphere prevails in the group. This means that the leader encourages participation and stresses individual initiative. Unlike the authoritarian and supervisory leader, the democratic leader is concerned with personalities as well as procedure.

Group-centered leadership is a type of leadership that offers the participants complete freedom to make procedural as well as policy decisions. This method of leadership is predicated on the belief that each person has the capacity to lead and, therefore, the ability to determine their own goals. Leadership duties are not vested in any one individual, but rather shared by all members. If the group would be aided by a running summary, any of the group's members could offer that summary.

The most permissive of all styles is called *leaderless*. This is really not a form of leadership, for when it prevails there is a total absence of leadership. Leaderless discussions are often characterized by a high degree of member satisfaction, but a low degree of productivity. It takes skilled participants to function in this type of anarchy.

LEADERSHIP IN THE GROUP

Research studies into group discussion and group dynamics have revealed that the so-called born leader is a myth. Leadership is composed of traits and characteristics that can be learned and cultivated. In an ideal or "perfect" group everyone would possess those traits and we would not have to worry about appointing someone to serve as "the leader." In this model situation, all the participants would act as leader. They would monitor the group's behavior as well as their own, the roles of leadership would be diffused throughout the group, and leadership tasks would be performed by any person who believed that a particular task would benefit the group. There are, however, many occasions when shared leadership does not work or is inappropriate. For example, the principal of a school would most likely lead the faculty meeting. In such instances, the group must rely on a single leader to guide it and to stimulate participation.

Because the duties of the leader can be shared by all members or vested in one person, the advice that follows applies to an appointed leader or to any participant who perceives a need for leadership in the group and attempts to fulfill that need.

1. The leader should create a cooperative, democratic climate. A group atmosphere characterized by demagoguery is less creative and quite often filled with discontent. You know from your own experience that if you feel uncomfortable due to the actions of an authoritarian leader, you will not do your best work.

2. The leader should try to remain impartial whenever possible. There is a tendency among members of a group to view the leader as a "boss" or someone of superior rank. Viewed in this way, the leader who states personal conclusions at the beginning of the discussion tends to close the door on free and open deliberation. This does not mean that as leader you cannot take part, it simply suggests that you see to it that all sides get presented and that you do not become a spokesman for one point of view too early in the discussion.

3. The leader has the responsibility of seeing that the discussion gets started. This often involves having the group get acquainted. We have all experienced that uneasy silence when forced to interact with strangers. The leader should help us over those periods by making sure there are some introductions and informal "chatting" before the group begins its serious deliberations.

The leader should also state the purpose of the meeting and mention the problem to be discussed.

4. The leader should try to get general participation among all members of the group. This includes changing the communication behavior of the monopolist as well as the shy member of the group. It is the leader's encouragement and attitude which often determines the frequency of participation among the individuals in the group.

5. The leader should see that a plan, an agenda, or an organizational pat-

tern is followed, and that the main phases of the problem get considered. If an agenda is used, it is the leader who becomes its particular guardian. In short, the leader must always be asking, "Where have we been?" "Where are we now?" and "Where are we going?"

6. The leader should make abundant use of transitions and summaries. By utilizing these two techniques the leader can keep the discussion organized and also keep everyone informed as to the group's progress. Try to visualize how helpful it would be to have someone say, "Now that we have seen the effects of overpopulation, it might be to our advantage to examine some of the causes of this problem."

7. In an ideal situation the leader would offer the encouragement and support that would allow all members to reach full potential. This would call for the supplying of extrinsic motivation to each and every person. Praise and reassurance are but two of the techniques available to the leader.

8. The leader should try to clarify details and contributions whenever possible. If necessary, contributions should be reworded or rephrased. There will be occasions when the leader might even ask someone else to clarify the point or evidence in question. For example, the leader might ask, "Janet, did your research support the notion just expressed by Paul?"

9. The leader should see to it that the group stays on the track and does not wander from point to point. Personal anecdotes may be interesting, but they seldom do much to keep the discussion moving. It is on these occasions that the leader must help the group return to the issue they were discussing before the irrelevant comment was made.

10. We have already alluded to the fact that a group must have successful interpersonal relations if it is to accomplish its goal. Personal hostilities and pettiness have no place in the problem-solving group discussion. A group of this kind cannot waste its time on therapy; it has too much to do. Therefore, the leader must set a tone that does not allow destructive behavior to develop. If, by chance, conflicts do emerge, the leader must resolve them. A leader may have to change the behavior of a troublesome participant, settle an argument, and at times even offer reprimands.

11. The leader should try to bring the discussion to a satisfactory conclusion. The solution can be summarized if one has been reached or a summary can be offered that highlights the points of agreement. The discussion can also be concluded by reviewing the questions and problems that still remain unanswered.

BARRIERS TO DISCUSSION

The most common barriers to successful group discussion can be found in the violation of the suggestions for participation and leadership. If the participant, either member or leader, manifests behavior opposite to that which we have just offered, he or she can contribute to the failure of the group.

There are three additional behaviors that are worth noting as we complete this section on group communication. We have already mentioned these barriers earlier in a slightly different context. However, they are important enough to warrant further consideration at this time.

Apathy among the group members is perhaps the most common barrier to successful group discussion. Apathy is a highly complex phenomenon. It can be brought to the group by specific members or it can even be generated by the group. In either case, apathy and all its external and internal actions, can literally destroy the group. Therefore, all members must seek to make the group an exciting and active encounter for all concerned.

Excessive formality, whether through rules or attitudes, hampers participation, and often increases tension. Although some rules might be helpful, too many rules appear restrictive and can keep the members stiff in both mind and communication.

Closely related to formality is the problem of control. A group that tries to control its members will be a group that has unnatural and rigid participation. A felt lack of freedom will destroy the flow of ideas, feelings, and information.

EVALUATING THE DISCUSSION

Most groups find it useful to evaluate the process they use and the effectiveness of their techniques. Evaluation of the group's behavior and actions can take place at any time and can take a variety of forms. The advantages of honest evaluation should be obvious. Most importantly, evaluation allows the group time to measure and isolate its successes and failures. Evaluation points out in a specific manner what happened and why.

Many groups find it helpful to evaluate periodically as they move through the discussion process. They simply stop and ask questions concerning what is happening, why it is happening, what the results are, and what should be done.

Evaluation can examine a host of variables. Members can evaluate group processes, participation, leadership, communication patterns and problems, interaction, tasks, and final products. These evaluations can be made by individual participants or by the group as a whole.

There are a large number of paper and pencil forms that can be used in group and individual evaluations. In the appendix of this book you will find some of the more common forms used in evaluation. Many groups also enjoy developing their own evaluation forms.

It should be remembered, in closing, that through evaluation and analysis of the group experience we are able to learn from that experience. The insights gained from each discussion can go a long way toward contributing to more effective participation in the next group in which we find ourselves.

SUMMARY

In this day of group consciousness we are constantly being asked to engage in group discussion. Whether simply to interact or to solve problems, we find ourselves participating in group deliberations. As discussants we may participate in encounter groups, lecture-forums, symposiums, panels, or in problem-solving groups. In all of these situations it is important for the participants to be well-informed and well-organized.

In problem-solving groups the topic must be selected, worded, and researched. John Dewey's five steps of reflective thinking constitutes one organizational scheme which is quite helpful in solving problems. Being able to define the problem, analyzing the causes and effects, suggesting solutions, and picking the best solution calls for deliberations that follow a clear-thinking pattern.

Each group member, whether participant or leader, should take an active role, be well informed, cooperate, listen, encourage others, develop empathy, and be brief.

Finally, most groups will find it beneficial to evaluate their efforts as a group and as individuals.

Suggested Readings

Bormann, Ernest G., and Bormann, Nancy C. *Effective Small Group Communication.* Minneapolis: Burgess Publishing Co., 1972.

Brilhart, John K. *Effective Group Discussion.* 2d ed. Dubuque: Wm. C. Brown Company Publishers, 1974.

Burgoon, Michael; Heston, Judee K.; and McCroskey, James. *Small Group Communication: A Functional Approach.* New York: Holt, Rinehart and Winston, 1974.

Cathcart, Robert, and Samovar, Larry. *Small Group Communication: A Reader.* 2d ed. Dubuque: Wm. C. Brown Company Publishers, 1974.

Gulley, Halbert E. *Discussion, Conference and Group Process.* New York: Holt, Rinehart and Winston, 1968.

Patton, Bobby R., and Giffin, Kim. *Problem-Solving Group Interaction.* New York: Harper and Row, Publishers, 1973.

Sattler, William M., and Miller, N. Edd. *Discussion and Conference.* 2d ed. Englewood Cliffs, N. J.: Prentice-Hall, 1968.

Appendix

Speech Evaluation Scale

Speaker _____ Date _____

Subject _____ Round _____

SPEECH PROCESSES	RATINGS AND COMMENTS

CONTENT: Purpose, thesis, analysis:
  Specific purpose: clear____ narrowed
   appropriate to audience _____
  Thesis: clear____ narrowed ____ appro-
   priate to audience ____ speaker ____
  Analysis of thesis: accurate ____
   Thorough ____
  Main points: directly support
   thesis ____ fully develop ____ thesis
	1 2 3 4 5

CONTENT: Development
  Supporting material: clear ____
   relevant ____ specific ____ adequate
   in amount ____ interesting ____
  Logical reasoning: accurate ____
   supported ____
  Facts: clear____ relevant ____
   adequate____ interesting ____
  Statistics: clear ____relevant ____
   adequate ____ correctly interpret-
   ed ____ interesting ____
  Examples: clear ____ adequate ____ in-
   teresting ____
  Testimony: clear____ adequate ____
   interesting ____
	1 2 3 4 5

ORGANIZATION:
   clear ____ effective ____
  Introduction: gets attention ____
   orients ____ thesis stated ____ par-
   tition ____ creates interest ____
   proper subordination ____
  Body:
   Main points: clear ____ pat-
    terned ____
   Sub-points: clear ____ pat-
    terned ____
  Conclusion: summary ____ effec-
   tive ____
  Transitions: smooth ____
   clear____ signposts ____
	1 2 3 4 5

LANGUAGE:
  Grammar: appropriate level
   errors ____
  Rhetorical qualities: oral style
   clear ____ appropriate ____
   interesting ____ concrete ____
	1 2 3 4 5

DELIVERY:

Physical presentation: appearance ___
poise ___ enthusiasm ___ directness ___ eye contact ___ posture ___
gestures ___ facial expression ___
Oral presentation: articulation ___
fluency ___ pronunciation ___
variety ___ pitch ___ rate ___
loudness ___ directness ___   1 2 3 4 5

SPEECH OUTLINE   1 2 3 4 5

Item markings: RATINGS:
   +   —very good   5 very good
(no mark)—average or better   4 good
   ✓   —needs improvement   3 average
                                            2 poor
                                          1 unsatisfactory

Speech Evaluation

I. DELIVERY
- A. Eye contact   good _____
  - 1. aimless _____   3. windows _____
  - 2. floor _____   4. other _____ .

- B. Posture   good _____
  - 1. stiff _____   3. aimless movement _____
  - 2. shifting of weight _____   4. other _____ .

- C. Gestures   good _____
  - 1. need more _____   3. poor timing _____
  - 2. larger _____   4. other _____ .

- D. Vocal variety   good _____
  - 1. change and vary your   2. pause _____
    - a. rate _____   3. enthusiasm _____
    - b. force _____   4. other _____ .
    - c. pitch _____
    - d. volume _____

II. CONTENT
- A. Audience analysis   good_____
  - 1. topic too general _____   2. not for this audience _____
  - 3. "feedback"_____
  - 4. other _____ .

- B. Imagery and Wording   good _____
  - 1. more detail _____   2. poor word choice _____
  - 3. other _____ .

- C. Support and evidence   good_____
  - 1. old sources _____   2. unrelated to issue _____
  - 3. weak ___, because _____ .

- D. Motivation (Motive appeals)   good _____
  - 1. poor audience analysis ____   3. more development _____
  - 2. more detail _____   4. other _____ .

- E. Introduction   good_____
  - weak, because _____ .

- F. Organization   good_____
  - 1. no clear pattern _____
  - 2. weak, because _____ .

III. OTHER

Speech to Convince

SPEAKER _____

RATING SCALE: 5—Superior; 4—Above Average; 3—Average; 2—Fair;
    1—Poor.

INTRODUCTION (cirlce one) 5 4 3 2 1

    Did the opening words get favorable attention?

    Was the issue under contention introduced tactfully?

    Did the speaker make you feel that the issue was worth considering?

BODY   5 4 3 2 1

    Was the central idea (proposition) clear?

    Were the purpose and central idea sufficiently narrowed?

    Did the main points suffice to prove the central idea?

    Were there too many main points? too few? satisfactory number?

    Was each main point supported by evidence?

    Were sources of evidence cited?

    Did the evidence meet the tests of credibility?

    Was the reasoning from the evidence sound?

    Was the speech adapted to audience interests?

    Was the speech adapted to existing audience attitudes toward the topic?

CONCLUSION   5 4 3 2 1

    Did the conclusion focus the whole speech on the central idea?

LANGUAGE USAGE   5 4 3 2 1

    Clear?

    Correct?

    Appropriate?

    Vivid?

DELIVERY   5 4 3 2 1

    Visual:

    Vocal:

        DOMINANT IMPRESSION OF THE SPEECH _____

Proposition of Policy

SPEAKER _____

RATING SCALE: 5—Superior; 4—Above Average; 3—Average; 2—Fair;
    1—Poor.

HOW CONVINCINGLY DOES THE SPEAKER SHOW:

That a problem exists? _____

That it is significant enough to warrant correction? _____

That it is caused by an inherent weakness in the present
system? _____

That the proposed solution will correct the problem? _____

That the solution will be feasible? _____

That any disadvantages will be outweighed by advantages? _____

That the proposed solution is the best solution to the
problem? _____

HOW EFFECTIVELY DOES THE SPEAKER EMPLOY:

Evidence of fact and/or opinion? _____

(Underline any appropriate categories: Evidence was
insufficient in quantity; poor in quality; improperly
applied; not clearly related to the point supposedly
being proved; sources not given; credibility of sources
not always established)

Forms of reasoning? _____

(Underline any appropriate categories: Faulty reasoning from examples; from axiom, from cause to probable
effect; from effect to probable cause; from analogy)

Factors of attention and interest? _____

Signposts for organizational clarity? _____

Language? _____

Visual aspects of delivery? _____

Vocal aspects of delivery? _____

    DOMINANT IMPRESSION OF THE SPEECH _____

Speech to Inform

SPEAKER _____

RATING SCALE: 5—Superior; 4—Above Average; 3—Average; 2—Fair;
   1—Poor

CHOICE OF SUBJECT   _____

INTRODUCTION

  Opening statements effectively gain attention?   _____

  Did the speaker make you feel a need for information?   _____

  Did he establsih his right to inform, directly or indirectly? _____

  Graceful transition into the body of the speech?   _____

BODY

  Clarity of organization?   _____

  Information made interesting?   _____

  Information made understandable?   _____

  Visual aid handled capable?   _____

CONCLUSION

  Speech gracefully concluded?   _____

LANGUAGE USAGE

  Clear?   _____

  Grammatically correct?   _____

  Vivid?   _____

  Appropriate?   _____

USE OF VOICE (Check the appropriate blank)

  Pitch level: Too high ____Too low ____ OK _____

  Variation of pitch: Varied ____ Monotonous to a degree _____

  Very monotonous _____

  Rate: Too fast ____Too slow ____ OK _____

  Variation of rate: Too little ____ Too much ____ OK ____

  Loudness: Too loud ____ Too soft ____OK _____

  Variation of Loudness: Too little ____ Too much ____ OK _____

  Pronunciation: Generally correct ____ Frequently faulty_____

  Words mispronounced: _____

  Enunciation (distinctness): Clear____ Slurring _____

VISUAL ASPECTS OF DELIVERY

  Posture: Alert but at ease ____ All weight on one foot _____

  Leaning on lectern ____ Stiff ____ Shifting weight constantly _____

  Gestures: Too few____ Too many ____ OK in quantity _____

  Quality of gestures: Properly motivated ____ Affected _____

  Clumsy _____

  Movements: Immobile _____ Distracting movements _____ Satisfactory in quantity and quality _____

  Facial Expression: Very animated____ Occasionally animated ____
Never animated _____

  Eye Contacts: Looked at everyone ____ Favored one section _____
Avoided audience _____

TOTAL IMPRESSION LEFT BY SPEECH (Use rating scale) _____

Evaluation and Criticism of Speeches

1. Has the speaker made an attempt to be objective and fair to himself, the audience, and the subject?

2. Did the speaker have a worthwhile purpose? Was it of college caliber? Was the purpose easy to follow and logically developed?

3. Was there evidence that the speaker had analyzed his audience and his speaking occasion?

4. Did the speaker know his subject? Did he seem to be prepared both in terms of research and in terms of oral practice?

5. Was the speech structurally sound? Did the subdivisions, both major and minor, relate to and support the main ideas? Were the transitions between ideas clear?

6. Did the speaker utilize language meaningfully? Did he employ words or phrases that were clear and adequately defined? Did he make effective use of imagery and word pictures? Did he avoid cliches, slang, and poor grammar? Was his usage appropriate to the audience, the occasion, and the subject?

7. Did the speaker utilize factors of attention and interest in both the content and delivery of the speech?

8. Did the speaker's illustrations, examples, statistics, testimony, and analogies meet the tests of sound evidence? Was enough evidence employed to support each point?

9. Did the speaker reflect a "sense of communication?" Did he maintain eye contact? Did he employ vocal variety? Was there adequate movement?

10. What was the *total* impression left by the speech?

11. How successfully did the speaker fulfill the demands of the specific speech assignment?

Understanding Your Receiver

The following factors are just a few of the characteristics that will influence an audience's perception and response to your message. (The term "audience" is used in this context to stand for one receiver or a large audience.)

Age _____ Sex _____ Approximately how many _____

Educational level _____ Occupation _____

Economic status _____ Group allegiances _____

_____

Political affiliation _____ Attitude toward me _____

Attitude toward the communication situation _____

Knowledge of the specific subject _____

Primary interests _____

Primary goals _____

Primary attitudes and beliefs _____

_____

Other important data _____

_____

_____

_____

Out-of-Class Listening Report

Supply the information requested below regarding a speech you heard presented before a religious, civic, or academic group, etc. Hand this report to your instructor during the first class meeting following the speaking event. DO NOT COMPLETE THE REPORT DURING THE SPEECH.

1. Speaker's name _____ Subject _____

2. General end _____ Specific purpose _____

3. Occasion_____ Time _____ Place _____

4. Type of audience _____ Number _____

5. How effective was he in beginning and ending his speech? _____

   _____

6. List the major points developed in the speech _____

   _____

7. How was the speaker's delivery? _____

   _____

   _____

   _____

8. Did the speaker adapt his speech to *this* audience? (explain) _____

   _____

9. Did he prove (or explain if informative speech) his main points? (explain)

   _____

   _____

10. Criticize his language in terms of clarity, interest, ambiguity, etc. _____

    _____

    _____

11. Did the speaker achieve his purpose? _____ Why or why not _____

    _____

    Note: Use the other side of the paper if needed.

Observation of a Formal Speaking Situation

Name _____ **Date** _____

Topic _____ **Date observed** _____

1. What was the speaker's key idea or thesis sentence?

2. What was the purpose of his speech (to inform or persuade?)

3. How did he explain or prove his main points? (Be specific.)

4. How did he maintain attention and interest?

5. What type of conclusion did he use?

6. Comment on his general effectiveness.

Evaluating Group Discussion

1. How effective was the group in accomplishing its *overall objective?*

1	2	3	4	5	6	7

very effective   moderately effective   not effective

2. Did the members of the group seem *well prepared?*

1	2	3	4	5	6	7

very well prepared   moderately prepared   not at all prepared

3. Did the group follow an *organizational pattern?*

1	2	3	4	5	6	7

very well organized   moderately organized   poorly organized

4. Was there an effective *flow of communication* between all participants in the discussion? Comment and evaluate.

5. What were the strong and/or weak points of the group in the area of *participation?*

6. What were the strong and/or weak points of the group in the area of *leadership?*

Observation of a Group Discussion

Name _____ Date _____

Place of observation _____

1. Describe the occasion, the subject under discussion, and the participants.

2. Type of discussion: (Problem/Solution?)

3. Why was the discussion performed and were the participants motivated?

4. Was this discussion effective in its pursuit? If so, how?

5. Was there evidence of good feedback between participants?

What was the effect of the feedback?

6. Did the discussion proceed in a purposeful manner?

7. Did all participants discuss? Why or why not?

8. Describe the leader's role.

Critic's Discussion Evaluation Sheet

Name _____ Date _____

Evaluation of individuals in group

Some criteria for evaluating individual participation:

1. Information (understanding facts and values involved in problem)
2. Analysis (use of evidence and ability to locate main issues)
3. Cooperative thinking (contributes to group opinion & synthesizes opinion)
4. Speaking (conversational attitude, clarity in voice and diction)
5. Courteousness (treatment of others, their opinions and attitudes)

Instructions: List participants, in column A, rate them; in column B, rank them in order of their effectiveness in the group.

	Name of participant	A rate 1, 2, 3, or 4	B rank 1, 2, 3, . . . 8
1.	_____	_____	_____
2.	_____	_____	_____
3.	_____	_____	_____
4.	_____	_____	_____
5.	_____	_____	_____
6.	_____	_____	_____
7.	_____	_____	_____
8.	_____	_____	_____

Rating: 1—Poor, 2—Average, 3—Good, 4—Superior

Evaluation of the Group

Some criteria for evaluating group participation:

1. Group Information. Does group possess extensive, comprehensive and accurate knowledge of the information on the discussion topic?
2. Group Processes. Does group exhibit knowledge of the basis of cause, generalization, theory, inference making and logical reasoning in the discussion process?
3. Group Relations. Does group demonstrate the ability to integrate and synthesize individual contributions into common purposes within the group?

Evaluation of this group _____

Rating: 1—Poor, 2—Average, 3—Good, 4—Superior

Comments: (over if you need more room)

End-of-Discussion Suggestion Slip

What is your over-all rating of today's discussion for each of the items?
Please circle appropriate number.

	Very Low	Low	Av	High	Very High
1. Physical arrangement and comfort	1	2	3	4	5
2. Orientation	1	2	3	4	5
3. Group atmosphere	1	2	3	4	5
4. Interest and motivation	1	2	3	4	5
5. Participation	1	2	3	4	5
6. Productiveness	1	2	3	4	5
7. Choice	1	2	3	4	5

Please answer the following questions:

1. How would you rate this discussion? (check)

   no good ____ mediocre ____ all right ____ good ____ excellent ____

2. What were the strong points?

3. What were the weak points?

4. What improvements would you suggest?

Index

After-dinner speech, 206–7
Analogy, 88–90
    figurative, 89
    literal, 89
    reasoning by, 184–85
    testing, 90
Anecdote, 90
Answering questions, 213–16
Antithesis, 137
Apparel
    influence of, 42–43
Arguments
    convincing, 181–85
Aristotle, 14
Articulation, 53–54
Attacking authority
    as humor, 205
Attention
    gaining, 117–21
Attitudes
    defined, 172
Audience analysis, 16, 27–38, 176–80
    defined, 28
Auer, J. Jeffery, 171
Aural dimensions of presentation, 50–56

Bandwagon, 68
Barnlund, Dean C., 10, 40
Barriers
    to discussion, 234–35
Behavior
    defined, 172
Belief
    defined, 172
Biological link, 31
Blackboards
    as visual aids, 165–66
Blair, Hugh, 55
Body
    informative speech, 157–59
Brembeck, Winston L., 170
Bryant, Donald, 93
Burke, Kenneth, 28

Card stacking, 68
Causal order, 109, 158–59
Channel, 5

Charts, 165
Chronological pattern, 158
Churchill, Winston, 89
Cicero, 14
Classical design, 112
Common ground
    establishing, 123–24
Communication
    context, 9
    defined, 4
    ingredients of, 4–5
    model of, 5–11
    nature of, 11–12
    taking part in, 8
    "what we bring", 6
Comparisons, 150
Conclusion
    challenge, 125
    declaration of intent, 125–26
    illustration, 125
    informative speech, 159
    preparing, 124–26
    quotation, 124–25
    summary, 124
Connotative meanings, 133
Contrasts, 150
Core statement, 102–3
Credibility, 190–92
Cronkhite, Gary, 171
Culture
    influence of, 31–33

Darrow, Clarence, 91
Decoding, 5
Deductive order, 109
Deductive reasoning, 182–83
Defining terms, 123
Definition
    in informative speaking, 148–49
Delimiting the topic, 122
Denotative meanings, 133
Descriptions, 146, 151
Detail
    in language, 136
Dewey, John, 225
Diagrams
    as visual aids, 165

Directness, 18
Discussion. *See* chapter 11
    barriers to, 234–35
    defined, 218
    evaluation, 235
    preparing for, 222–25
    types of, 218–21
Distinctness of utterance, 53–54

Empathy, 35
    defined, 36
    gathering data for, 36–37
    interference with, 37–38
Emphasis, 151–52
Encoding, 5
Entertaining speech
    characteristics of, 204
    development of, 205–6
    presenting, 206
    sample subjects, 23
Enumeration, 152
Enunciation, 54
Ethics, 12–14
    the receiver, 14
    the sender, 12–14
Evidence. *See* chapter 5
    in persuasive speaking, 181–82
Exaggeration, 204
Examples, 81, 149–50
Explanations, 146
Expository designs, 112–13
Extemporaneous delivery, 26–27
Extended illustration, 112
Eye contact, 18

Fable, 90
Facial expression, 43
Fallacies
    begging the question, 97
    detecting, 96–99
    hasty generalizations, 96–97
    irrelevant evidence, 98–99
    non sequitur, 97–98
Feedback
    defined, 10
    use of, 10, 66, 73
Festinger, Leon, 188
Figures of speech, 136–37
Fishbein, Martin, 172
Freeley, Austin, 99
Freud, Sigmund, 41

General purpose
    formulating, 21–23
    patterns, 106
Gestures, 46–47
Glittering generality, 68

Graphs
    as visual aids, 165
Grooming
    influence of, 42–43

Howell, William S., 170
Humor
    use of, 156, 204–5

Illustration, 81–84
    factual, 81–82
    hypothetical, 82–83
    as introduction, 119
    testing, 83
Imagery, 136
Impromptu delivery, 25–26
Impromptu speech, 207–10
Incongruity, 205
Indexes, 93–94
Induction, 183–84
Inductive Order, 109
Informal groups, 220
Informative speaking
    defined, 145
    material of, 148–52
    organization of, 156–62
    step in preparation, 146–48
Informative speeches. *See* Chapter 8
    sample outline, 159–61
    sample subjects, 22
    types of, 146
Institute of Propaganda Analysis, 67
Instruction, 146
Interest, 152–56
Interviews, 92–93
Introduction
    illustration, 119
    informative speech, 156–57
    preparing, 116–21
    promise of reward, 120
    quotation, 117
    reference to occasion, 121
    reference to recent event, 119
    reference to subject, 120–21
    rhetorical question, 119–20
    startling statement, 120
Introductions
    making, 210–11

James, William, 152
Jargon, 138–39
Journals, 95
Justifying topic, 121

Language. *See* chapter 7
    accurate, 134–35
    appropriate, 137

Language—*cont.*
   clear, 134
   distractions, 138–39
   importance of, 128
   improving, 139–41
   simple, 135
   static, 133–34
   vivid, 135–36
Language to induce desired responses,
   134–39
Language to represent reality,
   129–34
Leadership
   in the group, 233–34
   styles of, 232
Lecture-forum, 220
Listeners
   age, 33
   group affiliation, 34
   intelligence, 34
   occupation, 34
   responsibility, 72–73
   sex, 33–34
   what they bring, 28–33
Listening. *See* chapter 4
   barriers to, 60–64
   common weaknesses, 57–58
   improving, 64–67
   poor habits of, 61–62
   purposes of, 58–60
   to speeches, 67–70
Logical patterns, 109–13
Loudness, 51–52

Magazines, 94
Main points, 102
   formulating, 103–6
Manuscript speaking, 24–25
   advantages of, 24–25
   disadvantages of, 25
Manuscript speech, 211–13
   delivering, 212–13
   preparing, 211–12
Material for speeches
   finding, 16
Meanings
   in people, 132–33
Memory
   speaking from, 25
Mental attitude in speaking, 17
Message, 5
Metaphor, 136
Miller, N. Edd, 232
Models
   as visual aids, 162–64
Monroe, Alan H., 111–12
Motivated sequence, 111–12

Movement, 43–47
   and attention, 44
   of the entire body, 45–46
   facilitating, 45
   of hands and arms, 46–47
   limitations upon, 47
   and meaning, 43
"Mystery of words" fallacy, 66

Name-calling, 67–68
Nervousness
   coping with, 18
Newspapers, 94
Nichols, Ralph, 64
Nonverbal communication. *See* chapter 3
   forms of, 41–54
   importance of, 40

Objects
   as visual aids, 162
Occasion
   analysis of, 55
Olbricht, Thomas, 170
Organization. *See* chapter 6, 15
Osgood, Charles, 188
Outline
   informative speech, 159–61
   persuasive speech, 194–95
Outlining, 113–16

Pamphlets, 94
Panel, 220
Parable, 90
Partition, 152
Patterns of relationship, 106
Persuasion. *See* chapter 9
   defined, 170–72
   means of, 180–93
   targets and topics, 172–74
Persuasive designs, 113
Persuasive speaking. *See* chapter 9
   importance of, 170
   organizing, 193–98
   preparing, 175–80
   sample subjects, 22–23
   types of, 174
Physical animation, 18
Pictures
   as visual aids, 165
Pitch, 52
Plain folks, 68
Plato, 92
Posters
   as visual aids, 164–65
Posture, 41–42
Preparing audience for speech, 121–24
Presenting your credentials, 122–23

Problem-solving groups
    characteristics, 221–22
Problem-solving order, 110
Promise of reward, 120
Pronunciation, 54
Propaganda techniques, 67–68
Providing background information, 123
Proxemic distance, 48
Psychological appeals, 186–90

Quality of voice, 52–53
Quintilian, 14
Quotation, 117

Rate of speaking, 53
Reasoning, 182–85
Receiver, 5
Reference books, 94
Reference to occasion, 121
Reference to recent event, 119
Reference to subject, 120–21
Reflective thinking, 225–28
Reinforcements, 151–52
Repetition, 151
Reports, 146
Restatement, 151
Rhetorical question, 119–20

Sattler, William M., 232
Self-focus, 63
Semantic distractions, 62
Sherif, Muzafer, 179
Simile, 137
Slang, 138
Small group
    communication, 228–31
Smith, Donald K., 178
Source, 4
Spatial communication, 47–49
Spatial pattern, 158
Spatial relationships, 107–8
Speaker responsibility, 73–74
Specific instances, 81
Specific purpose
    formulating, 23–24
    persuasive, 180
Specimens
    as visual aids, 162
Speech
    organizing, 16–17
    practicing, 17

purpose, 15
title, 38
topic, 15–16
Speech criticism, 68–71
Startling statement, 120
Statistics, 84–86
    in informing, 150–51
    suggestions for using, 85
    testing, 85–86
Subpoints, 102
    formulating, 103–6
Suggestion, 189–90
Summary, 152
Support
    verbal, 79–91
    visual, 91
    when to use, 95–96
Symposium, 220

Tannenbaum, Percy, 188
Testimonial, 68
Testimony, 86–88
    guidelines for using, 87–88
    testing, 88
Therapy groups, 220–21
Thinking-speaking time, 65–66
Time-binding, xi
Time relationships, 106–7
Topical pattern, 159
Topical relationship, 108–9
Triteness, 138

Visual aids, 162–68
    types of, 162–68
Visual dimensions of presentation, 41–49
Vocal variety, 19
Voice, 50–55
    and attention, 51
    controllable element, 51–54
    and personality, 50–51
    and word meaning, 50

Wallace, Karl R., 93
Winans, James, 152
Words
    "Big", 139
    empty, 139
    loaded, 139
    many uses, 129–30
    as symbols, 129
Words omit details, 130–31